Praise for Everyday Life Among the American Indians

"When I have a research question that no one else can answer, I ask Candy Moulton. She has done historical novelists and historians, both amateur and professional, a tremendous service."
— Lucia St. Clair Robson, author of *Ride the Wind*

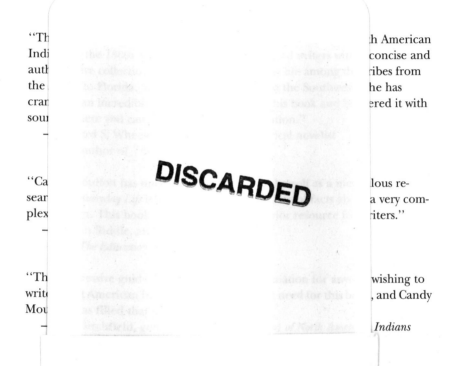

"Th ... h American Indi ... concise and auth ... ibes from the ... he has cran ... ered it with sou ...

"Ca ... lous research ... a very complex ... iters."

"Th ... wishing to writ ... , and Candy Mou ... *Indians*

EVERYDAY LIFE AMONG THE
AMERICAN INDIANS

EVERYDAY
LIFE
AMONG THE
AMERICAN
INDIANS

DISCARDED

CANDY MOULTON

WRITER'S DIGEST BOOKS
CINCINNATI, OHIO
www.writersdigest.com

Other fine Writer's Digest Books are available from your local bookstore or direct from the publisher.

Visit our Web site at www.writersdigest.com for information on more resources for writers.

To receive a free weekly e-mail newsletter delivering tips and updates about writing and about Writer's Digest products, send an e-mail with the message "Subscribe Newsletter" to newsletter-request@writersdigest.com, or register directly at our Web site at http://newsletters.fwpublications.com.

05 04 03 02 01   5 4 3 2 1

Library of Congress Cataloging-in-Publication Data

Moulton, Candy Vyvey
   Everyday life among the American Indians / by Candy Moulton.
    p. cm.
   Includes bibliographical references and index.
   ISBN 0-89879-996-1
    1. Indians of North America—Social life and customs. 2. Indians of North American—History. I. Title.

E98.S7 M68 2001
973'.0497—dc21   00-068666
                                           CIP

Editor: Brad Crawford
Designer: Sandy Conopeotis Kent
Cover designers: Melissa Wilson and Michelle Ringshauser
Production coordinator: Mark Griffin
Cover photograph courtesy of the National Museum of the American Indian, Smithsonian Institution (20.3035). Photo by David Heald. (See page xiii for original image.)

DEDICATION

To the spirit of the Indian woman whose burial site
is on the hill above my house and the belief that
Penny and I will again find the tipi rings of our youth.

ACKNOWLEDGMENTS

I would have never attempted this book without the encouragement and help of my friend D. L. Birchfield. Don, *kahoke*. Further, I am deeply indebted to the scholars who have in many cases spent their careers researching and writing about specific Indian tribes. Thanks also to these people who constantly inspire me and personally help me to broaden my base of knowledge about the American History and the American West: James A. Crutchfield, W. Michael and Kathleen O'Neal Gear, Lori Van Pelt, Richard S. Wheeler, Sierra Adare, Mike Blakely, Robert Conley and Win Blevins. I could write no book without the support of my family, Steve, Shawn and Erin Marie. I also appreciate Marcy Posner and Eric Zohn of the William Morris Agency and Dave Borcherding, Brad Crawford and the staff at Writer's Digest Books for their efforts to put this volume onto the bookshelf.

I have been fortunate to travel to many important American Indian sites with Indian guides to show me their ways. I've spent time at a Blackfeet Sundance site with Curly Bear Wagner, and I've slept alone in a Blackfeet lodge as the cold winds of late September swept across the plains near Browning, Montana. I've walked the ancient community of Walpai placing my feet in the stone indentations made by generations of Hopis. I've ridden a wiry Indian pony beneath the eight hundred foot-high cliffs of Canyon de Chelly and traced my finger over petroglyphs in my native Wyoming. I've stood where Chief Joseph surrendered his people in 1877 and where families died at Wounded Knee in 1890.

To write about Indian people, you must connect with such natural places, for Indian lifestyle and culture in the 1800s was completely and irrevocably tied to the land. If you fail to understand the land and its power, you will never completely grasp the meaning it gives to the lives of Indian people.

ABOUT THE AUTHOR

Candy Moulton is the author of nine nonfiction books on the West, including *The Writer's Guide to Everyday Life in the Wild West, Roadside History of Wyoming* and *Roadside History of Nebraska*. She is also the editor *Roundup,* the magazine of the Western Writers of America, and has written articles on the West for *True West, Wild West, Old West, American Cowboy, Persimmon Hill, Sunset, Southwest Art, Western Horseman, Travel + Leisure* and many other publications. Moulton lives with her family near Encampment, Wyoming.

TABLE OF CONTENTS

PART THREE:

AMERICAN INDIAN SOCIETY

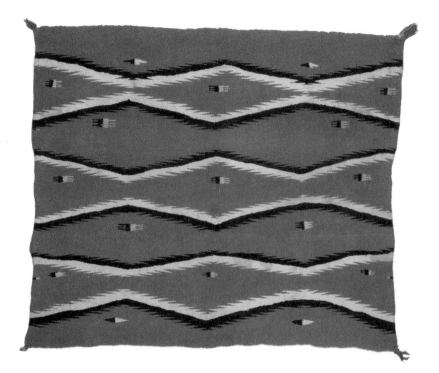

Navajo blanket (National Museum of the American Indian, Smithsonian Institution, 20.3035). Photo by David Heald.

INTRODUCTION

On 30 September 1800 Robert R. Livingston and James Monroe, serving as minister plenipotentiaries of the United States on behalf of President Thomas Jefferson, agreed to a treaty with Francis Barbe Marboios, minister of the public treasury of France, to purchase Louisiana from France for sixty million francs, with the exchange of property to occur on 30 April 1803.

It was an event that changed the course of settlement for North America and that had an impact on every Indian tribe on the continent. The purchase of Louisiana Territory was the first major expansion for the United States, which heretofore had grown slowly, moving ever westward from the Puritan colonies over the Allegheny and Blue Ridge mountains and toward the Mississippi.

By nearly doubling the land mass of the young republic, the Louisiana Purchase heralded an accelerated push to the West. By midcentury, politicians and practical farmers alike espoused the concept that it was Manifest Destiny for the United States to expand. It did so with the addition of Texas, the Spanish regions including California, and in 1867 with the purchase from Russia of the land up north—the region that became Alaska.

INDIAN REMOVAL

Simultaneous with the purchase of Louisiana, President Thomas Jefferson voiced the policy that was ultimately implemented by President Andrew Jackson: Indian Removal. With all the new land west of the Mississippi, Jefferson and Jackson reasoned, the Indians could relocate to Indian Territory; they would be out of the way of settlers.

But the expansionist attitudes of the century defeated that premise of separation. By midcentury, settlers were crossing the Mississippi and the Missouri in droves, bound for land in Oregon as the United States made its claim for the Pacific Northwest from the British while wrangling over the northern boundary and squabbling with Mexico over California. Mormons flooded west starting in 1847 to settle in Ute/Paiute country, and gold-crazed miners poured over the roads and trails in 1849 headed for California's treasure. They forever changed the lands of the California Indians, in many cases exterminating entire tribes within a few short years.

The Southeast tribes, removed to Indian Territory in the 1830s, found themselves sharing their new lands with other tribes forced from home regions to reservations in the Indian Territory—an area that became known as The Nations. Dozens and dozens of treaties promised annuities and lands and opportunity to live unfettered lifestyles; most were never honored even though the Indians relocated.

By 1890 all Indians in the United States had been affected. That year the U.S. Census Bureau declared there was no more frontier.

OUTSIDE INFLUENCES

Many outside influences affected Indian lifestyle during the 1800s. Though Indian people's lives changed dramatically as a result of Manifest Destiny, military conflict, gold exploration and exploitation, even without all of those outside influences Indians would have been different in 1900 than they were in 1800.

Change is the only constant thing in life. All people change and evolve as they grow older, as they learn more, as they find or make different opportunities.

An example of change can be shown through the appearance of the horse. Prior to having horses, Indian people moved their camps by loading supplies onto small drags, called travois, that dogs pulled; they put their possessions in boats and other watercraft; or they carried them on their own backs. They hunted and fought on foot. Then the Spanish introduced the horse to the tribes in the Southwest.

Though we might like to think they did, the fact is Indian people *did not* live in a vacuum, seeing only those people in their own camps. Many of them traveled widely in search of food; they had extensive trade networks. So when the Indians in the Southwest obtained horses, they took them over those trade routes to the Northwest and to the region that became Texas. From there they spread across the country. Nez Percés obtained horses, exchanging them along with fish for bison robes and other hides from the Shoshones, who subsequently traded with the Mandans, Sioux or Arikaras for food like corn, beans or squash or other supplies.

Once the Indians had horses, they could hunt bison and other game more easily, and they could haul bigger quantities of goods from one camp to the next, using the horses as draft animals pulling travois like dogs had done for generations. Among the results: lodges were enlarged, and people obtained and kept more goods like cooking pots, clothing and weapons. Even the size of families shifted; many Plains warriors had more wives because one man who had a good bison-hunting horse could kill more bison than one wife could process.

None of that change had anything to do with white expansion. But beginning with the explorations of land included in the Louisiana Purchase by Meriwether Lewis and William Clark in 1804 and continuing through the century, outsiders did impact Indian lifestyle in the nineteenth century.

TRADERS, MINERS AND THE RAILROAD

French, Spanish, British and American traders supplied a variety of goods to Indians ranging from metal needles and guns to trade cloth (material used for clothing and blankets that was obtained from traders, primarily stroud, a coarse woolen material), beads, kettles, whiskey and rum. Indians no longer relied on hide or clay pots, or on bone awls or porcupine quills for ornamentation of clothing. Along with horses, Indians obtained carts and, later, wagons. They used fewer hides and plant materials for clothing, and wore more garments of cloth.

Gold has always fueled imagination and greed, and its presence affected Indians across the country. Gold discoveries in the Cherokee Nation in 1819 accelerated the desire to remove that tribe from its homeland in Georgia and the Carolinas. California's rush in 1849 led to almost immediate extermination of some Indian tribes there. Subsequent impacts reverberated through tribes after discovery of gold and silver in what became Colorado, Idaho, Montana, South Dakota's Black Hills, Alaska and the Yukon.

Expansion and trade over trails and roads—Oregon Trail, Mormon Trail, California Trail, Santa Fe Trail, Whoop-up Trail, Natchez Trace and the like—further reduced Indian territory and changed lifestyle. The final flurry of Indian treaties resulted because of the desire to obtain rights-of-way for various railroad projects, which led to an influx of new settlers that eclipsed the numbers who had headed west with wagons. For about thirty years, from their arrival in Indian Territory after Removal until the Civil War, the Choctaws had little involvement with outsiders. But in 1866 a new treaty provided for a railroad to cross their new land, and within four years whites outnumbered Choctaws by three to one in their own country, leading to subsequent breakup of the Indian Nations, which were simply overwhelmed by outsiders.

REALITY AND POPULAR PORTRAYAL

For those writers whose subject matter involves stories of American Indians during the 1800s, there is rich material from which to draw. And there are many land mines as well. Indian people today are extremely sensitive about how their story—and their history—is told. Though they are critical of each other, they are even more critical of non-Indian writers. Many writers give them much fodder to chew by failing to accurately portray a particular tribe.

Some of that inaccuracy can properly be laid at the door of Hollywood filmmakers who stereotypically depicted all Indian warriors as wearing large feathered headdresses and few clothes, and talking in monosyllabic sentences or screaming unintelligible war cries as they raced their horses around an enemy—often a wagon train of emigrants or soldiers—shooting arrows and scalping victims. Some of it comes from writers of romance novels who consistently have story lines revolving around a white woman captured by a virile Indian man who seldom ravishes her but instead treats her kindly (the innuendo being that no Indian man could be kind) until she falls in love with him and learns he is not really a "savage" as she had been taught.

To be certain, both of those scenarios happened occasionally. There are cases when Indian warriors attacked and scalped foes. There are cases where Indian men captured white females (the tales of Cynthia Ann Parker and Olive Oatman come to mind). But by far the majority of Indian raiding involved members of one tribe attacking those of another tribe. Whites scalped Indians just as Indians scalped whites. Far more Indian women married white men (primarily traders) than Indian men took white women as wives.

Though Plains Indians wore feathered headdresses, Cherokees or Choctaws were more likely to wear top hats or turbans. California Indian women wore skirts woven of plant materials very early in the century, but replaced them with cloth garments by midcentury. Indians living in the extreme northeastern United States lived in frame houses or log cabins by the early 1800s; Hopis occupied the same adobe-style homes their families had used for centuries.

MAKING DISTINCTIONS

When writing about Indians in the 1800s—or any time period, for that matter—it is important and necessary to research the specific tribe you intend to depict. For example, although both are Plains tribes, Comanches and Cheyennes have different customs and traditions. There are differences in family relationships, in the types of food they ate, how it was prepared and how they taught their children. There are fundamental differences in their religious beliefs. There are even more significant differences between some Indian people. For example, at the same time Paiutes were subsisting on rabbits and grasshoppers, on roots and plants, Choctaws were sending their brightest young people to universities like Princeton and Yale.

As you write, even names can be a concern. All too often writers use names like Brave Wolf, Charging Falcon or Falling Star, irrespective of which tribe the individual represents. Many Cherokee and Choctaw Indians in the 1800s had English or European names—John Ridge, Elias Boudinot, Peter Pitchlynn or Samuel Coles—from their trader fathers/grandfathers. One writer who depicted the Choctaw tribe had characters named Brave Bear and Pretty Cloud. Actual Choctaw names in the nineteenth century included To Seize The Day And Kill, The Sapling Is Ready For Him and To Lie In Wait And Kill. Actual Comanche names included The Amorous Adulterer and The Man Who Marries His Wife Twice. To find real Indian names, read them on treaty documents or in contemporary accounts such as autobiographies or newspaper reports of treaty conferences.

Bear in mind that people who are Lakota, Dakota and Nakota are part of the Sioux confederacy and in the 1800s were most often lumped together as Sioux. Likewise the people referred to by outsiders as Eskimos (sometimes spelled Esquimaux) in the 1800s, really are Inuit. And remember, also, that though some tribes truly were exterminated prior to or during the 1800s, most are still viable. Indian people did not disappear with the frontier in 1890.

This book is a resource guide to help you write about Indians. It is impossible to include all the incredible detail of Indian lives in one volume, and I make no presumption that mine is the only book you will need. Even as I complete the final words, I feel as if I have just begun to provide the type of detail needed to write accurately about Indians in the 1800s. I have divided the more than four hundred tribes into nine cultural areas and have subsequently given specific details about the food, clothing, customs and other lifestyle elements for each of those areas and certain tribes within them.

Given space constraints the information in this book is limited, and in all likelihood you will want and need to do further research; therefore, I have provided bibliographic sources.

As you research and write, bear in mind the differences in attitudes from the 1800s and today. What is correct and appropriate today likely wasn't in 1865. For example, at that time white people and military leaders called warriors "braves" or "bucks" and Indian women "squaws." These words were primarily used by outsiders; in most tribes never by Indians.

So if you are writing about that time frame and in those contexts, use of such terminology is accurate. Be forewarned, that doesn't mean today's Indian critical reviewers won't criticize your work if you use such wording. They are extremely sensitive to what they perceive as Eurocentric bias, stereotyping and racism.

Fortunately there are many established and emerging native writers who share their culture in books and articles. Such works mean we are now learning the "other side of the story" in many situations and we have the opportunity to better understand Indian people. In the same way, members of one tribe can learn more about a different tribe. By the way, Indians usually prefer to be called by their tribal name. It is best to say, "He is Arapaho," or, "She is Tlingit." They are collectively known as American Indians. Though the term Native Americans can be used, it came from the U.S. Census Bureau, not from Indian people, and is not usually preferred by Indian people.

For all of us, there is much material to draw from when writing about North American Indians. Far too often, individual tribal stories are told only from the perspective of conflict. That is, when a certain tribe is in the limelight, as the Cherokees and Choctaws were in the 1830s during Removal or as the Sioux or Comanche were during the Plains Indian wars. That means there is a plethora of stories yet to be written. Like those of off-reservation boarding schools or other educational achievements.

To begin to understand Indian people, to learn the subtle differences between Creeks and Cherokees or Choctaws, study the specific Bureau of American Ethnology bulletins, found at libraries and research institutions, that deal with the tribe you're writing about. That's where you can find the terminology and the uniqueness of each tribe. In those bulletins you will also learn about core belief systems. Hopis, for example, and most other Pueblos, have ceremonies designed to try to bring rain, help the crops, etc. But for their neighbors, the Navajos, the thought of trying to intervene with nature is something that would never occur to them; they want to get themselves in sync with nature, not the other way around.

Even allies had differences. The Kiowas and Comanches had constant problems because the Comanches thought the Kiowas wanted to talk a problem to death and the Kiowas thought the Comanches were too volatile and too unwilling to consider all sides of a question. As Choctaw writer D.L. Birchfield put it, "I don't see how anyone could find out about the characteristics and unique practices of the tribe they want to write about without delving into that particular tribe in some depth; otherwise they're apt to have some Navajo doing a rain dance or have a bunch of hot-headed Kiowas suddenly deciding to do something."

In the introduction to his epic novel of the Comanches, *Comanche Dawn,* author Mike Blakely, wrote, "I read every book in the University of Texas library system that involved the Comanche, the Shoshone, or any number of other Plains Indian nations. I read every book I could find on the Spanish presence in New Mexico and Texas around the turn of the eighteenth century. I simply read every available source that in any way pertained to the subject of this novel, and this is in addition to interviewing anthropologists and Indian peoples and putting many miles of travel behind me in geographical research."

That is exactly what every writer should do when writing about American Indian subjects. Unlike the romantic images given to us in film and many books, the true images of Indian people are more complex and more compelling. And many of their stories are just waiting to be told.

PART ONE

GOVERNMENT AND WAR

CHAPTER ONE

TERRITORIES
AND LEADERSHIP

T hroughout their histories Indian people have been relatively mobile; as various culture groups would establish themselves in a certain region for a period of time—in many cases for multiple generations—before relocating to a new area. However, by 1800 most of the major culture areas had long been established. Within each of the major cultural regions, individual tribes established their own territorial boundaries—borders that changed and evolved as some tribes were forced to relocate by aggressive behavior of other tribes within the same cultural group.

Though tribal territories had constantly changed and shifted since the earliest aboriginal people lived in North America, during the 1800s those territorial changes not only affected almost every tribe on the continent, they also became more permanent, particularly due to the ceding (often under duress) of territorial lands to the federal government and the subsequent establishment of reservations.

Many tribes that had earlier moved to follow game migrations, or because other tribes forced their territorial change, found themselves relocated due to the policies and practices of the United States government. In some cases law or decree brought about the relocations—such as removal of the Cherokees from Georgia and North Carolina to land that is now within the states of Arkansas and Oklahoma. In other instances they were implemented through war, such as battles between the army and the Santee Sioux who were removed from Minnesota to Nebraska and South Dakota following an 1862 uprising.

Some tribes—particularly those in the Northeast and Southeast—had already ceded much of their land, and in some cases, such as with the Cheraw, Moneton, Tutelo, Waccamaw, Waxhaw and Yadkin had even become extinct as viable tribes by 1800. Almost every other tribe in the United States, and many in Canada, saw territorial changes during the nineteenth century. The ever-expanding United States population further eroded tribal identities and numbers as well. For instance, diseases such as smallpox and measles devastated certain tribes, such as the Mandans who were so powerful in 1804. And once-populous California tribes became virtually extinct immediately following the 1849 California Gold Rush.

For purposes of this book North American tribes are divided into these major cultural groups: Arctic and Subarctic, California, Northeast, Southeast, Great Basin, Interior Plateau, Northwest Coast, Plains, Prairies and Woodlands and Southwest. Those regions are generally identified by geographic boundaries and individual tribes as outlined below:

CULTURAL DIVISIONS

Arctic and Subarctic

The Arctic is the region generally consisting of present-day Alaska, extreme northern Canada and the Aleutian Islands involving the Eskimos and the Aleuts of the Aleutian Islands. The Subarctic cultural area, involving tribes throughout portions of central and eastern Alaska and extending across central Canada, is dealt with only in a limited way in this book due to space constraints.

California

This is the region generally including the present-day state and comprising these tribes:

Chumash	Pomo
Costano	Salina
Maidu	Wintun
Miwok	Yana
Modoc	Yokuts
Patwin	

as well as those known as the Mission Indians:

Cahuilla	Luiseno
Diegueno	Serrano
Gabrileno	Yuki

Northeast

Generally this is the region delineated by the border between the United States and Canada, with the Great Lakes to the west, the Tennessee River to the south and the Atlantic Ocean on the east. Tribes within the region included the

Abenaki	Cayuga
Algonquian (or Algonkin)	Delaware

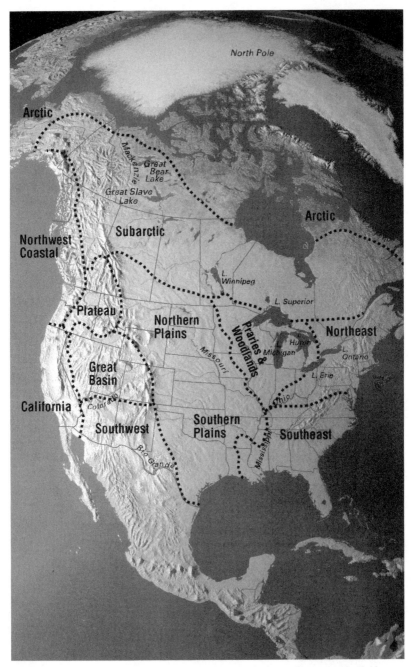

American Indian cultural regions. Cultural boundaries/map illustration by Bobby Daniels.

Erie	Passamaquoddy
Huron (earlier called Wyandot)	Pennacook
Kickapoo	Penobscot
Mahican	Pequot
Malecite	Piankashaw
Massachuset	Potawatomie
Miami	Powhatan
Micmac	Seneca
Mohawk	Shawnee
Mohegan	Shinnecock
Montauk	Susquehannock
Narraganset	Tobacco
Neutral	Tuscarora
Nipmuc	Wampanoag
Oneida	Wappinger
Onondaga	Wea
Ottawa	

Southeast

In the area roughly bordered by Kentucky and Virginia on the north, the Mississippi River to the west, and the Gulf of Mexico and Atlantic Ocean on the south and east lived the tribes that became known after the 1830–38 Removal period as the Five Civilized Tribes: Cherokee, Chickasaw, Choctaw, Creek and Seminole, as well as the

Ais	Monacan
Alabama	Natchez
Apalachee	Ofo
Atakapa	Pedee
Bidai	Pensacola
Biloxi	Quapaw
Caddo	Saponi
Calusa	Sugeree
Catawba	Taensa
Chiaha	Tamathli
Chitimacha	Timucua
Cusabo	Tunica
Eno	Tuskegee
Guale	Waccamaw
Hasinai	Wateree
Hitchiti	Woccon
Houma	Yamasee
Koasati	Yazoo

Some of these were extinct or nearly extinct by 1800.

Great Basin

The region lay west of the Continental Divide, generally east of the Sierra Nevada and bounded on the south roughly by the Colorado River and on the north roughly along the Snake River, comprising the western half of the present-day states of Wyoming and Colorado, all of Utah and Nevada, the southern half of Idaho and the southeastern quarter of Oregon. Major tribes within the cultural area include the Bannock, Gosiute, Paiute (spelled Piute by the tribe itself during the era), Panamint, Shoshone, Ute and Washo.

Interior Plateau

This area comprises western Montana, the Idaho panhandle, the eastern two-thirds of present-day Washington and a region of present-day Oregon, generally in the northeastern third of the state, and extends north into British Columbia, Canada. Among the tribes in the region are the

Cayuse	Okanogan (also spelled
Chelan	Okanagan)
Coeur d'Alene	Palouse
Columbia	Sanpoil
Colville	Shuswap
Flathead	Spokane
Klamath	Tenino
Klickitat	Thompson
Kutenai (also spelled	Umatilla
Kootenay)	Walla Walla
Lillooet	Wanapam
Methow	Wenatchee
Molala	Wishram
Nez Percé	Yakima

Northwest Coast

This tribal region lies along the Northwest Coast from southern Alaska, across western British Columbia, Canada, and extending through the western third of both Washington and Oregon. Tribes within the region include the

Alsea	Comox
Bella Bella	Coos
Bella Coola	Cowichan
Chastacosta	Cowlitz
Chehalis	Duwamish
Chimakum	Eyak
Chinook	Gitksan
Clallam	Haida
Clatskanie	Haisla
Clatsop	Heiltsuk
Coast Salish	Humptulips

Kalapuya	Semiahmoo
Kwakiutl	Siletz
Kwalhioqua	Siuslaw
Lumni	Skagit
Makah	Skokomish
Nanaimo	Snoqualmie
Niska	Takelma
Nisqually	Tillamook
Nooksack	Tlingit
Nootka	Tongass
Puntlatch	Tsimshian
Puyallup	Tututni
Quileute	Twana
Quinnault	Umpqua
Seechelt	

Plains

One of the largest tribal regions extending from Canada to near Mexico, the Plains are further divided into the Northern and Southern Plains. The region includes the southern portions of three Canadian provinces, Alberta, Saskatchewan and Manitoba, and more than a dozen states, including the eastern portions of Montana, Wyoming and Colorado and the extreme eastern part of New Mexico; all of North and South Dakota, Nebraska, Kansas and Oklahoma; and most of Minnesota, Iowa, Kansas, Missouri, Arkansas and Texas. Tribes within the region included the

Arapaho	Missouri
Arikara	Omaha
Assiniboine (also called Stoney)	Osage
Blackfeet	Oto
Blood	Pawnee
Cheyenne	Piegan
Comanche	Plains Ojibwa
Crow	Ponca
Gros Ventre (also called Atsina)	Quapaw
Hidatsa	Santee Sioux
Iowa	Sarcee
Kansa	Tawakoni
Kichai	Teton Sioux
Kiowa	Tonkawa
Kiowa-Apache	Wichita
Lipan Apache	Yankton Sioux
Mandan	Yanktonai Sioux

Prairies and Woodlands

This small region is a transition zone between the eastern tribes and the plains tribes. It is defined generally by Lake Michigan and Lake Superior on the east, the Missouri River to the west and includes the present states of Illinois, Wisconsin and portions of Iowa as well as parts of Canada. Tribes within the region included the

Chippewa (United States)	Miami
Fox	Ojibwa (Canada)
Illinois	Peoria
Kaskaskia	Sauk
Menominee	Winnebago

Southwest

This area in the United States includes most of the present-day states of Arizona and New Mexico, as well as part of western and southern Texas. This cultural area also includes the tribes of northern Mexico; however we are not including any significant amount of detail about those tribes due to space limitations. Among the tribes within the Southwest culture area were the Apache (including the Chiricahua, Coyotera, Jicarilla, Lipan, Mescalero, Mimbreno, and many other bands), and the

Cocopa	Pima
Havasupai	Piro
Hualapai (or Walapai)	Seri
Mohave	Walapai
Navajo	Yaqui
Opata	Yavapai
Papago	Yuma

and the Pueblo tribes including the Hopi in Arizona and the nineteen contemporary Pueblos in New Mexico such as Cochiti, Laguna, Taos and Zuni.

POLITICAL ORGANIZATION

Indian life can most often be viewed as an inverted pyramid. At the top is the tribe. Below the tribe are usually divisions or subtribes, which are comprised of several bands. The bands themselves are comprised of smaller groups of peoples, such as those sharing camps, villages or even family groups. At the very bottom of the structure—but certainly the foundation of all Indian organization—is the nuclear family: parents and children. Though some very poor Indians, such as those in the Great Basin, seldom if ever organized to the main tribal level, most had complex organizations and forms of self-government.

Within each tribe there were further divisions. Most often tribes separated themselves into hunting bands, which had their own territories within the larger tribal territory. The smaller bands often were a family group, and they seldom joined together with other bands, generally congregating only for two major purposes: to participate in major religious rituals or in war parties. Tribal leadership varied as well. Some had well-established central governments (such as the Iroquois Council), while in others leadership was vested in the local band leader or at the village level, and there was no general overall tribal government.

Though some leaders served throughout most of their lives and their son or nephew or other close relative inherited the leadership position, others served only as long as the people endorsed them. In some tribes women had powerful roles, such as the clan mothers of the Iroquois. War chiefs often led only for a single raid or two, taking charge of planning and carrying out an attack as led to do in visions and other solitary religious rites. In tribes where leadership relied on support of the people, a "chief" could never direct any-one to do a certain thing. He could only suggest it, and people often followed him because he had earned their respect.

Most tribes practiced democratic principles with all adults having the oppor-tunity to speak to issues and to vote in important situations. Though most chiefs had prestige, few had dictatorial powers. Most chiefs were elected (though a few were inherited positions, particularly among the Northwest Coast tribes). Few chiefs ruled outright; most held their positions because of past experience and success in situations ranging from war to diplomacy. The Great Sun of the Natchez was one of the few absolute rulers in North American Indian country, though his reign ended long before 1800. The Creeks had village kings whose word remained absolute. Some of the chiefs among the Northeastern and Woodland/Prairie tribes, including the Mohegan, Miami and other Algon-quian tribes, served so many years they also became autocrats. Few tribes had any class systems though some tribes had slaves (who were most often captives from another tribe).

Most tribes had many societies including those that were private and others that were public. They ranged from warrior, singing and dancing societies, to "clubs" for men and women. Among the many societies were these: Grand Medicine Society (prevalent among the Omaha, Winnebago and Ojibwa tribes), Crazy Dogs or Dog Soldiers (Blackfeet), Black Mouth or Bull Buffalo (warrior societies of the Mandans), Head Man's society (Oglala Sioux) and False Face Society (Iroquois).

In most tribes there were two chiefs, the civil chief who handled routine village affairs and the war chief who served during fighting. Among the Osages, such division was further exploited so there were both war towns, where individ-uals who provided military might for the tribe lived, and peace towns, which were home to all others in the tribe. Some Southeastern tribes had Red Towns (war) and White Towns (peace).

Traditionally the Aleuts and Eskimos—known today as the Inuit—had chiefs who protected hunting grounds, commanded in war if necessary and controlled the behavior of people under their leadership. Chieftainship generally passed from father to son (as did special rights and powers of whale hunting, particularly among Aleuts). After the Russians made their way to the region, Aleut communities developed a system of first, second and third chiefs. There are many Eskimo tribes and though they have similar lifestyles, there also are certain practices specific to individual tribes that do not carry over to all Eskimo people.

Mohaves had a head chief and subchiefs, but no single individual had much authority over other members of the tribe. As in many other tribes, people listened to the wishes of the chief out of respect, not because of authority.

After the Navajos returned to their homeland in 1868 from their exile at Bosque Redondo in eastern New Mexico as part of the forced "Long Walk," they had a head chief who was appointed by the Indian Agent and approved by the Secretary of the Interior, as well as regional leaders. After Indian Removal in the 1830s, the Five Civilized Tribes became constitutional republics with executive, legislative and judicial branches modeled after the U.S. government.

EXPANSION POLICY

The expansion policies of the United States during the century eroded lands of all Indian tribes, many of whom fought on the land or in the courts to retain their territory. The United States' population was expanding ever westward during the century, first by tiny steps and by the middle of the century by leaps and bounds. As a result, during the 1800s all cultural groups saw some changes in their territories, though not all Indian tribes were affected.

The Northeastern Indians, for instance, had already seen significant change, and many tribes there had been voluntarily or forcefully relocated to new lands by 1800. They had already felt the effects of white encroachment, so the 1800s brought seemingly fewer changes to their territories than it did to some other regions, such as the Plains. There free-ranging tribes in 1800 were first affected by disease carried to their country by explorers and settlers and then forced onto ever-smaller parcels of land, until by 1890 all were relocated to reservations representing a fraction of the land base the tribes had once used.

During the same period that Indian tribes were engaged in a struggle to keep their land under Indian domination and not the control of the U.S. government, they also had routine conflicts with other Indian tribes. Throughout the generations tribes had contested with each other over territory. The larger, stronger tribes generally fought with smaller, weaker tribes subsequently enlarging their own territories. The Sioux tribes are a good example of this practice. They had been in the region east of the Mississippi River and particularly around the Great Lakes until the 1700s, when they gradually began making their way westward, pushing tribes such as the Cheyennes, Kiowas and Crows out of the area presently known as the Dakotas. By 1800 the Sioux (both Lakota and Dakota) were powerfully ensconced around the Black Hills region and extending west into the Powder River Basin country of present-day Wyoming.

The Northern Cheyennes, meanwhile, had been pushed westward and southward into present eastern Montana, Colorado and Kansas, and the Crows were moved into present central Montana, while the Kiowas moved south toward the region of present Oklahoma and Texas. Then as the 1800s progressed, the Sioux were engaged in battles of their own to retain the territories they considered theirs. Their fighting, however, was primarily against the U.S. Frontier Army and in the battles the Cheyennes, whom they had earlier fought, became their allies.

LAND OWNERSHIP

Indian maps of their territories or to explain where a place was to strangers such as explorers Lewis and Clark were often drawn into the dirt, or perhaps they were sketched onto pieces of hide. Lines drawn into the sand could represent a stream or river, a chain of mountains, or even a well-used trade route or war trail. Indians had no real conception of north-south-east-west, but rather referred to direction by such terms as *above* and *below*, or toward *sunrise* or *sunset*. They identified regions by mountain ranges, water courses and the like.

In most cases Indian tribes did not consider the land that was their territory to be land they owned. Many tribes, and specifically the Plains tribes, did not believe they could own the land. Instead they believed they could live on the land and use the products available from it—like crops or game animals such as deer, elk or bison (commonly called buffalo but technically the species known as *bison bison*). Because they had no concept of ownership of the land, the tribes did not understand when they allowed settlers to move into their lands that they were actually giving those people ownership rights.

Sauk leader Black Hawk expressed the feeling of many when he said:

> Here, for the first time, I touched the goose quill to the treaty— not knowing, however, that by that act I consented to give away my village! Had that been explained to me, I should have opposed it, and never would have signed their treaty.

"No tribe has the right to sell, even to each other, much less to strangers," the Shawnee Tecumseh said. "Sell a country? Why not sell the air, the great sea, as well as the earth? Didn't the Great Spirit make them all for the use of his children?"

Exceptions to the land ownership philosophy of American Indians lay within the Five Civilized Tribes of the Southeast and the California tribes. The Cherokees, for example, did believe that the tribe, and subsequently individual tribal members, in their case the women, could actually own the land. Cherokee women owned and controlled garden plots, passing the land down to their daughters, or in the event that they did not have a daughter, to a sister or niece who was from their same tribal clan. The Cherokees were one of the most advanced tribes during the early 1800s, having their own alphabet and their own newspaper. When governmental leaders forced them to leave Georgia, Tennessee, Kentucky and North Carolina, the Cherokees fought the orders, not on the battlefield, but in the courts.

REMOVAL

From the first landing of Columbus on the North American continent, a common impact to the native people involved the concept of "removal." During the earliest years of the Plymouth Colony and continuing through the American Revolution, American Indians were systematically pushed from their territories to new areas. When one tribe was forced to move, it subsequently displaced another tribe so—like a stack of dominoes—the movement continued, ultimately affecting thousands of people.

By 1800 tribes in the Northeast had been moved around, in some cases consolidated with other tribes, and generally those left in the region had achieved some degree of permanency. The Arctic people were never systematically forced to move, though certainly some groups of people did relocate to better hunting areas.

In most other cultural regions, however, the 1800s saw great change in the distribution of native people. As the United States' population spread westward during the century, tribes felt the direct impacts. Tribes whose historic territories lay east of the Mississippi, like the Cherokee, Chickasaw, Choctaw, Creek, Delaware, Fox, Potawatomi, Santee, Sauk, Seminole, Sioux and moved west of the river to reservations or Indian Territory. The region included land in the present states of Oklahoma and Kansas and was commonly called The Nations because so many Indian nations were forced to relocate there during the 1800s.

Settlers claiming land in Oregon and Utah, as well as gold seekers in California, displaced tribes in those regions, as did people moving into Texas and the Dakotas. By 1850 more than half of the North American Indian people had been displaced from their traditional homelands; by 1890 virtually all of them were either living in new areas or confined to reservations that were tiny remnants of their once-large territories. Throughout the country and the century are instances where tribes were forcibly removed from one locality to another.

One Indian, whose name has not followed his words, in 1876 said:

> Tell your people that since the Great Father promised that we should never be removed we have been moved five times. I think you had better put the Indians on wheels so you can run them about wherever you wish.

The Cherokee Trail of Tears—1838

Small, round, red rocks abundantly found in Oklahoma are known as Cherokee Tears. They are the reminders of a major relocation of Indian people in a two-pronged removal that affected not only the Cherokees but also members of other Southeastern tribes, including the Creeks, Choctaws, Chickasaws and Seminoles.

Discussion began early in the century, first suggested by President Thomas Jefferson shortly before the Louisiana Purchase of 1803, about having the Indians who then lived in Georgia, North Carolina and Florida, relocate farther west. Once the Louisiana Purchase was consummated, Jefferson's talk of removal had a more concrete focus as there was then land controlled by the United States where the Indians could go. The preferred location: across the Mississippi River in country nobody seemed to want, in the place dubbed "Indian Territory." It included all of present-day Oklahoma and a portion of present-day Kansas. Jefferson recognized it as a place where Indians could be relocated.

Removal discussions were set aside during the presidency of James Monroe, but by 1830 the removal talk shifted into high gear under the leadership of President Andrew Jackson. He was determined to clear the Southeast of Indians so industrious white people could have free access to the land and to the mineral deposits underlying it.

That the tribes had been in the region for generations had little bearing on his expansion policies. It also mattered little that the five major tribes involved in the removal plans were highly efficient farmers; some were businessmen. The Removal affected all five of those tribes, but it is the story of the Cherokees that captured the attention of the nation at the time and subsequently.

The Cherokees were arguably the most progressive of all the Indian tribes. By 1830 they had their own alphabet. They had a newspaper, *The Cherokee Phoenix*. They had schools and organized towns—sixty-four of them. The women owned the land—the garden plots where they raised crops for their families—and in this matrilineal society, they had great power, including the right to vote on tribal issues. The Cherokees even had a constitution, patterned after the United States' Constitution. They were progressive farmers and knew mining techniques, learned in gold operations throughout their Georgia homeland.

President Jackson signed the Indian Removal Act in 1830. The Cherokees resisted. Leader John Ross took their case to court, eventually winning a Supreme Court decision, but Jackson ignored the courts and ordered troops to make the Indians leave. All of the tribes resisted removal to some extent.

Nevertheless, the Choctaws relocated first, ceding lands in the Treaty of Dancing Rabbit Creek in 1830. From 1831 to 1834 groups of five hundred to one thousand Choctaws made their way west to the new territory in forced winter migrations, during which an estimated thirty-five hundred of them died.

The Creeks went next, under terms of an agreement in 1836. More than thirty-five hundred Creek men, women and children died either during or immediately after their removal.

The Chickasaws then followed the pathway west in 1837, but because for them the journey was shorter, fewer of their people died as a result of the relocation.

The Seminoles, who had already been forced into Florida, strongly resisted removal, engaging in three separate wars with the United States including one seven-year fight from 1835 to 1842. Ultimately about three thousand Seminoles moved to Indian Territory, but many remained in Florida.

Simultaneous with the efforts by the Seminoles to remain in Florida, the Cherokees pursued efforts to retain their homes in Georgia, Kentucky, Tennessee and North Carolina. As noted, they first sought relief from the courts— and actually won their case. But Jackson's Removal policy overran that legal ruling. With full backing from the president, the State of Georgia began selling Indian lands.

The Cherokees' cultural and learning center at Spring Place Mission was sold in a lottery and converted into a tavern; the Georgia militia attacked the Cherokee capital at New Echota (the original Echota had already been usurped by whites), in the process destroying the printing equipment for the *Cherokee Phoenix*. Then the militia constructed twenty-three log stockades and rounded up the Cherokees, placing them in the outdoor holding pens until they could be sent west. Generally the Cherokees had with them only the limited amount of clothing and personal belongings they had managed to carry as they were forced into the stockades from their homes.

As George Hicks wrote to John Ross in November 1838:

> We are now about to take our final leave and kind farewell to your native land, the country that the great spirit gave our Fathers. . . . It is with sorrow that we are forced . . . to quit the scenes of our childhood . . . we bid a farewell to all we hold dear.

The first wave of Cherokees went west in 1838 in a river removal that took them by boat on a network of waterways including the Mississippi and Arkansas Rivers; subsequently others walked over an eight-hundred-mile route to Indian Territory through intense heat and extreme cold with insufficient food and clothing. About four thousand Cherokees died on the journey. The Cherokee Removal became known as the "Trail of Tears."

Indian removal issues captured ink in the nation's newspapers during the period. A few, mainly religious publications sympathized with the Indian plight and urged compassion. Others provided basic reporting of the removal including numbers and type of transportation with few details that humanized the event.

The *Niles Weekly Register* in Maryland on 10 May 1834 quoted the *Arkansas Gazette*:

> About 540 emigrating Cherokees, from the old nation, east of the Mississippi, passed up the Arkansas a few days ago, in charge of lieut. Harris, U.S.A., on board the steamboat Thomas Yeatman, on their way to join their brethren west of this territory.

The *Constitutional Journal* of 24 November 1836, had this to say about the Creek Removal:

> Emigrating Creeks—The Steamboat Daniel Webster, arrived here on Tuesday last, with a small party of Creek Indians, mostly women and children with wagons. They have encamped a short distance from this place, awaiting the arrival of the balance of their party, with horses, to convey them to their destination.

The term "Trail of Tears" came to symbolize all Indian removals, including the other Southeastern tribes. After the Cherokees, Creeks, Choctaws, Chickasaws and Seminoles had been relocated, they became known as the "Five Civilized Tribes." They had already partly assimilated into white culture, and after Removal they continued earlier efforts to provide education and business opportunity to tribal members.

Subsequently other Indian tribes also were forced to relocate to reservations in Indian Territory.

TRIBES REMOVED TO INDIAN TERRITORY

Arapaho	Iowa	Oto
Caddo	Kansa	Pawnee
Cherokee	Kickapoo	Ponca
Chickasaw	Kiowa	Quapaw
Choctaw	Kiowa-Apache	Seminole
Creek	Lipan Apache	Seneca
Delaware	Missouri	Shawnee
Huron	Modoc	Tonkawa
Illinois Confederacy:	Nez Percé	Wyandot
Fox, Ottawa, Pota-	Omaha	Yuchi
watomi, Sauk	Osage	

The Navajo Long Walk—1864

The United States Army and the Navajos had long-standing disputes that led to the incident known as "The Long Walk." In August 1849 Indian Agent John Calhoun and Col. John Washington met in the Chuska Mountains with Navajos under the leadership of Narbona. As the Indians started to leave, a Mexican with the American troops accused the Navajos of horse theft. The military subsequently fired on the Navajos, killing Narbona.

In September 1861 soldiers at Fort Fauntelroy shot and killed a dozen Navajo women and children. The incident started when the Navajos and the soldiers engaged in a wager on a horse race. When the race started, the horse ridden by the Navajo racer quickly went out of control because the bridle rein had been partially slashed with a knife, so that one pull on it caused it to break.

The Navajo horse subsequently lost the race and the Indians protested. But the race judges, who were all soldiers, ruled against them. The incident escalated until shooting started, leading to the deaths of the Indian women and children.

During that same period slave traders often raided the Navajo camps resulting in thousands of Indians being captured by New Mexicans. The Navajos and some Indian agents attempted to stop the slave trade, but they had little success. Eventually on 30 April 1860, the Navajos attacked Fort Defiance in retaliation for the slave trading. Though the Indians did not capture the fort, they came close.

By the fall of 1862, Brig. Gen. James Henry Carleton and New Mexico Gov. Henry Connelly wanted to stop Indian hostilities, so they agreed to start a war against both the Mescalero Apaches and the Navajos. Col. Christopher "Kit" Carson was assigned as field commander of the troops. The war against the Mescaleros lasted about five months before those Indians were placed on a military reserve at Fort Sumner on the Pecos River (known as Bosque Redondo).

In April 1863 Carleton told the Navajos they needed to relocate at Bosque Redondo by 20 July. After that date any Navajo not at Bosque Redondo would be considered hostile. Carson made his way to Fort Defiance arriving there on 20 July and beginning his military operation against the Navajos just two days later. Employing a scorched-earth policy, troops destroyed peach trees, hogans, water holes, animals and cornfields. Troops were paid a bounty for captured sheep, horses and mules.

On 6 January 1864 Carson raided the starving Navajos at Canyon de Chelly (Arizona). Subsequently some nine thousand Navajos surrendered at Fort Wingate and at Fort Canby. From January through March 1864, about eight thousand of them were forced to march to the Bosque Redondo Reservation (New Mexico). The march became known as "The Long Walk," and hundreds of Navajos died en route. The Navajos remained as prisoners at Bosque Redondo until 1868 when they were finally allowed to return to their traditional homeland, though some had earlier escaped and returned to their territory.

As discussions started about moving the Navajos from Bosque Redondo in 1868, there was talk of sending them to Texas or to Indian Territory. Navajo spokesman Barboncito told peace commissioners Gen. William T. Sherman and Col. Samuel F. Tappan: "I hope to God you will not ask me to go to any other country except my own. . . . We do not want to go to the right or left, but straight back to our own country."

The Flight of the Nez Percé—1877

The Nez Percé tribes had received a reservation in the Wallowa Valley of Oregon under a treaty in 1855, but in 1877 they were ordered onto the smaller Lapwai Reservation in Idaho. Five bands of the Nez Percé refused to go; they became known as the nontreaty Nez Percé. Some of the young men killed settlers in Idaho and the five bands then decided to leave the region.

They had various battles with federal troops (see Nez Percé War of 1877 on page 57), as they made their way north and east. They intended first to go to the eastern plains of Montana Territory, to take refuge with the Crows. However, by the time the Nez Percés reached the Crow country, they had had too many run-ins with the army, and the Crows did not want them to stay. So the Nez Percés continued on the move, heading north to Montana's Judith Basin. They were headed toward Canada, where they hoped to find refuge with Hunkpapa chief Sitting Bull, of the Lakota, who had gone there in 1876 following the Battle of the Little Bighorn.

The Nez Percés believed they had outrun the army and in northern Montana, just forty miles from the Canadian border, they slowed to allow the women, children and elderly people an opportunity to rest. However, the military had sent another detachment their way, and on 30 September the soldiers attacked. The battle and subsequent siege lasted five days, until finally on 4 October Chief Joseph surrendered at the Bear Paw Battlefield in northern Montana.

Nez Percé Chief Joseph, before 1877.
(William H. Jackson, National Archives,
106-IN-205)

In his celebrated speech Joseph said:

> Tell General Howard I know his heart. What he told me before I have in my heart. I am tired of fighting. Our chiefs are killed. Looking Glass is dead. Toohoolhoolzote is dead. The old men are all dead. It is the young men who say yes or no. He who led on the

young men is dead. It is cold and we have no blankets. The little children are freezing to death. My people, some of them, have run away to the hills, and have no blankets, no food; no one knows where they are—perhaps freezing to death. I want to have time to look for my children and see how many of them I can find. Maybe I shall find them among the dead. Hear me, my chiefs. I am tired; my heart is sick and sad. From where the sun now stands I will fight no more forever.—Harper's Weekly, *17 November 1877*

Upon surrendering, Chief Joseph and the Nez Percés were first taken to Fort Benton, Montana Territory, then loaded onto steamboats and taken down-river to Indian Territory. They were forced to share lands there, primarily a two-square-mile reservation of the Modocs, until finally returned to the Colville Reservation in Washington. Chief Joseph was never allowed to return to his home country, the Wallowa Valley of Oregon.

Some of the Nez Percés did make it to Canada. Though many of them eventually returned to join other tribal members at Colville, others continued to live in Canada through the rest of the century.

Dawes Severalty Act of 1887
Affecting tribes throughout the West, the Dawes Severalty Act provided for division of Indian Lands in 40-, 60-, 90-, or 120-acre allotments, based on family size. Once Indians had been allotted their lands, the remaining area could be distributed to whites under provisions of the Homestead Act of 1862.

The allotment process divided the land into Indian-owned property or individual allotments, tribal trust property, non-Indian fee lands and lands controlled by missions or the federal Bureau of Indian Affairs. Therefore, in addition to reducing the amount of land owned and controlled by Indian people, the Dawes Act implementation created problems because Indians then owned land in many cases in a checkerboard pattern with non-Indians. There also were problems associated with heirship interests, distribution of income from leased lands or development of resources such as minerals or timber, as well as misuse of lands by nontribal leaseholders.

GENERAL TRIBAL CONDITIONS

Arctic
In 1741 Vitus Bering first encountered native people in what became Alaska, when he met Aleuts on the Shumagin Islands. Russian fur traders also made their way to the Arctic region, eventually claiming it for Russia. Russian Orthodox missionaries followed Russian traders to the region, exposing local residents to Orthodox Christianity by the middle of the nineteenth century, except in the extreme northeastern area, where missionary influence didn't begin until late in the century, after the Americans had obtained control of the region in 1867.

After 1850 whaling ships routinely worked and traded in the region, supplying natives with a variety of goods such as firearms, ammunition, lead, matches, flour, crackers, molasses and tobacco. Commercial salmon fishing began in the 1880s and continued through the century.

California

The lifestyle of several of California's Indian tribes was altered as a result of mission establishment by Spanish friars who encouraged the Indians to live and work at the missions, in certain cases making the native people virtual slaves to the missions. In 1834 California's governor secularized the Indian missions. The grounds were converted into towns or pueblos, and the land was to be distributed among the neophytes, with each head of a family to receive thirty-three acres as well as a portion of the mission livestock, seeds and tools. However, in reality few of the Indians ever obtained or kept any land.

Some of the Indians gambled and lost their land. Others moved to towns such as Los Angeles, where they began drinking alcohol and where they had difficulty finding work. Indian *alcaldes*, or judicial officers, attempted to protect the rights of the Indians, but many Indians were forced to work on public projects. In essence they became slaves to the system working for the government. By 1847 the Indian district in Los Angeles was torn down. Residents of that district who had jobs as servants moved in to live with people for whom they worked. Other Indians established residences outside the city or were forced to live in jails or public works facilities.

The native people of California fared no better under the United States, which successfully took California from Mexican control in the Mexican-American War of 1846. The 125,000 or so Indians in the region when the Americans claimed California soon saw their homelands overrun with gold seekers. Many Indians in the gold region were simply exterminated by the gold miners. Some Indians actively mined for gold, though they often suffered from lack of knowledge about white measurements. For example, gold merchants used a two-ounce counterweight when determining the value of gold brought in by Indian miners (rather than the standard one-ounce counterweight), calling the Indian amount a "Digger ounce." The name "Digger" came from the word used to describe many of the tribes, who relied on digging sticks to procure much of their food supply.

By the end of the nineteenth century, many California tribes had been pushed to the brink of extinction.

Northeast

The five tribes of the Iroquois League—the People of the Longhouse—were the Senecas, known as the Keepers of the Western Door (for their tribal location at the western side of the region); the Mohawks, known as the Keepers of the Eastern Door (for their location in the east); and the three central tribes: Cayuga, Oneida and Onondaga. Because the five tribes represented the longhouse, they were said to be the five fires (and they in turn called the original thirteen American colonies the thirteen fires). Later the Five Fires became the Six Nations with involvement from the Tuscarora.

String and wampum belt. (National Archives, 106-IN-18A)

All great councils of the confederacy took place at the Onondaga fire, and they subsequently became known as the "firekeepers." They also maintained the League's archives and thus became the "wampum keepers." The tribes of the Iroquois practiced a custom of including a gift at any time an important statement was made. Wampum (tubes or disks of shell strung together like belts or necklaces) became the preferred gift, and ultimately it was exchanged on the occasion of any important statement or whenever a treaty was negotiated. Wampum eventually became a type of currency and was particularly used during the fur trade period of the 1800s.

The Iroquois League decided important issues in council, which comprised chiefs from the tribes, with the chiefs designated to differing groups or classes. All the tribes had clans or kinship groups descended from a common ancestor.

By 1800 most of the tribes in the Northeast were located on lands that were regions smaller than their ancestral territories, and they engaged in farming or subsisted on the money they obtained from white farmers who rented reservation lands. The tribes no longer relied on hunting to provide food for their families, though whaling provided jobs for those living near the coast. Population declines were significant in many cases through the century and actually resulted in the extinction of some tribes during the period. Indians of southern New England and Long Island by 1800 lived a lifestyle similar to English people in the region. English-style houses and household goods replaced their wig-wams, and they wore clothes in the English style as well. By 1786 most Mahicans had established farms; the women raised sheep, spun wool and wove cloth to provide for their families and earn funds for other goods. By 1800 the Stock-bridge Indians lived in villages modeled after rural white communities.

The Delaware Indians of the Northeast by 1800 had been pushed west, establishing themselves on reservations in present Kansas, Missouri and Okla-homa. There they raised crops and became involved in frontier occupations such as stock raising, army scouting and fur trapping.

The fire of the Iroquois League, which had been at Onondaga, in the latter part of the eighteenth century was rekindled in two locations: at the Buffalo Creek Reservation in the United States (in present New York State) and at the Six Nations Reserve in Canada. Establishment of the reservations—and requirements that the tribal members live on reservation lands—reduced the importance of the tribe and confederacy. Following the Compromise Treaty of 1842, tribal lands were further reduced, leading to additional changes in tribal governing. In 1848 the Senecas on the Allegany and Cattaraugus reserva-tions, threatened with removal to Kansas, adopted a constitution that estab-lished an elected council to replace the traditional council of chiefs.

The tribal members became divided in their religious practices as well. Some practiced the Longhouse religion as advocated by Handsome Lake start-ing in 1799, and others followed the teachings of Christian missionaries or Quakers.

As a result of both the development of reservations and the general en-croachment of whites onto their traditional lands, the Iroquois after 1820 found themselves relying less on traditional lifestyle practices and more on modern practices. Women had traditionally tended fields and harvested crops while men spent their time engaged in war or hunting. The restrictions on movement and subsequent decline in game left men unable to continue their traditional activities at the same levels; therefore, some men began working fields (previously women did field work). Further, they used plows, wagons and oxen, rather than planting by hand.

Annuities paid as part of treaty stipulations gave the people funds to pay for work by blacksmiths or gunsmiths and to purchase goods such as blankets, cloth, guns, powder, axes, hoes, shovels, knives, lead and flints, chisels, nails, scissors, needles, sheet iron and kettles. They also bought yarn, thread, beads, ribbons, vermillion, spoons, plates, mirrors, tobacco, paper, shawls and even silk handkerchiefs. Previously they had traded for those items or not had them at all.

Southeast

These tribes had similar cultural traits. For the most part they lived in towns or chiefdoms located on or near the banks of streams or rivers so they could plant crops in the fertile bottomlands. Larger towns spread back into the woods along the rivers with a series of trails connecting the residential areas. Towns had central plazas that were the ceremonial center of the town. Each plaza had a flat field where ceremonies and ball games took place, a summer council house and a circular town house. The Cherokees called that circular house a *tcokofa* and used it for winter meetings and some celebrations. Visitors to the Cherokee communities also stayed in the tcokofa as did elderly people who had no kin.

Cherokee communities had town councils, which made decisions regarding everyday life of the residents. Sometimes towns formed alliances with other towns and some of the alliances involved the entire nation. At that highest level of government, major debates occurred related to trade, war or peace. Generally anyone could speak at a council meeting.

Cherokees began assimilating—much of it by force—into white culture in the early 1800s. The tribe accepted missionaries, who established schools where the children learned English, geography and arithmetic. The tribe created a new central government with the power to override town councils, and the people abandoned the practice of blood revenge (where someone killed another to atone for a killing or other misdeed) in exchange for judicial power vested in the central government. Even property ownership changed under the new government so a man's property could be inherited by his wife and children (similar to European practice), rather than by his sister and her children under matrilineal rules.

In 1827 the Cherokees adopted a new constitution—modeled after the Constitution of the United States—that provided for executive, legislative and judicial branches of government. With the Indian Removal Act of 1830, most Cherokees were ultimately forced to leave their homes in Georgia, Kentucky, Tennessee and North Carolina and reestablish themselves in Indian Territory. The removal divided the Cherokee people into two different factions, with bitterness remaining throughout the century. John Ross led the National Party, which opposed removal, while John Ridge led the pro-removal Treaty Party.

Ridge, one of the Cherokee leaders who supported removal in part to avoid conflict with whites, pointed out to a northern audience:

> You asked us to throw off the hunter and warrior state: We did so. You asked us to form a republican government: We did so— adopting your own as a model. You asked us to cultivate the earth, and learn the mechanical arts: We did so. You asked us to learn to read: We did so. You asked us to cast away our idols, and worship your God: We did so.

Cherokees who voluntarily moved to the West when first asked to do so became known as the Cherokee of the West, the Arkansas Cherokee or the Old Settlers.

The Creeks (also called Muskogee) had warriors; a group called the second men, who were responsible for internal affairs at a town such as taking care of the square ground, building houses and cultivating gardens; and the beloved old men, who were the elders, valued for their wisdom. At council meetings the warriors, second men and beloved old men each had the opportunity to express opinions. Additionally the *yatika* or "interpreter" and the *holibonaya* or "war speaker" could address the council. Prior to any council meeting, those present drank a ritual tea made from the twigs and dried leaves of the holly shrub, which they called "white drink" though it later became known as "black drink." They also smoked sacred tobacco.

Creeks belonged to one of two sides or "fires" known by their colors: red or white. Someone from the same fire would be *anhissi* or "my friend" while someone from the other fire was *ankipaya* or "my enemy." The Red towns and the White towns had competitive ball games each summer, preceded by ritual observances. If a Red town lost three years in a row to a White town, it might be required to convert—thus becoming a White town.

Southeastern tribes also had clans, which were more important even than towns because clan ties were as strong as family ties. The clans served as both police and court systems, and a clan could be counted on to help in times of need. Southeastern clans were matrilineal, so children became members of their mother's clan. A girl learned skills from her mother, while a maternal uncle taught boys. Clans held annual meetings, generally in the fall. Creek clans included turkey, bear, alligator, beaver, deer, panther, wolf, wild potato, eagle, raccoon and supernatural beings called wind people. Cherokee clans were wolf, wild potato, bird, blue, deer, paint and twisted or long hair.

Like the Cherokees, the Choctaws had taken advantage of opportunities advanced by whites. The Choctaws in the early 1800s believed education was a key to their survival, and in 1816 they signed a treaty ceding land along the Tombigbee River, their eastern boundary. Funds derived as a result supported schools and that, leaders believed, would help with future relations involving the United States government; the United States, however, saw it as a lever. Those Choctaws who refused to assimilate into white culture would be removed to the Indian Territory. Traditionally, the Choctaw leadership was vested in all adult men of the tribe, but changes approved in the 1820s called for an elected, representative government. The result was near civil war among the tribe that culminated in the Treaty of Dancing Rabbit Creek (1830), which ceded tribal lands, forcing the Choctaws to take the Trail of Tears west.

In 1818 the first Protestant missionaries had arrived among the Choctaws and established schools, a total of eleven by 1830. The Choctaws already had influential, educated mixed-blood families descended from white traders who intermarried within the tribe, and the mixed-blood families produced tribal leaders who were loyal Choctaw patriots in disputes and negotiations with the United States throughout the nineteenth century.

In 1824 the first Choctaw lawyer, James Lawrence McDonald, was admitted to the bar, after studying law in the office of Judge John McLean in Ohio (who later became a justice of the Supreme Court). The Choctaws had sent McDonald to the East when he was fourteen to be privately tutored by the Rev. Dr. Carnahan (who later became president of Princeton College). McDonald negotiated the Treaty of Washington of January 1825 for the Choctaws, prompting Commissioner of Indian Affairs Thomas McKinney to say, "I found him so skilled in the business of his mission . . . as to make it more of an up-hill business than I had ever before experienced in negotiating with Indians. I believe Mr. Calhoun [U.S. Secretary of War] thought so too." McDonald refused to listen to new United States treaty demands until the government had first fulfilled all its unmet obligations from previous Choctaw treaties, many of which were satisfied by new monetary awards to support Choctaw schools.

Also in 1825 a young Choctaw named Peter Perkins Pitchlynn lead the first group of Choctaw boys on horseback to the Choctaw Academy in Kentucky. Many future Choctaw leaders were educated there until 1841, when the Choctaws began building nine similar academies in the Choctaw Nation in Indian Territory for both boys and girls. Choctaws sent their most promising graduates to Dartmouth, Union, Yale and other colleges.

In 1834 the Choctaws established a new tribal constitution; in 1841 they took over control of schools that had been run by missionaries; and by 1861 had a representative form of government in place. The divisions that led to the Treaty of Dancing Rabbit Creek remained, however, and not all members of the tribe resettled in Indian Territory, creating two distinct bands: The Mississippi Band of Choctaw Indians and the Choctaw Nation of Oklahoma, which developed separate governments.

The Seminoles, meanwhile, established towns and had social structures that were identical to those of the Creeks. They relied on farming, fishing and gathering of wild plants for sustenance and relocated to Indian Territory only following long and harsh warfare with the U.S. army.

Great Basin

For the most part, Great Basin tribes were poor people who lived in a harsh climate that required most of their energies for survival. They lived in simple, seldom permanent houses, wore clothes made of furs and natural fibers and ate such foods as grubs, insects, rabbits and occasionally larger animals.

The Western Shoshones lived mainly in small bands and had loose organization involving no true tribal leaders. Without military or political structure, they seldom engaged in warfare, but spent most of their time simply obtaining food, clothing and shelter needed for mere survival. They became known by a variety of names such as Seed Eaters, Earth Eaters, Root Eaters, Sheep Eaters, and Diggers.

The Northern Shoshones, however, were more influenced by the tribes of the Great Plains and the Rocky Mountains, and they did have some limited tribal structure even though, like their Western cousins, resources were sparse and life a constant struggle. They did engage in some tribal gatherings, including holding Sun Dances each year (for more information on Sun Dances, see page 225).

Jesuit priest Fr. Pierre De Smet observed some of the Indians in the region in what is now northern Utah, writing of them:

> There is not, very likely, in all the universe a more miserable, more degraded and poorer people. . . . The land they inhabit is a veritable waste. They lodge in crevices of the rocks, or in holes dug in the earth; they have no clothing; their only weapons are a bow and arrows and a pointed stick; they range the barren plains in search of ants and grasshoppers, on which they feed, and they think it a feast when they come upon a few tasteless roots or nauseous grains. . . . Their number is unknown, for they are seldom seen more than two, three or four together. They are so timid that a stranger would have a good deal of trouble to approach them.
> —The Life, Letters and Travels of Father Pierre-Jean De Smet, S.J. *by Hiram Martin Chittenden and Albert Talbot Richardson, 1905; from* American Indian Almanac, *Terrell, 385.*

The Utes ranged in a territory that is now western Colorado, eastern Utah and portions of New Mexico along the San Juan River. More organized than some of their other Shoshonean cousins, they routinely raided Spanish and Mexican pueblos and ranchos, and later raided the farms and settlements of the Mormons in Deseret (Utah). Closely allied (and intermarried with) the Jircarilla Apaches, they regularly joined in attacks with that tribe. They became involved in slave trading when they captured Western Shoshones and traded them to the Spanish in New Mexico where they received knives, guns, ammunition and clothing in exchange. Eventually the Utes expanded their slave raids as far west as California and east onto the plains of Colorado and Kansas.

Each Ute band was autonomous with no central tribal government, though they did have a military organization (particularly in the 1800s when they regularly raided to obtain slaves).

The Pyramid Lake Paiute tribe was placed on a reservation in 1858–59, which led to the brief Pyramid Lake War of 1860. Non-Indian ranchers took some productive farmland and others grazed cattle on the reservation without authority to do so. Other developments occurred as well, including fishing, hunting and settlement of towns that had not been approved by the tribe.

Interior Plateau

The basic social units in the Plateau area were the village and band. Tribal development occurred after contact with whites. Among most tribes there were no clans, so the main unit of the people was the band. For most Interior Plateau tribes, chieftainship generally descended from father to son, though local opinion could change the selection in some cases. A chief had little or no authoritative power, though people would follow his wishes because of his character and past accomplishments.

Cataclysmic events affected the tribes during the 1800s, including encroachment by explorers, fur trappers and traders and other whites who brought with them deadly diseases: smallpox, measles, influenza and fevers, so that by 1850 tribal populations had declined by about half from their number in 1800.

Perhaps more than in any other region, Plateau society involved significant intermingling among tribes as individuals intermarried, routinely traded with each other, joined together in seasonal tasks ranging from fishing to gathering food, spoke each other's languages and even lived in each other's villages.

From their willingness to assist Lewis and Clark on their expedition in 1805–6, the tribes showed their peaceful tendencies. They usually avoided confrontation with each other and with Europeans; they reserved fighting efforts for conflicts with the Crows, Blackfeet and Shoshones.

Development of both Protestant and Catholic missions in the 1830s and later years affected village lifestyle, and after 1843 travelers (settlers) on the Oregon Trail further impacted the tribes.

Northwest Coast

Northwest Coast tribes had highly organized communities divided into three classes: chiefs, commoners and slaves. It was unlikely anyone born into one class could ever rise to the one above it, and there were no clans, except among the Haidas. Initially Haidas also had villages comprised of a single clan, though by the end of the 1800s more than one clan shared a village. Salishan chiefs had little or no authority because rank was social; there were no political ties between different small settlements. In most cases all people in a Kwakiutl village were descendants of the same man. Though chiefs had little real authority, succession was hereditary.

These were among the most prosperous of all Indian tribes in part due to the rich bounty of the land, which had abundant game, fish and plants, and a mild (though wet) climate. Outside traders established regular routes to the region providing a conduit of goods from European and Russian suppliers, so by the early 1800s Indians in the region could obtain such goods as knives, cooking pots and cloth or non-native clothing.

Plains

Plains Indians were highly democratic people without heredity classes who relied primarily on hunting and gathering, though a few of the tribes on the fringes of the plains and prairie spent considerable time and energy on growing crops. The primary food supply for Plains tribes was bison, abundant across the region and an animal that met many other needs, such as providing materials for shelter and clothing. Most Plains Indian settlements were tightly clustered groups of lodges made of hides (primarily) or other materials such as grass, earth and the like. Some settlements had "fortresses" such as palisades or even waterways like moats around them to provide security for inhabitants. Other settlements were situated along streams and rivers.

The Plains people had organization in tribes, with individual groups or bands led by leaders who served at the will of the people. The earth lodge village people (such as the Mandans and Hidatas) had common social and ceremonial organizations, and they routinely saw each other. The nomadic Plains tribes, however, gathered villages or bands together only during spring and summer ceremonials to participate in the Sun Dance and to reorganize military societies. Otherwise they remained in smaller band units, which could more easily find food and shelter.

Plains tribes had military and social societies. Though some tribes warred against others from their cultural groups, alliances also were formed, particularly after struggles involved the frontier army.

Plains tribes had large horse herds in the 1800s providing them with mobility and wealth. They had regions or territories to rely upon for hunting, and some tribes had fairly permanent village sites where they raised crops. But most did not believe they owned the land, instead they lived from it and used it as needed.

The Arikaras held land in family groups or as corporate property. As Meriwether Lewis and William Clark reported: "They claim no land except that on which their villages stand and the fields which they cultivate." Their fields were plots of about one and one-half acres with each family marking its own plot through the use of pole-and-brush fences.

Leadership was vested in individuals who had won respect for their deeds. Intertribal warfare predominated in the early part of the century and continued throughout most of it with members of one tribe raiding and attacking those of another tribe. Each tribe had men who stood out as leaders. Though not all tribes referred to such individuals as chiefs, some did have organized chieftainships. In almost all cases a chief served only because others wanted to follow his leadership; he could not compel anyone to obey. Some chiefs served many years, others might be leaders only for a single battle or raid.

The Cheyennes had a system of forty-four chiefs including an executive chief, four head-chiefs (representing each of the four directions) and forty men of authority or counselors. Initially chiefs were elected every eight years, but later they were chosen every four years. When discussing issues, the executive chief sat by the lodge door listening to the comments of all others in the lodge; when he spoke and made a decision it was final. Though the Cheyennes were once together, in the early 1800s they divided into two groups, the Northern Cheyenne and the Southern Cheyenne.

The Wichita tribe had four bands (Isiis, Tawakoni or Tawakudi, Wichita and Waco or Weeko), each with a chief and subchief. Wichita chiefs were elected, but their rule was primarily a parliamentary position and subchiefs likewise served at the will of the people. The Wichitas relied on agriculture for subsistence and erected permanent lodges known as grass-houses; thus they became the "Grass-House People."

The tribe referred to as the Sioux throughout the century originally lived in the Upper Midwest, relocating to the plains in the 1700s. They belong to three dialect groups and are from several tribes. The eastern group, or Santee, are Dakota and include the Wahpekute, Sisseton, Wahpeton and Mdewakanton tribes. The middle group, or Nakota, includes the Yankton and Yanktonais tribes (Ihanktonwan and Ihanktonwanna) as well as the Assiniboines during the prereservation era. The best-known group is the western or Teton Sioux or Lakota, which comprises the Oglala, Hunkpapa, Miniconjou, Sans Arc (Itazipacola), Brûlé (Sicangu), Sihasapa (Blackfeet) and Two Kettle (Oohenunpa) bands. The name Sioux comes from the Chippewa (or combined French and Ojibwa) name for them—*Nadouessioux*—meaning "adders" or "little snake."

Though called Sioux throughout the 1800s, they are more properly addressed as Dakota, Nakota or Lakota, or by individual tribal names. Thus the Sioux chief Crazy Horse is most properly called Crazy Horse, leader of one band of the Oglala Lakota. Red Cloud led a different band of Oglala Lakota.

The first major treaty with Northern Plains Indians was negotiated at Fort Laramie in 1851, and it established territorial boundaries. The Southern Plains tribes had in 1835 agreed to the treaty of Camp Holmes that likewise identified Indian territories. Subsequent treaties—none of which were fully followed—diminished those same territories and required the Indians to move onto reservations. Though some remain on smaller portions of their original territorial lands, others are far removed from such locations.

Prairies and Woodlands

Forests and water bodies provided for the Prairie and Woodland tribes who hunted, fished and gathered a variety of foods and building materials from both. In an intermediate zone between the Northeastern tribes and the Plains groups, those of the Prairies and Woodlands also farmed, raising corn and squash. They assumed an important place in the trade relations of many nations due to their middle position between western tribes, which were the first to have horses, and eastern tribes, which first had guns.

The tribes had clans and bands that often revolved around the nuclear family. And all Prairie and Woodland tribes had formal leadership with legislative, executive and judicial authority vested in chiefs, subchiefs and leading men. They had both civil and war chiefs, and some chiefly positions were hereditary. In addition, there were tribal councils and military societies that maintained order in villages and on hunting expeditions.

Through the 1800s the Prairie and Woodland tribes were relegated to reservations and in many cases removed from their traditional territories to resettle in Indian Territory. By the end of the century most of their lands had been divided by allotment, so individuals rather than tribes owned it.

Though closely related to the Chippewas, the Crees had no clans. Chippewa bands and groups in larger geographical regions had individual chiefs who served based on ability, not inheritance. In large camps the Unimihituwuk (soldier societies) maintained order, especially during tribal ceremonies.

Southwest

In 1812 a Spanish constitution provided that pueblos should be allowed to elect their own municipal governments. Though the Spanish constitution considered a pueblo simply a Spanish town, Spain's governor in New Mexico interpreted it to include the Pueblo Indians. This meant that Indians, who had earlier been classified as inferior citizens, now had equal standing with other Spaniards, including the right to vote or run for office. By the late 1820s, most pueblos had elected municipal governments, although those governments were short-lived. Earlier Pueblo tribal leaders had been given canes of authority from the Spanish government; the holder of the cane served as the leader of the pueblo. (The authority of the canes was reiterated by the United States after it claimed the region in 1846.)

On 24 August 1821 the Treaty of Cordoba provided for Mexican independence and guaranteed personal rights, racial equality and the preservation of private property. Indians received Mexican citizenship, and their lands were to be protected. By the 1830s the Pueblo Indians began practicing rituals in public that had been conducted in hiding and in secrecy due to Spanish rule. By 1837 all of the municipal governments—or home rule—of the pueblos were abolished and a new system was implemented. It divided the province into districts that were governed by appointed prefects, but traditional Pueblo government continued under the *caciques* (chieftain).

The cacique, according to trader Josiah Gregg, had a significant role in Pueblo administration:

> When any public business is to be transacted, [the cacique] gathers together the principal chiefs of the Puebla in an *estufa*, or cell, usually underground, and there lays before them the subjects of debate, which are generally settled by the opinion of the majority. No Mexican is admitted to these councils, nor do the subjects of discussion ever transpire beyond the precincts of the cavern. The council also has charge of the interior police and tranquility [*sic*] of the village.

The cavern referred to was the *kiva* (a circular worship area) at the pueblo.

As a result of territorial changes—when the Southwest passed from Spanish control to Mexican dominion—Pueblo tribes lost some of their land and water rights. In the arid region concerns over land and water rights continued after 1846 when the United States obtained control of the region. (Some of those same issues are still tribal concerns.)

Village organization was fairly structured for the Pimans and Papagos. Agricultural lands generally surrounded compounds of houses causing a certain amount of settlement sprawl. That was held in check by the need to use common wells or water sources, the desire to build on ridges and high ground to avoid floods and the need to stick close for security reasons. In the space between the houses and other structures—which never touched each other—

and the fields, the tribes had cleared areas used for ceremonies, collectively called "The Ceremonial Cycle." The areas were never crossed or stepped onto except for ritual and ceremonial use.

The Pima and Papago people had meeting areas in each village—typically a round house similar to a dwelling, but one where no one lived. An open-roofed sunshade stood to the east of the dwelling, and even farther east was a fireplace where nightly meetings took place. No meetings actually took place inside the house, but it needed to be close enough to the family dwelling so those people the farthest from it could hear when someone hollered that there was to be a meeting—since that was the way tribal members were summoned. Some Pimans called their meeting house the "smoking house" since "smoking" also meant "to have a meeting."

The Apaches generally had no chief or organized political authority, though individual bands or local groups had a leader or "chief." Among the local chiefs were Mangas Coloradas, Cochise, Naiche and Victorio. Usually a band involved from three to five local groups.

Attributes of Western Apache chiefs included industriousness, generosity, impartiality, forbearance, conscientiousness and eloquence. Chiefs never traveled alone, and they did not do menial work such as collecting firewood. Often their homes were larger than those of other people.

ADDITIONAL READING

Barrett, S.M. *Geronimo's Story of His Life*. Harrisburg, PA: The National Historical Society, 1994; originally printed by Duffield & Company, New York, 1906.

Burton, Jeffrey. *Indian Territory and the United States, 1866–1906*. Norman: University of Oklahoma Press, 1995.

Gilbert, Joan. *The Trail of Tears Across Missouri*. Columbia: University of Missouri Press, 1995.

Gregg, Josiah. *Commerce of the Prairies, Vols. 1 and 2*. Norman: University of Oklahoma Press, 1990; originally published by Henry G. Langley, New York, 1844.

Kissinger, Rosemary K. *Quanah Parker Comanche Chief*. Gretna, LA: Pelican Publishing, 1991.

Larson, Robert W. *Red Cloud: Warrior-Statesman of the Lakota Sioux*. Norman: University of Oklahoma Press, 1997.

O'Brien, Sharon. *American Indian Tribal Governments*. Norman: University of Oklahoma Press, 1993.

Paul, R. Eli, ed. *Autobiography of Red Cloud: War Leader of the Oglalas*. Helena: Montana Historical Society, 1997.

Waldman, Carl. *Atlas of the North American Indian*. Rev. ed. New York: Facts on File, 2000. An indispensable guide with concise commentary, maps and timelines.

CHAPTER TWO

TRADE

T he first white people to settle in North America eased their harsh lives by trading with the native inhabitants of the region for food and other products. But as time passed the Europeans imported goods that were useful to the Indians, ranging from clothing to cooking implements and even to weapons. By 1800 Northeastern and Southeastern tribes had well-established trade practices, including centralized trade centers. Many women from Southeastern tribes even married white traders in order to further trade relations.

When Meriwether Lewis and William Clark made their way into the country of the Louisiana Purchase in 1804, they had several goals. One of them involved establishing trade with Indians in the region. Though Lewis and Clark and subsequent American traders did bring a wide variety of goods to the tribes along the Missouri River and in the Pacific Northwest, the tribes there had already established trade with whites—primarily the French traders of the North West Company and the British traders of the Hudson's Bay Company. These traders had worked their way west across Canada and then South into the region encompassing the northern reaches of the Louisiana Purchase. The Indians also had established relations with Spanish traders who had made their way north from Mexico.

Besides those trading opportunities, Indians had routinely traded with each other, and there were solidly established trading locations and routes used by Indian people throughout the country. In the region west of the Mississippi River, in a very general sense, the agrarian tribes traded products they raised such as corn, beans and squash with the hunting tribes who had bison and other furs. Indians from the Southwest brought such items as turquoise or metal bells, while those from the Northwest often traded horses and dried salmon for different food products or bison hides.

Indians of almost every tribe at one time or another engaged in trade practices with other tribes. There were some specific trading locations and routes.

The Old Spanish Trade Route was a trail linking the northeastern Plains region (North and South Dakota, Nebraska and Wyoming) with the Southwest (primarily the Santa Fe region). Indian trade rendezvous were conducted regularly along the Missouri in present eastern South Dakota; on the James River at the Dakota Rendezvous involving the Teton, Yankton and Yanktonai Sioux, along with the Sissetons; in present southwestern Wyoming involving the Utes, Nez Percés, Shoshones and Flatheads; and at various locations in the Southwest.

Indian gatherings for trading purposes were conducted on a routine basis—often annually—and were the forerunner to the mountain man trading opportunities known as rendezvous. Of course, the Indians also participated in those mountain man rendezvous (1825–43) routinely exchanging such things as furs, or even the use of their women, for such products as kettles, guns, ammunition and blankets.

Trade items available at the centers were diverse because a variety of tribes not only made pilgrimages to those trading centers to exchange goods, but also conducted trade in other regions. For example, the Crees routinely made trades with the North West and Hudson's Bay companies in Canada, and then brought some of the items they obtained there (such as Hudson's Bay point blankets) to use in negotiating further trades at Knife River (in North Dakota) or the Arikara villages. Apaches or Indians from the eastern Pueblos in the Southwest likewise brought goods north bartering deer hides, turquoise and Spanish or Mexican trade bells for blankets or corn. Such exchanges meant goods primarily available in Canada could eventually reach the Southwest tribes who brought their own trade items north.

Trading also created a movement of goods between tribes in the east and west. Catlinite (red or black pipestone) used in manufacture of pipe bowls, for example, was a popular trade item from its primary location in present Minnesota. It could be exchanged for any variety of trade goods, such as shells from the Pacific coastal tribes, turquoise from the Southwest or blankets from Canada. Little of the early trade involved furs, more of it was an exchange of food and leather goods such as moccasins, leggings or skin shirts.

When Pierre la Verendrye explored the upper plains in 1738–39, he found the Mandans trading "grain and beans of which they have an ample supply" for dressed skins and porcupine quills. He noted that the trading began "every year, at the beginning of June [lasting] over a month." (Pierre G.V. la Verendrye, *Journals and Letters of Pierre Gaultier de Varennes de la Verendrye and His Sons*, 336–38)

By the time Lewis and Clark made their way to the Mandan villages in 1804, they found the Indians routinely trading there for riding gear, horses, mules, tools, household utensils, weapons and clothing.

Horses became important trade items in the period between 1739, when la Verendrye visited the region, and 1804 when Lewis and Clark were there. The horse, which was first obtained by tribes near Mexico, had been brought to that region by Spanish conquistadors. Then the horse moved north via two major trade routes. The main one extended across the western high plains involving the Arapahos, Cheyennes, Kiowas, Kiowa-Apaches and the Comanches. A second trade route for the horse involved the Shoshonean tribes west of the Continental Divide, as well as the Nez Percé and Flathead people. Mules and Spanish gear, such as saddles, bridles and bits, also made their way from the Southwest and West to the northern plains over the same two trade routes.

Once horses were available, they became important trade items. One report shows the Crows trading 250 horses to the Hidatsas in June 1805 for 200 guns. Horses also were commonly used as trade items for wives, or as payments (similar to a dowry) to a husband or his family from a bride's family.

Ships from a number of countries, including Britain and the United States, routinely visited the Northwest Coast prior to 1800, bringing with them a variety of goods that became trade items such as cloth and metal objects including knives, axes, pots and kettles. After 1800 fewer ships reached the Northwest Coast and those that did were primarily American. They carried such items as copper, brass, iron, cloth, rum, trinkets and muskets, which they traded with the Indians for furs. (Subsequently the American ships went to China, where the furs were traded for tea, porcelain, silk and spices.)

As fur traders and trappers moved into the Canadian and American West, they established trading forts or posts. Among them were posts started by the North West Company: Flathead House on the Snake and Blackfoot rivers in present western Montana; Spokane House on the Spokane River; Fort Colville west of the Pend Orielle River in present northeast Washington (abandoned in 1825); and Fort Nez Percés, located at the confluence of the Columbia and Walla Walla rivers in present southeastern Washington. Other trading posts included Fort Piegan, along the Missouri River at the mouth of the Marias River, which opened for business in 1831, and Fort Union, also along the upper Missouri.

Plateau Indians routinely traded at various other forts and posts including these: Kootenai House (1807), Kootenai Falls (1808, temporary site), Kullyspell House (1809, on Pend Orielle Lake), and Saleesh House (1809, on Clark Fork River).

The trade goods available at mountain man rendezvous and at fur trader posts included blankets and beads and modern implements such as cooking pots, which the Indians soon obtained. They also traded for fabric, particularly calico and red felt trade cloth; the former was used for shirts or dresses and the latter for breechclouts.

The three items that became standard trade gifts for Indian chiefs were flags, ornate, semimilitary coats (called chief's coats) and medals.

At The Dalles (Oregon) the Chinookan tribes along the Northwest Coast traded such items as iron knives, hatchets, and files, copper goods, blankets, wool and cotton cloth and clothes with Plateau tribes who had bison robes, camas root, dried salmon and beargrass.

Plains Indians traded sweetgrass, bison robes and pipestone to the Plateau Indians in exchange for dried salmon and horses or dentalium shells. At trading opportunities in the Boise Valley (Idaho), Plateau tribes met Ute traders who had knives, mules, saddles and other goods from Spanish settlements in New Mexico. In California the Plateau Indians traded such items as dentalium shells, salmon, horses, parfleches and bison robes for such items as metal goods, beads, bows and slaves.

Throughout Indian America, trade practices provided goods and products that made life easier for the native people. As the nineteenth century passed, most tribes included among personal possessions metal cooking and eating utensils, in addition to (in some cases in lieu of) traditionally made pots, kettles and the like. Trade practices also affected clothing styles as Indians began intermixing calico or stroud with buckskin.

Arctic

When Russians established trade relations in western Alaska, they did so to encourage fur trading. They attempted to identify community leaders in the native villages, whom they appointed *toions*. The Russians presented each toion with a silver medal. The toion was expected to encourage his village people to obtain furs for trade with the Russians. The Russians provided glass beads, iron axes, copper bracelets, metal tools and clothing as trade items. The emphasis on fur trading caused Arctic men to engage in that pursuit more and more, while doing less hunting, which ultimately affected the amount of food they could provide for their families. As a result there was increasing dependence for food upon trading posts established by the Russians, and later the Americans, though it was very late in the century before Eskimos became dependent upon such trade.

The variety of trade items increased greatly after the United States obtained Alaska in 1867 and particularly after whaling increased in the 1880s. Items available for trade in 1891 among the Nunivak Eskimos were seal oil and fox and seal skins, which could be exchanged for matches, gunpowder, lead, knives, needles, tobacco, flour and calico.

California

The items most often traded by California Indians were salt, acorns, fish, miscellaneous vegetables, marine shell beads, dentalium shells, clamshell disk beads, whole or broken marine shells, miscellaneous beads (such as those made of stone, berries, nuts or mollusk), baskets and basketry materials, hides and pelts, pigments and paints, bows and obsidian.

The California tribes had regular north-south trade routes that ultimately linked Mexico with Oregon, as well as east-west trade routes linking the Pacific Coast with the Great Basin.

Northeast and Southeast

In the Northeast, regular trade occurred along river routes by Indians who hauled goods in their birchbark canoes. They exchanged copper from the southern shore of Lake Superior for tobacco and wampum. Other trade items included red pipestone (catlinite) from Minnesota, brown pipestone from the Chippewa River (Canada), flint from Ontario and obsidian from the Rocky Mountains to be exchanged for furs, fish and crops. Ultimately the furs were traded with the French.

Indians in the Southeast lowlands traded with those in the uplands, while those along the coast traded with others living in the interior of the region. The Mississippi River became an important trade artery. The single most important trade item in the region was salt. Trading fairs were held, routinely drawing people from a region about sixty miles in circumference. By the 1800s the tribes regularly traded European goods.

Indians throughout a large part of the Southeast used a trade language called Mobilian Trade Jargon, which was a simplified form of Choctaw.

Great Basin

Tribes in the Great Basin engaged in little trading. They lived in a harsh climate and used most of their resources for simple survival. The Shoshones, however, did exchange horses for other goods, since they were able to obtain the animals before other tribes due in part to their cultural connections with the Comanches. The Shoshones regularly participated in the trade rendezvous on the Green River in present southwest Wyoming.

Interior Plateau

The Columbia River trade network that Lewis and Clark tapped into involved several major routes and trade locations. The area of The Dalles (Oregon) was one primary trading spot, as were the Lower Columbian Villages near the mouth of the Columbia at the Pacific. Other trading took place near Kettle Falls (in extreme present northeastern Washington). Of course trade occurred up and down the Columbia River, and along both the Willamette and Deschutes rivers. People of the Eastern Plateau as well as Shoshones traded at a site in present eastern Oregon, along the Snake River (near Farewell Bend, Oregon). Trade routes extended from near that site to a location in present southwestern Wyoming.

Introduction of the horse had a tremendous impact on the Columbia trade network. Early trade items were transported in canoes on rivers or carried overland, but the horse made it possible to haul a much wider variety of goods as well as more of them. Before horses were available, traders carried smaller, lightweight, valuable trade items, but with the horse they could transport even raw or semiprocessed foods and other items. The trade routes no longer followed rivers; instead they went overland in more direct paths. Trading parties increased in size, and the horses themselves became important trade items.

English traveler Henry J. Coke in 1850 wanted to purchase a horse from a Cayuse, showing the Indian some five-dollar gold pieces. The Indian had his own gold pieces, and Coke reported, "The Kayuses were very rich, and wanted nothing. They had plenty of cattle, plenty of corn, plenty of potatoes. When they wanted money, or cloth, or blankets, or paint, they bartered their horses at [Fort] Wallah-Wallah or [settlements along the] Wilamette."

Explorer Wilson Price Hunt in 1811 noted that the Snake Indians had good buffalo robes that they had traded salmon to obtain. With Hunt they traded a horse for glass beads and an old pewter kettle. They refused a gun.

Northwest Coast

Trading between people on the Northwest Coast occurred up and down the coast from Vancouver Island to the mouth of the Columbia. Among the commonly traded items were dentalium shells, copper (from the Copper River in southern Alaska), furs and eventually European goods. The trading along the coast was so widespread that there was a trade language, Chinook Trade Jargon, composed of mostly Chinook words with a few French and English words. Regular trading rendezvous took place near the coast involving several days of trading, feasting, singing and dancing. In 1811 Wilson Price Hunt traded a horse for a canoe noting that the Indians had many canoes, some of them capable of carrying three thousand pounds of gear.

Plains

Plains Indians developed a sign language used in trading between different tribes. Two primary trade centers in the upper plains included the Mandan and Arikara villages along the Knife River (North Dakota) and the Arikara villages at the confluence of the Grand River and Upper Missouri River (South Dakota).

Plains tribes exchanged a variety of products including crops they grew and/ or harvested and products obtained through hunting. Goods included fat, dried meat, prairie-turnip flour, lodges, buffalo robes, furs, dressed hides, and moccasins, shirts and leggings made of buckskin and decorated with quillwork or beadwork, which were often exchanged for tobacco or foods such as corn, pumpkins and beans. After 1800, the agricultural tribes living along the Missouri River had a variety of goods for trading purposes including knives, awls, glass beads, mirrors, guns, powder, bullets and metal kettles.

Horses were traded initially, but by 1800 they had became the most valued form of merchandise or currency for all tribes, so they more often exchanged hands through theft rather than trade (it being the highest honor for a warrior to steal an enemy horse).

In 1811 Wilson Price Hunt explored throughout the West, reporting that the Cheyennes were honest and clean, hunting bison and raising horses to trade to the Arikaras for corn, kidney beans, pumpkins and other merchandise. Hunt gave the chief presents of tobacco, knives, a piece of scarlet cloth, some powder, and bullets.

By the 1800s trading played an important role in the Comanche economy. Comanches established major trade routes, rounding up both horses and slaves to use in trade. Traders from various pueblos or Mexico routinely visited the Comanche camps, and the Comanches made their way to places like Santa Fe and San Antonio missions to engage in trading. In 1789 New Mexican Governor Concha placed restrictions on trade allowing only licensed traders to make their way to the Comanche camps, and then only at the request of the Comanches themselves. Those traders, first known as "viageros" or "travelers," by 1813 became known as "Comancheros."

Among the items traded in the early 1800s were blue and red cloth, blankets, gold wire, vermillion, rifles, knives, needles, scissors, small bells, jingles, beads, ribbon, tobacco, lead, powder, flint, gun rods, mirrors, sombreros and metal buttons.

As Jean Louis Berlandier reported in *The Indians Of Texas in 1830*, Comanches traded with the presidios in the Southwest and Texas. "They bring bear grease, buffalo meat and various furs. They used to go to Santa Fe in New Mexico each year to do their trading. . . . From the villages and presidios they get shot and powder, loaves of sugar called piloncillos, silver ornaments for themselves and their horses and sometimes weapons such as swords which they use to make their lances, or cheap cloth ornaments."

Comanche trade patterns sustained a major change with the establishment of permanent or semipermanent trading posts that were controlled by Europeans rather than by the Comanches. The posts included one started by Thomas James on the North Canadian River in 1823; various forts operated by the Bent family, including the Stockade built about 1825 and the Old Fort established about 1832 in the region of the Upper Arkansas River. The Bents then began sending trading expeditions into Comancheria. In 1842 they built a wood post on the South Canadian River. Meanwhile Holland Coffee had a post on the Red River in 1834, and Auguste Choteau established a post in 1835 at Camp Holmes on the South Canadian River and one on Cache Creek (near Fort Sill) in 1837. The Cache Creek post of Abel Warren at the confluence with the Red River was in operation from 1840 until 1846.

Items traded at Warren's post included red and blue blankets, strips of bright blue cloth, gingham handkerchiefs, hoop iron, glass beads, vermillion and other face paints, calico and brass wire. The latter was twisted around a warrior's forearm to protect it from the recoil when shooting his bow.

Comanches (and other Indians in the region) could obtain a wide variety of products at the Torey Brothers' Trading house in 1844–45 including ticking, brown and blue cloth, calico, broad cloth, stroud (a course woolen cloth), blankets, hats and bonnets, boots and shoes, fringe shawls, combs, brass kettles, drugs and medicines, hair pipes, sugar, coffee, tobacco, flour, salt, fishhooks, hoes, pins, Indian bells, buttons, files, pocket and butcher knives, coffee mills, tinware, skillets, pans, looking glasses, powder, lead, percussion caps, gun tubes, steels and flints (for use in starting fires), soap, rice, beads, brass wire, awls, crockery ware, axes and jews harps.

Prairies and Woodlands

Prairie and Woodland tribes traded food products such as corn, beans and wild rice. Those living near deposits of catlinite (Minnesota) had a valuable commodity to trade since Indians used the unique stone for a variety of pipe bowls. They traded it throughout the continent. These Indians also served as middlemen, trading guns and other European products obtained from Northeastern and Southeastern tribes for horses and furs made available by Plains tribes.

Southwest

The Southwest Indians, who had long had access to Spanish goods, began receiving trade goods from American traders in 1821 with the opening of the Santa Fe Trail from present-day Kansas to Santa Fe. Subsequently they could purchase manufactured goods from the United States including tools, household articles and food items. Because they could obtain such items, some tribes relied less on traditional tools, clothing and the like. For example, weaving was less often used for making cloth for clothing, though it remained in use for sashes and belts, because the Pueblo people could purchase or trade for inexpensive wool and cotton. Likewise, Pueblo people could obtain milled wood and other products—such as glass for windows—that were used in homes and other structures.

The Southwest tribes also traded with each other. The Hopis routinely obtained salt from the Zunis. The Havasupais traded buckskins, baskets and food with the Hopis, Navajos, Walapais and Mohaves for such items as cotton goods, pottery, jewelry, horses and bison hides.

After 1867 trading posts affected the Navajos as traders mediated problems within the tribe and families, bought and sold goods, buried Navajo dead, and filled out forms and wrote letters for the tribal members. The Navajo traders promoted development of crafts, particularly the weaving of Navajo rugs, which they sold in ever-increasing numbers. Among the trading posts were Round Rock, opened in 1885, and the Hubbell Trading Post, opened in 1871 by Charles Crary, but owned and managed by Lorenzo Hubbell after 1876. The Indians traded such items as food, tobacco, goatskins and harnesses for wool and woven blankets. Both locations are still open and operating as traditional Navajo trading posts.

Trade items became common forms of ''currency'' for tribes who had no other type of money. Strings of shell beads known as *hishi* could be exchanged

COMMON TRADES AMONG TRIBES
IN THE SOUTHWEST

Items Traded	*Tribes Involved in Trade*
1 buckskin for 1 blanket	Yavapai—Navajo
2 large buckskins for 1 saddle blanket	Paiute—Havasupai
1 chief's blanket for 1 horse	Navajo—Ute
1 buffalo robe for 1 horse	Hopi—Havasupai, Paiute
1 buffalo robe for 1 chief's blanket	Ute—Navajo
1 long string shell beads for 2 mantas	Eastern Pueblos—Hopi
1 string turquoise for 1 large blanket	Pueblos—Navajo
Few strands of beads for 1 horse	Cochiti—Navajo
1 strand of beads for 1 buckskin	Zuni—Western Apache
1 burden basket of corn for 1 horse	Havasupai—Hopi
3 buckskins for 1 big blanket	Walapai—Havasupai

for other commodities at any time. Certain values were placed on specific items and though some bargaining may have occurred, it was probably fairly limited. For example, in the Southwest a bison skin, a horse, a burden basket filled with corn, a large blanket or a buckskin were all of equal value. And any one of those items was also valued the same as one gun. Goods that had "added value" also were recognized, so that buckskin that was properly tanned was worth generally twice as much as a raw hide. Most trading in the Southwest occurred in the late fall and winter, after harvest and before time to prepare fields for a new year of production.

ADDITIONAL READING

Berlandier, Jean Louis. *The Indians of Texas in 1830.* Edited by John C. Ewers. Washington, DC: Smithsonian Institution Press, 1969.

Braund, Kathryn E. Holland. *Deerskins and Duffels: Creek Indian Trade with Anglo-America, 1685–1815.* Lincoln: University of Nebraska Press, 1993.

Jablow, Joseph. *The Cheyenne In Plains Indian Trade Relations 1795–1840.* Lincoln: University of Nebraska Press, Bison Books, 1994; originally published by University of Washington Press, Monograph 19, American Ethnological Society, 1950.

CHAPTER THREE

WARS, WEAPONS
AND TREATIES

I n reading historical accounts it is easy to reach the conclusion that Indian conflicts primarily involved disagreements with white intruders, particularly the U.S. government and its Frontier Army. Though there certainly were instances when those factions faced off with weapons, intertribal warfare was even more common. Long before the era covered by this volume—the 1800s—tribes had attacked and raided each other. There were long-standing tribal conflicts as well as long-standing tribal alliances.

By the early 1800s tribes in the Northeast and Southeast had already been forced from their homelands in many cases, resettling in regions farther west. And as the United States spread west, tribes there were impacted not only by fur trappers and traders, emigrants and even the army, but also by other Indian tribes who abandoned—either willingly or by coercion—ancestral lands. The movement led to inevitable conflicts as tribes established themselves in new regions.

There were really two types of Indian wars in the nineteenth century—those that are well known and highly documented involving the various tribes and the Frontier Army and those that involved fighting between tribes. Not as documented by media of the era or Western historians of today, the latter conflict was in actuality the more prevalent type of fighting engaged in by Indians.

Some tribes formed alliances with each other—such as the Sioux and the Cheyenne—while others remained on opposite sides of all conflicts. The Lakotas (Sioux) and the Pawnees, for example, were historic enemies who raided each other's camps routinely. The same goes for the Lakotas and the Crows.

Though the Lakotas and Dakotas could have forged an alliance with the Pawnees and the Crows, they didn't, and instead both of those traditional enemy tribes sided with the Frontier Army in fights involving the Lakota and Dakota tribes.

Pawnees became scouts for the military under the leadership of Frank North, serving in a number of engagements throughout Nebraska and the high plains, while the Crows also served as army scouts and fought on the side of the military at the Battle of the Little Bighorn (also known as the Custer Battle by whites and as the Battle of the Greasy Grass by the Sioux).

In an interesting twist, Indians who fought valiantly against the military, often—sometimes within months of a defeat or violent battle—then served as scouts for the army. A case in point involves Lakotas who were with Crazy Horse at the Little Bighorn in June 1876 and who ultimately surrendered at Fort Robinson, Nebraska. Some of those same individuals served as scouts with General Nelson Miles in the Battle of the Bear Paw in northern Montana Territory in October 1877, where he subdued the Nez Percés who had engaged in a running flight—and several bloody battles—across Idaho, Montana, and through Yellowstone National Park.

Though some tribes did form alliances and were effective—at least in specific situations—in repelling people from their tribal lands, there was no widespread or universal joining of the tribes, no pan-Indian organization. Had the Indians set aside their tribal conflicts and cohesively worked to stop white encroachment into their lands, they no doubt would have changed some of the historical record.

While it may seem that all Indian fighting occurred in the West, actually there were many conflicts east of the Mississippi River. However, most of those situations occurred prior to 1800. Even so, some of the major Indian engagements in that earlier period will be outlined briefly to provide an understanding of Indian fighting, battles and tribal alliances.

In all Indian fighting, whether against encroaching whites or other tribes, several rules applied. The first was that there were no rules regarding Indian participation in a battle. An individual could break off an engagement at any point and return home, with no concern about disgrace. Anyone participating in a war or raiding party was there willingly, no one could be required to participate. But in many tribes a young man could not marry until he had proven himself as a hunter and warrior, so participation in war parties was an important and integral part of his development. Indian people did not generally fight to defend "the sacred soil of the homeland," because such a concept wasn't understood in Indian culture. Though Indians fought to obtain or retain hunting grounds, they had no concept of land sovereignty.

Indian-against-Indian fighting generally involved raids on camps to steal goods (primarily horses after they were a common item of wealth) and to take captives. Some were revenge raids, undertaken to avenge the death of a clan member or fellow tribesman. Raiding generally took place at night or in early morning; fires were often scattered to provide illumination and destroy lodges and goods in the enemy camp. Men usually undertook the raids and provided the primary defense, but women would defend their homes using various weapons at their disposal, and women participated in revenge raids as well.

In almost all situations the decision to go to war was made by the war council, or elders, though the dream or vision of a warrior often precipitated their ruling. Because most tribes were scattered in different villages, when general war was declared, runners went from one band or village to another informing the people of the plans and seeking warriors to participate. Warrior parties usually had from thirty to forty participants. Women often accompanied war parties to cook and provide other services, and in some tribes women also fought as warriors. Preparation for going to war varied according to tribe, but could include war dances and singing, ceremonies involving war bundles, smoking of the war pipe and preparation of war clothes, weapons and horses. In the horse tribes of the Northern and Southern Plains particularly, warriors had special war horses, used only for battle and never for day-to-day work or activities. The war horse was treated as a member of the family and often tethered near the family lodge (sometimes with a tether tied to the warrior at night to prevent theft.)

Those participating in war parties did not wear their war clothes and paint when traveling. Instead, prior to going into actual battle, warriors donned special clothing and paint and prepared their horses (if they used them) as well. They undertook such preparations to invoke protection from the spirits.

Principal weapons included bows and arrows, spears, lances, shields and war clubs or tomahawks. As they became available, warriors also used guns, knives and even swords.

War parties often left their home camp at night, traveling generally only at night, with each member carrying his or her own food. Though some war parties lasted only days, others extended over weeks or even months (especially among the Iroquois). Attacks took place when the enemy was least prepared to provide defense: during the evening meal, at night or at dawn. Any tribe concerned about an attack would post sentinels. Some Indians, such as the Shoshones, feared the dark and would never raid an enemy camp at night; others preferred such attacks because of the advantage it gave them.

Plains warriors fighting on horseback might wrap their horse's hooves with leather to soften their footfalls. They could shield themselves by hanging to one side of the horse and were able to retrieve a fallen comrade by riding near, reaching down and hauling the wounded individual up behind them on the horse. Most attacks were hit-and-run affairs where warriors quickly moved in and then quickly retreated.

Captive women and children were usually treated as slaves and sometimes later adopted by enemy tribes; captive warriors were almost always tortured before they were killed.

Victory in war generally resulted in a celebration at the home camp involv-

San Juan, a Mescalero Apache chief, holding a spear and shield. (National Archives, 111–SC–82324)

ing feasting, dancing and singing. After a defeat tribes reacted differently: some simply returned home, others remained away for a period of time before eventually making their way back to camp.

MAJOR INDIAN CONFLICTS

Within the scope of this book, it is impossible to provide detailed information about all of the major Indian conflicts both leading up to and during the 1800s; however, a brief synopsis of some of them follows:

PRE-1800 CONFLICTS

The wars fought prior to 1800 set the stage for attitudes and actions in the nineteenth century conflicts. In all cases the end result was dispossession of people, loss or cession of millions of acres of land, tribal relocation and development of policies that permanently altered Indian culture. For Eastern culture areas most fighting—both intertribal and with foreign enemies—occurred prior to 1800.

Powhatan Wars: The Powhatan Confederacy involved 32 tribes and 200 villages, which could easily have annihilated the members of Jamestown Colony, which was established in 1607 and which three years later had only 150 mem-

SCALPING

Though not necessarily a part of Indian warfare in earlier centuries, by the 1800s scalping was common.

To take a scalp, an individual cut around the temples of the victim and then peeled the scalp back, slicing it away from the skull. Some tribes took the entire scalp; others the entire head. Southeastern tribes retained an arm or leg instead of the scalp, or took women's scalps, indicating they had penetrated the enemy camp. Plateau tribes simply sheared the hair. Some Indians cut off fingers of enemy people.

In most cases, once taken, the scalp was dried and then attached to a scalp pole, the medicine lodge, or the warrior's lodge, war horse or weapons. Scalp locks also could be attached to eagle feathers and used in the war bonnets of Plains Indians.

Counting Coup

For Plains Indians, touching or striking an enemy—not necessarily killing one—was an important act of bravery. Known as counting coup, it was a recognized war honor. Each of the first few men (the number varied according to tribe) to strike an enemy could claim coup. Other war honors involved capturing a horse, taking a scalp and killing an enemy. If a Sioux warrior counted coup, was wounded, had his horse killed or injured or if he served as a chief of scouts, he then could wear a shirt (or feathers) decorated with scalps. Any Sioux who led four war parties, striking or touching an enemy during each, was thereafter regarded as a chief.

---

bers out of the original 900. The Powhatan Confederacy did not instigate any hostile acts toward the English colonists, primarily because of the policies of Wahunsonacock, known as King Powhatan. However, four years after his death in 1618 violence erupted. On 22 March 1622 warriors led by Opechancanough (Wahunsonacock's brother) attacked and killed 347 members of the Jamestown colony. The colonists retaliated by attacking and burning Indian villages. The two sides agreed to a peace treaty in 1632, but on 18 April 1644 the Indians led another raid, killing 400 to 500 settlers. Two years later the colonists successfully captured Opechancanough, eventually shooting and killing him and bringing about a tenuous peace.

Bacon's Rebellion: In 1675 Nanticoke Indians became involved in a dispute with English settlers over an unpaid bill. The Nanticokes stole some hogs, and the Englishmen captured and killed the Indians responsible. Other Indians killed a herdsman, then the English colonists formed a militia and attacked the Nanticokes, killing eleven before attacking some Susquehannocks, who had had nothing to do with the unpaid bill, theft of the hogs or the death of the herdsman. Widespread fighting broke out, and Nathaniel Bacon ultimately became involved along with a group of vigilantes who attacked the peaceful Ocaneechi and Monacan tribes. Bacon was arrested, but he was released and he obtained a commission from the House of Burgesses as commander in chief of the Indian war. Though his commission was ultimately rescinded and Bacon was labeled a traitor, he still led his rebel army to Jamestown intending to use wives of the aristocratic leaders as shields while his men prepared for a defense. The rebels successfully captured Jamestown and then burned it. The Indians involved in the initial fighting and the subsequent actions by Nathaniel Bacon had unwittingly been drawn into a colonial dispute.

The Pequot War: In the 1630s the Pequots of the Connecticut River Valley were involved in fighting colonists who continued to settle on the Indian lands.

King Philip's War: Like the Pequot War, King Philip's War was a dispute over land as the whites encroached on Indian territory. This war began in 1675 and fighting continued until the summer of 1676. By then hundreds of Indians had been captured and sold as slaves in the West Indies and Spain. When combined with the death of many more, the war losses led to the virtual extermination of the Narraganset, Wampanoag and Nipmuc tribes.

French and Indian Wars or Imperial Wars: Colonial powers fought several wars over control of North America in the period 1689–1763 including King William's War (1689–97); Queen Anne's War (1702–13); King George's War (1744–48); and the Great War for Empire or French and Indian War (1754–63). Indians were often involved in these conflicts as they attempted to ally themselves with factions in order to protect their lands and position. Among the many conflicts involving Indians during the same period were the Tuscarora War (1711–13); Yamasee War (1715–28); Cherokee War (1760–61); Natchez Revolt (1729–30); Chickasaw Resistance (1720–63) and the Fox Resistance (1720–35). Indians from various tribes also participated in the American Revolution, largely on the side of the British.

CONFLICTS IN THE 1800s

Arctic

Aleut and Tlingit people in Alaska and the Aleutian Islands had no conflicts with American authorities—who did not obtain possession of Alaska until 1867—but they were involved in various confrontations with Russians. The *promyshlenniki* (Russian fur trappers and traders) made their way to the Aleutian Islands and Alaska shortly after Vitus Bering explored the region in 1741 and forced native people to begin trading with them. Typically, the Russians entered a native village, took hostages, handed out traps to the men and then demanded furs in exchange for the hostages (usually women and children). This practice continued yearly and proceeded from one Aleutian Island to the next, until in the early 1760s Aleuts and Eskimos rebelled, killing traders rather than working for them or allowing the Russians to use the native women as concubines. Further conflict occurred including an attack in 1766 by Russian trader Ivan Solovief, who led a force against the Aleuts, killing many living along the chain of islands. By the end of his attack the Aleuts were no longer any threat to the Russian traders.

Tlingits, meanwhile, first traded with the Russians, then became concerned about the value of products traded, and in the 1790s they attacked the Russians. The Tlingit raiding on Russian traders continued sporadically until 1867.

California

Miwok War (or Mariposa Indian War) of 1850–51: California Indians suffered dramatically following the discovery of gold in 1848. The hoards of miners who rushed to the region disrupted the Indians' hunting and gathering practices and killed many Indians without provocation. The extermination was so widespread that within a few years the California Indian population dwindled by nearly two-thirds of its pre-gold discovery numbers. In 1850 the Miwoks and Yokuts rose against the miners, attacking prospectors and burning trading posts operated by James D. Savage. The Mariposa Battalion, organized by Savage to quell the disturbance, was involved in several minor fights in 1851.

Modoc War of 1872: The Modocs signed a treaty in 1864 that gave them lands on the Klamath Reservation in southern Oregon. Due to conditions on the reservation and poor treatment from the Klamath Indians, however, the Modocs, led by Kintpuash (Captain Jack), left the reservation and returned to their California homelands where they lived without conflict for several years. Then in 1872, cavalry troops under the command of Capt. James Jackson were ordered to round up the Modocs and return them to the Klamath Reservation. The effort to negotiate a quiet return shifted when fighting broke out between the soldiers and the Modocs, leading to a death on each side. Kintpuash led his people to a refuge in a volcanic lava bed and another band of Modocs led by Hooker Jim joined them there. Additional fighting in the lava beds led to further deaths on both sides of the battle. Eventually the Modocs surrendered, though several of them were executed for their roles in the fighting. The remaining Modocs were removed to Indian Territory (Oklahoma) where they were given a small reservation, only about two miles square—which they later shared with Nez Percés.

Northeast and Southeast

Among Southeast tribes, intertribal warfare occurred seasonally, usually in the late spring, summer or early fall. War parties generally included forty or fewer men. The reason for raiding and war often revolved around killing or capturing enemy people, ideally without suffering any (or at least, significant) casualties. Attacks generally took place at night or from ambush, with warning given by lighting an enemy house on fire. Warriors used clubs and knives, which were

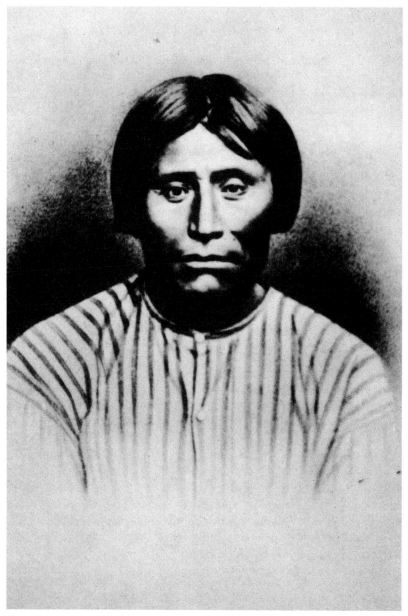

Captain Jack (Kintpuash), a Modoc subchief, executed 3 October 1873. (Louis Heller, 1873; National Archives, 165–MH–404)

effective at close range. They scalped the fallen enemies, hanging the scalps on pine tree boughs.

Sometimes they took live captives, adopting children and women, while torturing and killing men or perhaps making them slaves. Though an Indian slave had considerable freedom to move around the town, it was almost impossible to escape because most had their feet maimed when they were captured. After Europeans settled near the tribes, Indian enemy men were often captured and then sold as slaves. Prior to European influence, most warfare involved blood revenge raids; after European settlement most warfare was purported to take captives who could subsequently be sold as slaves. Due to the intensified raiding, by the early 1800s many of the Southeastern tribes had been either exterminated or absorbed into stronger tribes.

Among the Cherokees, fighting and warfare involved only men, though women occasionally accompanied war parties in order to cook or do other domestic chores. The Beloved Mother (who was a retired war woman), or Ghighau, "War Woman" or "Pretty Woman" determined the fate of war captives. She could order their deaths, make them slaves or allow them to be adopted by clans who had lost members.

Creek tribes had three grades of warriors: war chiefs, big warriors and little warriors. One of the war chiefs became the *tastanagi tako* or "great warrior" who led the town in war.

Standard war gear for the Delawares included extra moccasins, a blanket, a tumpline used as a prisoner tie, and a rifle, powder horn and bullet bag. After they were relocated to Indian Territory and started fighting western tribes, Delawares also began carrying a coup stick.

Tecumseh's Rebellion and the War of 1812: Tecumseh and his brother, the Prophet, who were Shawnees, lost their father in the Revolutionary War, lost a brother in Little Turtle's War (which was fought in the 1790s), and believed that Indian people should not cede any more of their lands without consent of all of the tribes. Tecumseh worked to unite the tribes into a military alliance that eventually included many tribes in the Midwest and some in the Southeast, while the Prophet provided spiritual leadership for the movement. When some of the chiefs who had not joined in Tecumseh's alliance were tricked into ceding three million acres of land for only seven thousand dollars and small annuities, Tecumseh protested though he didn't launch any attack. However, before long the situation became more tense, and while Tecumseh was away from Prophetstown, Indians led by his brother, the Prophet, attacked soldiers who had camped within three miles of the Indian village. The premature attack and resulting defeat of the Indian forces significantly damaged Tecumseh's ability to rally the Indians into a united confederacy. Ultimately on 18 June 1812, when the United States declared war on Great Britain, Tecumseh saw it as an opportunity to forge a new Indian homeland for all tribes. He joined the British in the fighting for the region then known as the Old Northwest, significantly thwarting efforts of the United States by participating in battles that included the capture of Fort Dearborn (Chicago) and the taking of Detroit. But the British ultimately lost the war, and Tecumseh himself died on the battlefield on 5 October 1813.

Indian Resistance: Following the War of 1812, the Kickapoos refused to leave their homelands. Though some of the Kickapoo bands left the region in 1819 to move west, others, such as the bands led by Mecina and Kenekuk, refused to relocate until after further conflict including the Black Hawk War.

Creek War: Tecumseh made several trips to the powerful Creek Nation to enlist their support for an Indian confederacy. Though the confederacy never truly organized, the Creeks supported Tecumseh during the War of 1812, participating in the Raisin River Massacre and the murder of settlers along the Ohio River. On 20 August 1813 William Weatherford, known as Red Eagle, organized a force of one thousand Creeks (known as Red Sticks or Upper Creeks) and advanced on Fort Mims, situated on the Alabama River. The Red Sticks succeeded in their attack, killing some four hundred settlers, most of them whites, while allowing most of the black slaves to live. As a result of the massacre, Gen. Andrew Jackson was authorized to outfit an army of thirty-five hundred men. That army ultimately attacked the Creeks and following a series of engagements defeated the Indians, who were forced to accept terms of the Treaty of Horseshoe Bend, in which Jackson demanded twenty-three million acres from both the Red Sticks and from the White Sticks (Lower Creeks who had supported Jackson's side in the fighting).

Seminole Wars: After his "success" with the Creeks, Jackson turned toward Florida and the Seminoles living there. In March 1818 he organized forces at Fort Scott, Georgia, and then made his way south. The Seminoles, having been warned of Jackson's intent, fled into the Florida swamps. Jackson subsequently marched toward the Spanish fort at Pensacola, capturing it and claiming it for the United States—a violation of international law and an action that was immediately protested by both Spanish and British leaders. U.S. President John Quincy Adams responded that Spain either needed to control the Seminoles or cede the land to the United States. In 1819 Spain and the United States negotiated for the sale of East Florida and the United States took possession in 1821. White settlers started pouring into the region, forcing the Seminoles into ever smaller regions. By 1829, Jackson had become president of the United States, and within a year he was calling for removal of all Southeastern Indians to the region west of the Mississippi. Though some Seminoles in 1833 agreed to resettle on lands in the Creek Nation west of the Mississippi, two years later none of them had actually left Florida. Instead they hid out in the Florida swamps and engaged in a number of battles that comprised the First Seminole War. Subsequently there was a seven-year period of fighting, known as the Second Seminole War. During the period 1835 to 1842, some three thousand Seminoles were relocated to Indian Territory, but a number of them continued to hide out in Florida's swamps, never formally surrendering to the U.S. government. A third Seminole uprising in 1855 involved a guerrilla-style war in which the Seminoles attacked settlers, traders and trappers, then fled to the swamps. In 1858 Billy Bowlegs and his band finally agreed to relocate to Indian Territory, though some of the Seminoles continued to hide out in the Florida Everglades.

Great Basin

Paiute War (or Pyramid Lake War) of 1860: This involved Paiutes and miners in a dispute over trading posts and operation of the Central Overland Mail and Pony Express stations in present-day Nevada. Two Paiute girls were abducted and raped by white traders at Williams Station, leading Paiute warriors to attack the station where they rescued the girls and killed five whites. In response to that attack Nevada miners organized under leadership of Maj. William M. Ormsby. They followed the Paiutes but were ambushed in the Truckee River Valley, where some fifty miners died. Additional volunteers from California as well as army regulars then joined the effort pursuing the Indians to Pinnacle Mountain where they were subdued.

Bannock War of 1878: Bannocks and Northern Paiutes along with some Cayuses and Umatillas became involved in the Bannock War of 1878 in Oregon and Idaho, sparked over the digging of camas roots on the Camas Prairie about ninety miles from Fort Boise (Idaho). Though an earlier treaty guaranteed the Indians the right to dig the roots that made up much of their diet, conflict arose when hogs owned by settlers began damaging the prairie vegetation. A Bannock wounded two whites in May 1878, and later a war party involving about three hundred Bannock and Paiute warriors gathered. Their leader, Buffalo Horn, died in a clash with volunteers and the U.S. Army mobilized under the leadership of Gen. Oliver O. Howard, Capt. Evan Miles and Capt. Reuben F. Bernard. A series of battles followed until both the Bannocks and Paiutes surrendered. As a result of the war, the Paiute reservation at Malheur (Idaho) was closed, and the Indians were resettled in Washington on the Yakima reservation. The Bannocks were first held as prisoners at military posts and later allowed to return to their Idaho reservation.

Interior Plateau

Coeur d'Alene War: Believed to be an extension of the Yakima War, the Coeur d'Alene War (sometimes called the Spokane War) involved the Northern Paiutes, Palouses, Spokanes and Coeur d'Alenes. The first battle took place in May 1858 between the Indians and federal troops led by Maj. Edward Steptoe. Though the war began partially due to encouragement by Chief Kamiakin of the Yakimas to unite the Columbia River tribes, the outcome, including the death or hanging of several tribal leaders, actually broke the power of the tribes.

Nez Percé War of 1877: Given a reservation in the Wallowa Valley of Oregon under a treaty in 1855, the Nez Percés in 1877 were ordered onto the Lapwai Reservation in Idaho. Five bands of the Nez Percé (who became known as the nontreaty Nez Percé) refused to go to Lapwai, and the attack and killing of whites in Idaho by some of the young Nez Percé warriors put the bands on the run. They fled across Idaho, engaging in a fight with federal troops under Gen. Oliver O. Howard at White Bird Creek (Idaho) on 17 June 1877. The Nez Percé then continued in their flight, battling troops again at Clearwater Creek (Idaho) on 11 July and engaging in a dawn battle at the Big Hole (Montana) on 9 August. The Nez Percés resumed their race for freedom after the Big Hole, staging a retaliatory attack against soldiers at Camas Creek (Idaho) on 20 August. Other battles occurred at Canyon Creek (13 September) and at Cow Island (23 September) both in present-day Montana, before the army finally squeezed hard enough and forced the Nez Percé to surrender at the Bear Paw Battlefield (30 September–5 October) in northern Montana—just forty miles short of their goal of joining Sitting Bull in Canada. The surrender came, in part, because the military successfully captured the Nez Percé horse herd.

Northwest Coast

Cayuse War, 1847: This is the first significant conflict between Indians and whites in the Northwest, and involved members of the Cayuse tribe and settlers at the Whitman Mission on the upper Columbia River. The mission, established by Marcus Whitman in the 1830s, had by 1847 established itself as a center for the Rocky Mountain mission. Cayuse children were enrolled in the school operated by Whitman and his fellow missionaries, and when many of the children contracted measles and died from the disease, Chief Tilokaikt and other Cayuses blamed Whitman and the other whites. They attacked the mission on 29 November 1847, killing Whitman, his wife, Narcissa, and ten others. They took some fifty men, women and children as hostages.

Oregon Territory quickly raised a militia to track the Indians, though Peter Skene Ogden of the Hudson's Bay Company successfully negotiated with the Cayuses for release of the hostages. The militia under leadership of Cornelius Gilliam, however, attacked an innocent band of Cayuses, killing about thirty Indians. That set off additional fighting, which had the potential to unite all of the Columbia Basin tribes. However, before that occured, leaders Tilokaikt and Tomoahas along with three of their companions surrendered. They were tried, convicted and hanged for their role in the Whitman massacre, as the initial battle became known.

Long-term repercussions of the Cayuse War included establishment of Oregon Territory, construction of additional military forts and the opening of Cayuse lands to white settlement. The outcome also led other Columbia Basin tribes—which had been peaceful—to fear their own lands would be taken by the whites.

Rogue River War: Fighting broke out in 1855–56 among the Takelma and Tututni Indians of southern Oregon and northern California. When rumors of war started circulating in the region, Capt. Andrew Jackson Smith, attempting to diffuse tension, invited the Indians to visit the fort. Many of the men did so, with plans for their wives and children to follow, but before the women and children could travel to the fort, Oregon volunteers not under Smith's command attacked their village. The warriors then retaliated by raiding a Rogue Valley settlement. In both attacks more than twenty-five persons died. Raids and counterraids continued through the winter and spring of 1855–56 until finally the Indians surrendered. They were removed to the Siletz reservation in the north.

Plains

General fighting age for Plains warriors was between ages fifteen and thirty-five. The leader of the war party was the pipeholder, or the man who carried the pipe. Generally a raiding or war party could consist of between four and twenty warriors, though in certain cases as many as one hundred to two hundred warriors rode together. Some were experienced, as in the case of the pipeholder, while others were young boys learning warrior ways. Those young boys provided assistance to the experienced warriors by carrying equipment and gear, and they did not always participate in the actual raid. Likewise, some women also often accompanied war parties, to cook, in most cases, though occasionally to also fight alongside the men, particularly to avenge the death of a spouse, a brother or other kinsman.

Prior to beginning on any war party, the members engaged in prayer. Generally a priest or medicine man led them in a "medicine sweat," and they often made sacrifices by cutting a piece of skin from their body; this was particularly done as they prepared for a revenge raid. When a war party was on the road, the medicine man would remind people in camp of their absence by riding around shouting their names, and he would also pray for their safe journey.

When traveling by horseback, the war party would cover about fifty miles a day, while a war party on foot generally went about twenty-five miles a day. The party almost always started before sunup. Though mounted war party members had with them their best war horses, they generally led them en route to the raid, to keep the animals fresh for the actual battle.

Traveling in single file and usually down ravines or coulees to avoid being seen, the war party usually had experienced men who served as scouts. Called "wolves" because they carried wolf skins to use as camouflage and disguises, they sometimes spread mud over their faces and bodies to further conceal themselves. When Plains scouts returned to the main band to make a report, they usually met at a planned site. Tribes had different methods of making scouting reports. Blackfeet scouts kicked a pile of sticks as they made their reports, some scouts of other tribes kicked at piles of bison chips. Kiowa scouts had the pipeholder put a straw in his hair, and the scouts told their story as they removed the straw. Assistants to the pipeholder were one or two men recognized by the crooked staffs they carried, which were generally green saplings often wrapped in cloth or fur.

Warriors often were nearly naked, wrapped in a blanket and perhaps wearing lightweight shirts and leggings to prevent sunburn in the summer and provide warmth in the winter. Northern Plains Indians in the winter would wear a blanket coat—called a capote—with yellow or red horizontal stripes, made of Hudson's Bay or other trade blankets. Warriors carried fine clothing and regalia such as war bonnets and coup feathers in a parfleche, or a rawhide case, tied to the saddle. When near the area where the party intended to attack the enemy, warriors might put on their regalia and war shirts. They often stripped the saddles from their horses, leaving them with extra gear at a designated place, such as a war lodge. See page 69.

> We wore only light shirts and leggings made from the skins of bighorns and carried nothing except our bows and shields. War-bonnets and bright colors were hidden away, because they can be seen easily, and no war-party wishes to be seen. Bonnets were never used by warriors until all chance of surprise was gone. Then they were brought out, if there was time. Our bonnets were in rawhide cases and might not be used at all.—*Crow chief Plenty Coups*

Prior to the raid the war party generally took the time to pray and smoke the sacred pipe. They generally killed game and dried it, so they would have food on their return trip to their home camps.

In intertribal battles, upon meeting the enemy, warriors from both sides often taunted each other for up to several hours before actual warfare broke out. As the fighting began, warriors on both sides sang their individual war songs, yelling loudly to work up their courage. Though war parties preferred to ambush enemies, or to attack them in their camps, certainly some encounters took place in the open. Generally fighting involved four passes before attackers broke away, either to regroup and attack again (four times) in a different location or to abandon the battle altogether. In some tribes the number of attacks varied, depending on each tribe's recognized sacred number.

When Plains war parties concluded a fight, individual members made their way back to the site of their war lodge, where they retrieved extra horses and gear and joined their companions. In the event enemies pursued, the warriors might quickly leave a message for companions and each then headed toward home. Eventually the warriors might regroup to return to their home camp.

Though Plains warriors were not afraid to die—in fact they preferred to die in battle if death was necessary at all—they were often extremely cautious. The Comanches, for example, would break off an attack if an enemy killed even one of their warriors, even in situations when the Comanches far outnumbered the enemy. Northern Plains warriors weren't so quick to break off a fight, but they also would leave the battlefield if several of their companions fell.

The Indians attempted to recover wounded and dead comrades. Wounded warriors would be transported home on a travois, while those who had died in battle most often were buried, perhaps in shallow graves or under rocks. Blackfeet warriors covered dead comrades with dead members of the enemy tribe.

Most tribes mutilated dead enemies either by scalping them or often by cutting off their fingers or other limbs. Arikaras practiced ritual cannibalism of enemies.

Though captive women and children often became part of the battle plunder, warriors were seldom taken captive. If a man was taken prisoner, he was generally tortured and then killed.

Upon returning home, warriors attracted the attention of people in the camp and then let them know about the success or failure of the raid through a series of signals. Crows, for example, painted their faces black if they had been victorious. Assiniboine warriors trotted in a zigzag fashion to indicate success.

If a war party had suffered a death of a member, it might attract the people's attention, then throw a robe wrapped into a ball. Each time the ball-shaped robe was thrown, it represented the death of a warrior. Crows attracted attention by firing a gun or some other method. Then they lifted a robe and dropped it, with each successive motion indicating how many warriors had died on the war trail. Crow elders would join the war party where it stopped away from the village to hear the story of the raid, then return to the camp to inform relatives who went into mourning while the war party members remained away for another ten days.

Some of the battles of the Plains Indian wars were these:

Grattan Massacre, 1854: War on the northern plains between the Frontier Army and various tribes began in August 1854 near Fort Laramie, when Lt. John Grattan attempted to arrest a Miniconjou for killing a cow that had wandered from its Mormon owner. The warrior didn't surrender, Grattan opened fire, and the Indians responded in kind. Grattan's entire command died as a result, as did several Indians, including chief Conquering Bear (sometimes called The Bear).

Battle of Blue Water (Harney Massacre), 1855: In August 1855, Gen. William Harney took revenge for Grattan in the Battle of Blue Water, which is also known as the Harney Massacre and the Battle of the Bloody Blue. The fight occurred near Ash Hollow, Nebraska Territory, on Blue Water Creek. It led to the death of more than one hundred Indian people, including women and children, none of whom had been involved in the Grattan battle of the previous year.

Sand Creek Massacre, 1864: Fighting with federal troops across the plains did not become widespread until 1864. On 29 November Col. John Chivington with troops from the Third Colorado Cavalry attacked the peaceful village of Cheyenne chief Black Kettle and about six hundred of his followers and some

Arapahoes. The Indians had camped on Sand Creek in eastern Colorado Territory, believing they were under no threat from soldiers. Chivington used four howitzers to fire upon the Indians, killing about two hundred of them, again including women and children. The Sand Creek Massacre, as the incident quickly became known, set off the Cheyenne-Arapaho War or the Colorado War of 1864–65, launching an era in 1865 that became known as the Bloody Year on the Plains.

Indians from various Plains tribes subsequently attacked individual travelers, took hostages, burned stage stations and generally created havoc across the region. To further chronicle the Plains Indian conflicts, we will look at each tribe and outline major engagements in which they participated.

Arapaho: Allies of the Sioux and Cheyennes, the Northern Arapahos were involved in fighting in Wyoming's Powder River country, while the Southern Arapahos took part in the battles that occurred in Colorado and Kansas. In August 1865, Black Bear's people were attacked by Gen. Patrick E. Conner as they camped on the Tongue River in northern Wyoming. Many Indian people of all ages died in the fighting, and the army destroyed their possessions. The attack by Conner, similar to the attack in November 1864 by Chivington at Sand Creek, involved Indians who were not engaged in any military action at the time. Both situations strengthened military alliances between the Arapaho, Cheyenne and Sioux tribes.

Blackfeet: Hostile toward most people—white or Indian—the Blackfeet and their kin, the Bloods and Piegans, who primarily lived in Canada, had no direct, organized conflicts with the United States military, though they were involved in Canadian battles.

Caddo: An agrarian tribe, the Caddos served as scouts for the United States military.

Cheyenne: As noted above, the attack on Cheyennes at Sand Creek precipitated the first major period of Indian Wars on the Northern Plains, and the tribe was involved in many significant battles throughout the next two decades. They engaged Lt. Col. George Armstrong Custer and his Seventh Cavalry in western Kansas, northeastern Colorado Territory and southwestern Nebraska in the summer of 1867 in a campaign known as the Hancock Campaign. Though Custer attempted to catch the Indians, they eluded him and he managed only to burn an evacuated village in Nebraska.

In September 1867, the Cheyennes fought with Maj. George Forsyth on an island of the Republican River that became known as Beecher's Island, for Lt. Frederick Beecher, who died in the several-day siege by the Cheyennes.

One winter later, Custer again engaged the Cheyennes, this time attacking a band that also included Arapaho chief Black Kettle, in the Battle of the Washita. Before the bullets stopped flying about one hundred Indians, including Black Kettle, were dead as well as five soldiers. But Custer failed to account for all of his men, and another fifteen were cut off from the army and subsequently killed by the Cheyennes. Further engagements soon led the Southern Cheyennes and the Southern Arapahos to take refuge on reservations.

The Northern Cheyennes, meanwhile, allied themselves with the Sioux and fought in the First and Second Sioux Wars. The most significant Northern Cheyenne battles included the Battle of Warbonnet Creek in northwest Nebraska in July 1876, just weeks after the Custer fight on the Greasy Grass, and the bitter struggle at the Dull Knife Battle in Wyoming in November 1876. In the Dull Knife Battle, Lt. Ranald Mackenzie and his Frontier Army troops surrounded the Cheyennes and other tribal members, routing them from their lodges and forcing them to flee across the bitterly cold, snow-covered landscape. After the Dull Knife battle the Cheyennes, led by Dull Knife and Little Wolf, surrendered at Fort Robinson, Nebraska, and they were subsequently sent to a reservation in Indian Territory. However, in 1879, they broke away from the reservation and fled north, eventually obtaining a reservation in Montana.

Comanche: Known as the Horse Warriors of the Southern Plains, the Comanches engaged in several battles with Texas Rangers as early as 1840. Fighting continued in such conflicts as the Battle of Soldier Spring on 25 December 1868 and during the Red River War of 1874–75, which is often called the Buffalo War. Lt. Ranald Mackenzie subdued the Comanches when his troops attacked them in Palo Duro Canyon in Texas. His method of controlling the Comanches involved capturing or killing their horse herd, estimated at fifteen hundred animals.

Crow: At the urging of Chief Plenty Coups, the Crows aligned themselves with the Frontier Army, serving as scouts. They participated in many of the battles on the northern plains, including those in both the First and Second Sioux Wars, but on the side of the military, rather than as allies of the tribes.

Kiowa and Kiowa-Apache: These tribes became allies of the Comanches and fought alongside them in various battles.

Osage: Traditional enemies of the Kiowas and Comanches, the Osages served as army scouts.

Pawnee: Traditional enemies of the Sioux, the Pawnees became the first Indians to scout for the Frontier Army in the West.

Ponca: The Poncas had no violent encounters with the United States military, but they did leave their reservation in Indian Territory (Oklahoma) without permission and became involved in a major decision in 1879 that established Indians as people under terms of the United States Constitution.

Sioux: Perhaps the most well known of all Indian-military battles are those related to the tribes of the Sioux confederation (Lakota, Dakota and Nakota).

STANDING BEAR VS. CROOK

In 1879 federal courts affirmed that Indians are "people" in *Standing Bear vs. Crook* when Ponca chief Standing Bear went to court. The Poncas in 1858 had negotiated a treaty with the United States, and in 1876 the government ordered the Poncas under Standing Bear and other chiefs to Oklahoma Territory.

> "We got ready and started, wishing first to visit the Omaha reserve, but this was not allowed us," the Ponca chiefs said in a statement published in a Sioux City, Iowa newspaper. "After some days we reached the country of the Osages, and looked over the country and found it stony and broken, and not a country we thought we could make a living in. We saw the Osages there, and they were without shirts, their skin burned, and their hair stood up as if it had not been combed since they were little children. We did not wish to sink so low as they seemed to be."

After the inspection trip the Ponca chiefs did not want to move to Oklahoma. They made their way home to Nebraska, where they intended to remain, but in 1877 the government ordered a forced relocation to Oklahoma, where many of the Poncas died. Unable to bear the hardships forced upon his tribe, in early 1879 Standing Bear broke away from the reservation in Oklahoma to return to Nebraska, where his people sought refuge with their friends and relatives, the Omahas.

When Gen. George Crook ordered troops to take the Poncas into custody and return them to Oklahoma, *Omaha World-Herald* editor Thomas Tibbles, a former abolitionist crusader in Kansas, heard of the plan and vowed to fight "for exactly the same principals [*sic*] for which he [had] fought twenty-four years ago, the equality of all men before the law," Kay Graber wrote in her introduction to *Standing Bear and the Ponca Chiefs: An Account of the Trial of Standing Bear.*

Attorneys John L. Webster and A. J. Poppleton filed a writ of habeas corpus in behalf of Standing Bear against General Crook, which centered on the issue of whether Indian people had the same basic civil liberties as all other Americans.

Crook's troops took the Poncas into custody and placed them in the Omaha Barracks. While there the Omaha tribe came to the aid of the Poncas, offering to share their reservation and to support the Poncas until they could provide for themselves. A letter signed by twenty members of the Omaha tribe dated 21 April 1879 spelled out the Omahas' concern for the Poncas:

> They are our brothers and our sisters, our uncles and our cousins, and although we are called savages we feel that sympathy for our persecuted brethren that should characterize Christians, we are willing to share what we possess with them if they can only be allowed to return and labor, improve and provide for themselves where they may live in peace, enjoy good health, and the opportunity of educating their children up to a higher state of civilization.

After hearing the testimony on both sides of the case, U.S. District Judge Elmer S. Dundy on 12 May 1879 filed his opinion in the matter, writing:

The reasoning advanced in support of my views, leads me to conclude:

First. That an *Indian* is a PERSON within the meaning of the laws of the United States. . . .

Second. That General George Crook . . . has the custody of the realtors under color of the authority of the United States, and in violation of the laws thereof.

Third. That no rightful authority exists for removing by force any of the realtors to the Indian Territory. . . .

Fourth. That the Indians possess the inherent right of expatriation as well as the more fortunate White race, and have the inalienable right to "*life, liberty* and the pursuit of happiness," so long as they obey the laws and do not trespass on forbidden ground. And

Fifth. Being restrained of liberty under color of authority of the United States, and in violation of the laws thereof, the realtors must be discharged from custody, and it is so ordered.

One early conflict occurred in present-day Minnesota when Santees raided trading posts and settlements on 18 August 1862. About four hundred white settlers died in the initial fighting, and the region became a war zone for several weeks thereafter. In late September, Gen. Henry Hastings Sibley followed the Santees to Wood Lake forcing them to surrender under the barrage of firing by his soldiers using various pieces of artillery. Though some of the Santees fled to Canada, many were arrested. Subsequent trials led to the execution of thirty-eight Santees in Mankato, Minnesota, on 26 December 1862. The remaining Santees were then removed to a reservation in eastern Nebraska.

First Sioux War

(Red Cloud's War), 1864–1868: The First Sioux War, called Red Cloud's War, broke out over a trail and forts established in the region north of the North Platte River and east of the Big Horn Mountains, in what is known as Powder River country of present-day Wyoming. John Jacobs and John Bozeman pioneered the trail that took Bozeman's name in 1864 following the discovery of gold in Virginia City, in what became Montana Territory. It would provide a shorter route from the major overland trail corridor along the North Platte to the gold fields.

But the land through which it passed had been set aside for the Sioux in treaties negotiated in 1851 at Fort Laramie. When travelers began using the road, and even more significant, when the military established forts in the region, the Lakota launched their first offensive. Among the battles in Red Cloud's War were these:

The Battle of Platte Bridge: On 25 July 1865, Lt. Caspar Collins and several companions were killed by combined forces of Sioux, Cheyenne and Arapaho warriors, with the fighting in view of soldiers at Platte Bridge Station (present-day Casper, Wyoming). The battle also included the attack and death of twenty members of an army wagon train led by Sgt. Amos Custard.

Fetterman Massacre: On 21 December 1866, Lt. William J. Fetterman and eighty of his troops were outmaneuvered and attacked by warriors led by Crazy Horse, resulting in the death of all the soldiers near Fort Phil Kearny north of present-day Buffalo, Wyoming.

Hayfield Fight: On 1 August 1867, warriors attacked soldiers near Fort C.F. Smith in southern Montana Territory.

Wagon Box Fight: On 2 August 1867, army woodcutters were attacked and surrounded by Sioux and Cheyenne warriors. The soldiers took refuge in a corral made of the boxes of their wood-hauling wagons. They had new breech-loading Springfield rifles, which allowed them to shoot more times before reloading, effectively repelling the larger force of Indians. It is fairly certain the Hayfield and Wagon Box fights were carefully planned by the Sioux since they occurred just one day apart. It's just as certain that the Indians were unaware the troops had the new Springfield rifles.

Following the Hayfield and Wagon Box fights, the United States military succumbed to Red Cloud's demands and abandoned the three forts—Phil Kearny, C. F. Smith, and Reno—and moved out of the Powder River Country. The Indians immediately burned the forts, and several months later Red Cloud went to Fort Laramie where he negotiated the 1868 peace treaty, which placed him on a reservation in northwestern Nebraska.

Second Sioux War

(Crazy Horse's War), 1874–1876: There was a period of relative peace on the northern plains for six years, until further fighting broke out in 1874. This time the primary war chief was Crazy Horse. Though there were numerous skirmishes during the next two years, the major battles of the Second Sioux War, or Crazy Horse's War, involved the Battle of the Rosebud and the Battle of the Little Bighorn (called Battle of the Greasy Grass by the Lakota), both in June 1876 in Montana Territory.

Though the tribes won both engagements, they ultimately surrendered. The Cheyenne allies turned themselves in following the Dull Knife Battle of

November 1876, and Chief Crazy Horse with 899 men, women and children, surrendered in the spring of 1877 near Hat Creek Station in Wyoming Territory. His people were sent to the reservation on the White River in Nebraska, but Crazy Horse spent little time there. In September 1877 he was stabbed and killed in an altercation with guards at Fort Robinson.

Brûlé chief Sitting Bull, who fought with Crazy Horse at the Custer Battle, fled to Canada, where he lived with his people for many years, before eventually returning to the United States and a reservation in South Dakota, where he, too, was killed in an altercation.

Wounded Knee: 29 December 1890 the final Sioux battle—which like Sand Creek and the Battle of the Washita was truly a massacre—occurred at Wounded Knee, South Dakota, when federal troops opened fire on Big Foot and his followers, killing more than 150 Indians and wounding another fifty.

Prairies and Woodlands

The Winnebagos, Sauks and Foxes refused to relocate when whites attempted to intrude on their lands, and in 1826 several Winnebagos attacked a family of maple sugar farmers near Prairie du Chien in Wisconsin. The only real engagement of the subsequent Winnebago Uprising occurred in June of 1827, when Winnebago warriors attacked boatmen on a keelboat that had stopped near Prairie du Chien. The boatmen drank rum and kidnapped several Indian women, whom they later raped. The warriors launched a raid that was not successful, but it did allow the women an opportunity to escape from the keelboat and it also resulted in the deaths of both Indians and boatmen. As a result of the melee, United States troops pursued the Winnebagos, arresting leader Red Bird and his followers.

Black Hawk War: The final war for the Old Northwest simmered for years. In 1804 some Sauk Indians killed settlers north of St. Louis, and not long afterward Indiana Territorial Governor William Henry Harrison received permission to negotiate with the Sauks and Foxes for tribal lands. He persuaded the tribal chiefs to turn over one of the individuals who had been involved in the settler killing, and then lavished liquor and gifts on the chiefs until the Sauks relinquished all tribal lands east of the Mississippi in exchange for just two thousand dollars and annuity goods worth about one thousand dollars. The Indian who had been turned over to authorities for his role in the settler killing was to receive an executive pardon, but before it could be granted he was shot and killed during an escape attempt.

Sauk Chief Ma-ka-tai-me-she-kia-kiak (Black Sparrow Hawk), who became known as Black Hawk, believed the 1804 Treaty was fraudulent. He and his followers staged sieges on Fort Madison in 1808 and 1811. They supported Tecumseh during the War of 1812. Unrest continued for years until in 1827 the federal government decided to remove all the Indians from Illinois. Though some of the Indians left, Black Hawk and his three hundred warriors and their families continued to live in the disputed territory. They drew back temporarily, delaying the conflict, but by 1832 the dispute had escalated into war. Black Hawk's band was ultimately joined by other Indians from various tribes including Potawatomis, Winnebagos and Kickapoos as well as by other bands of the Sauk and Fox tribes. When the warriors under Black Hawk ultimately made their way west, as many as three hundred Indians died in the Massacre at Bad Axe—where Sioux Indians attacked members of the other tribes who believed they were crossing the river from "White lands" to "Indian lands."

Southwest

Tiwa: On 19 January 1847, Tiwa Indians at Taos Pueblo revolted, killing Charles Bent, then the territorial governor for the region, and twenty other individuals. Militiamen from Santa Fe responded to the uprising at Taos, surrounding the pueblo and shelling the pueblo church in which the Tiwas had taken refuge. In the fighting more than two hundred Indians died, many of them women and children who had sought sanctuary in the church.

Apache Wars: In 1861 rancher John Ward wrongfully accused Chiricahua Apache Cochise of stealing cattle and abducting his children. Lt. George Bascom at Fort Buchanan sent word to Cochise requesting a meeting, and on 4 February, Cochise and several family members met with Bascom. The army officer accused Cochise of the raid on Ward's family and livestock and arrested the chief, who cut his way out of a tent with his knife and escaped. But Bascom took Cochise's family members hostage. Cochise responded by ambushing travelers on the Butterfield Trail and taking his own hostages. Joined by White Mountain Apaches and members of the Mimbreno Apaches led by Cochise's father-in-law, Mangas Colorado, Cochise continued attacking stagecoaches on the trail. Both sides eventually killed their hostages, escalating attacks by the Apaches.

Though some of the conflict diffused with the beginning of the Civil War, fighting between the Apache bands and the military continued through the 1860s and early 1870s. Eventually, in the spring of 1873, the military broke Apache resistance and settled most of the Indians on reservations. However, Victorio, then leader of the Mimbreno Apaches, and Geronimo, who had fought beside Cochise, reprised the Apache resistance in uprisings that lasted from 1877 through 1886, when the last holdout, Geronimo, surrendered at Skeleton Canyon (Arizona).

The Apaches were then transported to Fort Pickens in Pensacola, Florida, for a year-long incarceration, followed by additional time at Mount Vernon Barracks, Alabama. In 1894 many of the Apaches were allowed to return to Fort Sill, Oklahoma, to share a reservation with the Comanches and Kiowas.

Apaches engaged in a number of violent practices including torturing prisoners by tying them in ant piles, castrating them while living (and after they had died), tying them to cactus plants or poking them with cactus spines, tying them and starting a fire near their head, or cutting the tendons in their heels.

WEAPONS

Indians had a variety of weapons ranging from guns to bows and arrows, lances, axes, war clubs, or pogamoggans, and knives. Though Indians early in the period relied on their bows and arrows, or even a well-thrown tomahawk or knife, tribes in the Northeast and Southeast were armed with guns before 1800, provided to them when they allied with either French or British troops during a variety of engagements. By the 1860s almost all Indians across the country had guns, which they had obtained in a variety of ways: through legitimate trade, as plunder during previous attacks and even as gifts from the U.S. government.

As First Infantryman James S. Hamilton noted in 1876:

> We were told that . . . Winchester rifles had previously been issued by our government to the Indians for shooting buffalo. . . . Indians had better rifles than our own men. . . . When they were disarmed at Standing Rock they had cap and ball Colts plus various kinds of rifles, but for the most part they carried good Winchester rifles.

An account published in *Frank Leslie's Illustrated Weekly Newspaper*, 26 June 1875, 247–3 (page and column numbers), shows how the Indians obtained some of their guns:

> Our Indian visitors of the Mineconjou tribe of the Sioux nation left New York, June 9th, after having enjoyed themselves at Gilmore's Summer Garden, at the races in Jerome Park, and at the various 'stores' in town—notably at Remington's where each Indian was presented with a rifle. If the Government would only distribute homesteads instead of rifles among Indians of every tribe, there might be some prospect of reaching, ultimately, a satisfactory solution of the Indian problem.

According to Kit Carson, Klamaths had arrows "all headed with a lancet-like piece of iron or steel—probably obtained from the Hudson's Bay Company's traders on the Umpqua—and were poisoned for about six inches."

Spokane bow types included the straight bow, sinew-backed bow and an elk rib bow used in brush. Favored woods for making bows were mountain mahogany, syringa and ocean spray, while arrows were made of dogwood or alder, and projectile points were of basalt, obsidian, chert, flint and metal. Flatheads and Pend d'Oreilles sometimes used compound bows. They also used a war club known as a pogamoggan, which had a stone inside a small bag that was attached to a staff about three feet long.

Warriors always carried their scalping knives, but they did not always take war axes on war parties. Blackfeet Warrior Weasel Head recalled, "We carried no axes on war parties. But our sharp scalping knives were as useful as any axe would be."

Among the types of weapons and gear warriors took on a raiding party were knives, shields (when on horseback; not always when walking), clubs and/or tomahawks, lances, guns and accessories for them (including powder horns, patch bags for bullets, patches and balls), bows and about twenty arrows for each warrior. They also carried rawhide cases for clothing and gear such as war bonnets, quirts (short whips), sinew and awls, war paint bags, extra moccasins, pipes and tobaccos, robes and blankets, and extra moccasins (and perhaps moccasins from an enemy tribe worn to decoy curious enemy bands).

Individual tribes had differing styles of moccasins, with the footprint of each known to other tribes. When in enemy territory, warriors often wore the moccasins of their enemies, in order to make them believe they were from the same tribe.

WAR LODGES

Northern Plains tribes used war lodges that provided protection from the elements and enemy attack. The war lodges were a base for operations and supplies and a communications center where warriors could leave messages for their comrades following an attack or raid. War lodges were used throughout the Northern Plains, particularly in the last days of intertribal warfare.

The Blackfeet generally constructed war lodges in heavily timbered areas along a known war trail, near where the warriors would attack an enemy camp. The lodges were used time after time. The war leader selected the site for construction of a new war lodge, and members of the party collected timber to build it. They used their scalping knives to cut timber if needed. Initially three or four heavy cottonwood logs were hooked together and set up to create a conical form, similar to a tipi. The butt ends of the logs rested against the ground, and lighter poles were stacked around the heavy framework, with slabs of bark placed over the entire structure to make it somewhat air- and watertight. If bark could not be obtained, the warriors used brush for the outer covering. The covering materials were not attached to the framework, though sticks might be placed over the covering to hold it in place. At one side of the circular structure—usually the east—the builders left a V-shaped opening. Then they used additional cottonwood logs, sticks, brush and bark to form an entryway that was several feet long. Once the entire structure was in place, the warriors put additional cottonwood logs or stones about two feet high around the base of the exterior structure. There were few interior furnishings. A central fire served for warmth and cooking, and warriors wrapped themselves in their robes and slept on a floor covered with pine boughs or brush covered with grass. Most war lodges were sufficiently large to house about a dozen men, though sometimes as many as eighteen men used a single lodge.

NORTH WEST TRADE GUNS

Indians desired no item as much as they did the gun when it first became available to them. Among the Plains tribes, even horses—another extremely valuable commodity—were traded for guns. French explorers introduced guns to Indians in the Great Lakes region. After 1670 when English traders established trading posts on Hudson Bay, gun trading began. Crees obtained guns from the Hudson's Bay Company posts and exchanged them for other goods with Indians living to the south and west on the Canadian plains and along the Upper Missouri River. The Crees first used guns in battle against the Assiniboines, but when the latter tribe had been subdued, the Crees formed an alliance with them and ultimately provided their former enemies with guns.

Eventually both the Crees and the Assiniboines became middlemen, trading guns with other tribes to the south and west. Among the tribes getting the powerful weapons were those of the Blackfeet Confederacy including the Piegans and the Bloods. They subsequently attempted to halt the sale and trade of guns in order to limit the firepower available to their enemies.

Nevertheless, other trading continued as both the Hudson's Bay Company and the North West Fur Company routinely gave guns in exchange for furs. Much of the gun trade occurred through the Mandans and Arikaras, who obtained them from the fur companies and distributed them to Plains tribes, such as the Crows and the Sioux.

When Meriwether Lewis and William Clark reached the Lemhi Shoshones in western Montana in 1805, they found that the Indians had "few small fusils [guns] of the North West Co. trade type."

The first gun obtained by the Indians, was the North West Trade gun, a weapon originally produced in England, made by companies in London and Birmingham, with the majority of the guns bearing a lock plate imprint "Barnett." Later weapons not made by those firms also had the name "Barnett" stamped on the lock plate, indicating that the Indians trusted that recognizable name and would only trade for weapons bearing it.

North West "Barnett" guns sold in 1810 at the Fort Osage trading post on the Lower Missouri for eight dollars each. By 1850 the Hudson's Bay Company traded North West guns to the Plains Cree for three silver fox pelts or five buffalo robes.

Though the first North West guns were made in England, or even Belgium, by 1843 they were manufactured by Henry E. Leman in Lancaster, Pennsylvania. In the 1850s the U.S. government purchased large numbers of the Leman guns, which were distributed to Indians as part of the annuities promised under treaty terms. In 1858 the U.S. government distributed 297 flintlock and 68 percussion-cap guns made by the Leman company to the Teton Dakota tribes. The $\frac{5}{8}$-inch smooth-bore guns had barrels ranging from 2'6" to 3'6", though many horseback riding Indians cut the barrels to shorter lengths for greater mobility. Some Indians used North West Trade guns even after more accurate, breech-loading, repeating rifles could be obtained.

Though Indians wanted guns, the plains tribal members did not always use them when hunting buffalo from horseback, finding that their shots were more accurate when they relied on their bow and arrows or lance.

During battles—either with other Indians or with the Frontier Army—Indians reduced reloading time by carrying bullets in their mouths and reloading without using wadding. Such a practice meant they could fire more shots in less time, but the lack of wadding affected bullet range and accuracy.

Some war lodges were not so sturdily built; they involved leaning poles against a nearly horizontal tree limb to form an enclosed area. Willow poles also were used for lodges of traveling war parties, particularly in areas or years when hostile attack was less likely to occur.

INDIAN TREATIES

Throughout the nineteenth century, before Congress ended all treaty making with Indian tribes in 1871, the American government instigated treaty conferences with tribes across the region, negotiating hundreds of treaties that, for the most part, restricted Indian territories and lifestyle. Most of the treaties, though initially approved, were later amended or never fully followed. In the vast majority of the cases, the Indians made significant concessions, and the federal government failed to hold up its end of the bargain. As a result there were often several treaties with the same tribe.

In the 1790s, for example, the government negotiated four treaties with the Cherokees—in 1791, 1792, 1794 and 1798. Each one not only added additional provisions for the Indians (many of which were never provided) but also stipulated more land cessions. In the 1800s, Cherokees were involved in thirteen additional ratified treaties that further eroded their lands and changed their lifestyle (eventually placing them in Indian Territory). Those treaties were negotiated in 1804, 1805 (two treaties), 1806, 1816 (three treaties), 1817, 1819, 1835 (two treaties), 1846 and 1866. Additionally there were two treaties with the Western Cherokees in 1828 and 1833. The number of treaties with the Cherokees is matched or exceeded by most tribes, giving an indication of the number of treaties negotiated during the period.

Treaty conferences had some similarities. Often more than one tribe was invited to each conference, which involved tribal leaders and high-ranking military and governmental officials. Negotiations took place with Indian spokesmen, often war leaders or chiefs, whom the federal officials believed spoke for their people and could make agreements. In reality the chiefs could not require their people to abide by any treaty decisions; individual bands within the same tribe might disagree on treaty provisions that were accepted by some leaders, and each Indian had the right to make his own individual decision with regard to whether or not he would abide by treaties.

In almost all cases interpreters served a vital role in explaining the positions of both Indians and governmental officials. The interpreters could be Indians, mountain men, traders or anyone, male or female, who knew a common language with the officials and the Indians.

Treaties established territories, made provision for payments to traders who had advanced goods to Indians, and usually provided other annual allocations of supplies—or annuities—to the Indians. The annuities generally included food, clothing and other material items, particularly those that would induce the Indians to rely less on hunting and gathering and more on farming and stock raising. As an 1855 treaty with the Gila Apaches, Mescalero Apaches, Navajos, Capote Band of Utes, Muache Band of Utes and Jicarilla Apaches said, the Indians received lands on which they could settle to "cultivate the soil and raise flocks and herds for subsistence." Treaty provisions often required Indians to establish schools and to refrain from use of alcoholic beverages; in exchange they received cows and plows.

In finalizing the treaties, governmental officials presented medals and gifts to the chiefs, and usually they also distributed gifts to the hundreds or thousands of tribal members who had come to the treaty conferences with their leaders.

George W. Manypenny, commissioner of Indian Affairs, noted in 1856 that there were three kinds of treaties:

> First, treaties of peace and friendship; second, treaties of acquisition, with a view of colonizing the Indians on reservations; and third, treaties of acquisition, and providing for the permanent settlement of the individuals of the tribes, at once or in the future, on separate tracts of lands or homesteads, and for the gradual abolition of the tribal character.

The final period of formal treaty making occurred during the 1860s, though other agreements came after that. While the earliest treaties sought primarily to establish peace, by the end of the period the tribes had been confined to reservations, and most of the tribal lands had been divided and allocated to individual members. In this space it is impossible to outline the hundreds of treaties negotiated during the 1800s—most of them never followed to the letter of the law—however, following are some of the key treaties and agreements.

TREATY TIMELINE

1814 August, Treaty of Fort Jackson: Creeks cede land in Georgia and Alabama, marking the end of Indian resistance south of the Ohio River.

1817, 0 July: Cherokees agree to exchange land in Georgia and North Carolina for equal amounts of land farther west along the White and Arkansas rivers, in the first treaty that allowed for exchange and *removal* rather than outright cession of land. This split the Cherokees into Eastern and Western bands.

1820, 18 October, Treaty of Doak's Stand: Choctaws cede some of their land in Mississippi for land in present-day Arkansas, Oklahoma, Texas and New Mexico. Some Choctaws move to the new land.

1830, 28 May: President Andrew Jackson signs the Indian Removal Act, which forces Cherokees to move from their lands in Georgia; the Cherokees take the law to the U.S. Supreme Court winning their case; ultimately they are still forced to move west to Indian Territory in 1838.

1830, 31 August: Chickasaws cede eastern lands in exchange for suitable lands in the West, conditional upon location of those lands (which did not occur until 1837).

1830 Prairie du Chien: Eastern bands of Sioux tribes agree to treaty provisions in an effort to end conflicts with the Sauks and Foxes.

1830: Choctaws agree to cede lands under the Treaty of Dancing Rabbit Creek, which provides for their removal from Mississippi to their land west of the river.

1831, 21 February: The Choctaw removal bill wins approval in Congress.

1832, 9 May, Payne's Landing: Seminoles sign a treaty that calls for their removal from Florida. They later refuse to acknowledge the treaty, and war breaks out lasting until 1842 when the Seminoles are either dead or moved (with the exception of a small band of holdouts who remain in Florida).

1832: Potawatomis agree to three separate treaties that reduce their territory and give them reservations in Michigan, Illinois, Indiana and southeastern Wisconsin.

1835, 24 August, Treaty of Camp Holmes: Nineteen Comanches sign the treaty that states "said Indians or tribes have free permission to hunt and trap in the grand Prairie west of the Cross Timbers, to the western limits of the United States." After the treaty signing, Auguste Choteau builds a trading post at Camp Holmes which soon does a brisk business.

1837: Chippewa western bands cede a large area in eastern Minnesota and north-central Wisconsin for cash, settlement of traders' claims and annuities; they retain fishing and hunting rights. Chippewas cede further lands in 1842 for similar consideration.

1838, 15 January, Buffalo Creek: New York Indians, including the Seneca, Oneida, Onondaga, Tuscarora, Cayuga, St. Regis, Brotherton, Stockbridge and Munsee tribes, agree to a treaty that parallels the removal treaties of the Southeastern tribes and calls for removal of the New York Indians to western lands. Congressional wrangling follows. Subsequently the tribes do not relocate to Indian Territory in Kansas as the treaty had stipulated when new treaties allow the tribes to remain in the Northeast.

1851: Sisseton and Wahpeton bands of Sioux make further land cessions at Traverse des Sioux while the Mdewakanton and Wahpekute bands make cessions at Mendota giving up most of their lands in Minnesota and eastern Dakota.

1851, 17 September, Fort Laramie: Sioux, Cheyennes, Arapahos, Crows, Arikaras, Gros Ventres, Assiniboines and Mandans surrender Indians lands for a fee of $50,000 each year for fifty years (later reduced to ten years) and establish new tribal lands at the treaty conference held on Horse Creek (Nebraska/Wyoming). The Indians agree to limit hostilities, to make restitution in the event of wrongs committed against whites by Indians and to allow roads through their territory (the Oregon-California-Mormon Trail, being the primary one).

1851–52: Indian commissioners negotiate a number of treaties with California tribes and with tribes in Oregon.

1853: Comanches, Kiowas and Apaches living south of the Arkansas River agree to treaties similar to the 1851 Fort Laramie Treaty.

1854: Chippewas negotiate another treaty that gives them permanent reservations in northeastern Minnesota, northern Wisconsin and Michigan's Upper Peninsula.

1854: Otos, Missouris, Omahas, Delawares, Peorias, Shawnees, Piankashaws, Weas and Miamis cede all but 1.34 million of their 15 million acres, opening most of eastern Nebraska to white settlement. They are promised annuities ranging from $5,000 to $20,000 to be paid for thirty-eight years with an additional $20,000 for the Indian removal to their new reservation lands, where land will be allotted to individual Indians in farm-sized plots.

1857, 24 September: Pawnees agree to the Table Rock Treaty at Nebraska City, signing away the last of their land; they move to a reservation at Genoa, Nebraska.

> It is expected that a treaty will be negotiated this summer with the Yorktown [Yankton] Sioux Indians, in Minnesota, for the extensive region of country bounded by the Missouri river and the Big Sioux on the West and East, and the 45th parallel of north latitude, on the North and South. This treaty will open up the best portion of the territory of Dacota to settlement.
> —Frank Leslie's Illustrated Weekly, *August 8, 1857, 155–3.*

1861: The Five Civilized Tribes negotiate treaties with the Confederate States of America, which grants fee-simple ownership of the land to be held in common "so long as grass shall grow and water run."

1863, 16 February: Congress voids all extant treaties with the Sisseton, Wahpeton, Mdewakanton and Wahpekute bands of Sioux following the 1862 Sioux Uprising in Minnesota.

> The President, in his instruction to Indian commissioner Dole, who is about to proceed to the Far West, for the purpose of effecting important treaties with the red men, directs him to press upon these wild and roving people the importance and necessity of abandoning their present savage and unsettled mode of life, and applying themselves to industry and the habits of civilization.
>
> —Frank Leslie's Illustrated Weekly, *15 July 1865, 259–2*

1865 October: Cheyennes and Arapahos sign away their lands in Colorado in exchange for a reservation in Kansas and Indian Territory, and the Kiowa-Apaches, Comanches and Kiowas agree to settle on a reservation in the Texas panhandle and in Indian Territory. But neither Texas nor Kansas will allow the agreed-upon reservations, so the treaties are voided.

1867: The United States creates an Indian Peace Commission, charged with settling the Indian conflict by negotiating treaties and requiring Indians to move to reservation lands and out of the path and settlement areas of whites.

> Our camp near Laramie was . . . located close enough for business, but far enough away to prevent the mingling of the troops and Indians for any purposes—thus avoiding the possibility of collisions growing out of trades in furs, beads, and other articles, in which the Indian is generally the unlucky one. . . ."
>
> —Margaret Carrington, *13 June 1867* (Absaraka, 75)

1867, 21 October, Medicine Lodge: Kiowas, Comanches, Apaches, Cheyennes and Arapahos gather at Medicine Lodge Creek, Kansas. The Comanches and Kiowas agree to reservations encompassing three million acres between the Washita and Red Rivers. Comanche leader Quanah Parker refuses to sign saying: "Tell the White chiefs that the Quohadas are warriors and will surrender when the bluecoats come and whip us."

Frank Leslie's Illustrated Weekly reported on the Medicine Lodge talks:

> The commissioners were seated upon camp stools ranged in a semi-circle, and the head chiefs squatted upon the ground forming a circle about them. A shady bower had been erected to shelter the party from the sun. Satanta, the chief of the Kiowas, secured a camp chair for himself, and occupied a position in front of his principal warriors. Little Raven, a very corpulent chief, filled the second station of honor. Facing the Commissioners was Mrs. Virginia Adams, the interpretess for the Arapaho tribe, attired in a bright crimson gown.
>
> General Harney, who is held in the utmost veneration by the Indians on account of having outrun their fleetest warrior, occu-

pied the position of grand chief in the council, and appeared in full-dress uniform. Upon the right of General Harney were Commissioner Tayler and Generals Auger and Terry, and upon his left, General Sandborn, Colonel Leavenworth, and McClosky who acted as the interpreter of the council.

Senator John B. Henderson, made known to the Indians the stipulations of a treaty between themselves and the Government, after which several prominent chiefs gave an expression to their views, which in the main were in opposition to their being settled upon reservations.

A subsequent meeting was held on the following day, at which there was a general interchange of sentiment upon the features of the proposed treaty, and on the 21st the Indians came to terms and the treaty was signed. . . .

. . . It may be well to state as an evidence of good faith on the part of the Government, that the Commissioners have distributed over $150,000 worth of provisions, besides a large number of blankets, suits of uniforms, tobacco, Indian cloth, axes, bed-tickings, revolvers, and sixteen elegant silver medals valued at $250. . . .

. . . On the 21st ultimo the Indian Commissioners and the chiefs of the Comanches and Kiowas signed a treaty of peace, which gives the Indians 6,000 square miles of land in the south-western corner of Indian Territory [Oklahoma]. Each Indian is to receive annually a full suit of clothes; they are to have farming implements, a teacher, miller, physician, warehouse, etc., and $25,000 per annum, or its value in such things as they may need. In consideration of all this, the Indians are to be peaceable and let all railroads be built across the plains.

—Frank Leslie's Illustrated Weekly, *16 November 1867, 135, 2 & 3*

Immediately after the talks the Indians received pots, pans, kettles, nails, brushes, sugar, coffee, flour, guns, powder and clothing.

The issue of clothing to the Comanche Indians after they had signed the treaty of peace was one of singular oddity, as many of the Indians forsook their old clothes immediately upon the receipt of new. The clothing issued consists of blankets, coats, shawls, calico, skirts, hats, pants, plumes, cords, beads, needles, pins, thread, yarn and woolens by the bale.

—Frank Leslie's Illustrated Weekly, *23 November 1867, 154-1*

1868 Spring: Peace Commissioners negotiate treaties with the Brûlés (29 April), Crows, (7 May), Northern Cheyennes and Northern Arapahos (10 May). Red Cloud's Oglala refuse to accept treaty conditions.

1868, 2 July: Hunkpapa chief Sitting Bull signs the Fort Laramie Treaty that sets aside the Great Sioux Reserve and establishes a reservation for the Hunkpapas.

1868, 3 July: Shoshones and Bannocks agree to treaties establishing reservations in Wyoming and Idaho territories.

1868, 3 August: Nez Percés agree to treaties and subsequent reservations.

1868, 6 November: Red Cloud ends his war and signs a treaty—the final formal treaty negotiated between tribes and the U.S. government—at Fort Laramie. The agreement said: "From this day forward all war between the parties to this agreement shall forever cease. The government of the United States desires peace, and its honor is hereby pledged to keep it. The Indians desire peace, and they now pledge their honor to maintain it."

1871: The U. S. Congress declares an end to all treaty making with Indian tribes. Indian affairs will now be legislated by Congress. The U.S. government will continue to negotiate some agreements with Indians, but they will not be considered treaties.

ADDITIONAL READING

Afton, Jean, David Fridtjof Halaas, and Andrew E. Masich. *Cheyenne Dog Soldiers: A Legerbook History of Coups and Combat.* Denver: The University Press of

Treaty signing by William T. Sherman and the Sioux at Fort Laramie. (Alexander Gardner, 1868. National Archives, 111–SC–95986)

Colorado and the Colorado Historical Society, 1997. Original drawings by Cheyenne warriors, known as Dog Soldiers, are reproduced giving a seldom seen perspective of Indian fighting.

Brady, Cyrus Townsend. *Indian Fights and Fighters*. Lincoln: University of Nebraska Press, Bison Books, 1971; originally printed by McClure, Phillips & Co., 1904.

Bruce, Robert. *The Fighting Norths and Pawnee Scouts*. Lincoln: Nebraska State Historical Society, 1932.

Carrington, Margaret Irvin. *Absaraka: Home of the Crows*. Lincoln: University of Nebraska Press, Bison Books, 1983; originally published by J.B. Lippincott and Co., Philadelphia, 1869. An account by an army officer's wife of events on the upper Plains during the 1860s.

Clark, Robert A., ed. *The Killing of Chief Crazy Horse*. Lincoln: University of Nebraska Press, Bison Books, 1988; originally published by Arthur H. Clark Co., 1976.

Crutchfield, James A. *Tragedy at Taos: The Revolt of 1847*. Plano, TX: Republic of Texas Press, 1995.

Dunlay, Thomas W. *Wolves for the Blue Soldiers: Indian Scouts and Auxiliaries with the United States Army, 1860–90*. Lincoln: University of Nebraska Press, 1982.

Forsyth, George A. *Thrilling Days in Army Life*. Lincoln: University of Nebraska, Bison Books, 1994; originally published New York: Harper & Brothers, 1900.

Frazer, Robert W. *Forts of the West*. Norman: University of Oklahoma Press, 1965.

Goetzmann, William H. *Army Exploration in the American West, 1803–1863*. Austin: Texas State Historical Association, 1991.

Greene, Jerome A. *Yellowstone Command*. Lincoln: University of Nebraska Press, 1991.

Grinnell, George Bird. *Two Great Scouts and Their Pawnee Battalion*. Lincoln: University of Nebraska Press, 1973.

Hampton, Bruce. *Children of Grace: The Nez Percé War of 1877*. New York: Henry Holt, 1994.

Hauptman, Laurence M. *Between Two Fires: American Indians in the Civil War*. New York: The Free Press, 1995.

Kenner, Charles L. *The Comanchero Frontier: A History of New Mexican-Plains Indian Relations*. Norman: University of Oklahoma Press, 1969.

Lavender, David. *Bent's Fort*. Garden City, NY: Doubleday, 1954.

———. *Let Me Be Free*. New York: Anchor Books/BDD, 1992; originally published by HarperCollins, 1992.

Mails, Thomas E. *Warriors of the Plains*. Tulsa, OK: Council Oaks Books, 1997. An excellent source.

———. *Mystic Warriors of the Plains*. Garden City, NY: Doubleday, 1972.

Marcy, Randolph B. *Thirty Years of Army Life on the Border*. New York: Harper & Brothers, 1866.

McDermott, John D. *A Guide to the Indians Wars of the West*. Lincoln: University of Nebraska Press, Bison Books, 1998. A concise view of Indian fighting techniques and individual battles.

Michno, Gregory. *Lakota Noon.* Missoula, MT: Mountain Press Publishing Co., 1997.

Miles, Nelson A. *Personal Recollections & Observations of General Nelson A. Miles Vol.1 and Vol. 2.* Lincoln: University of Nebraska Press, Bison Books, 1992; originally published Chicago: Werner Brothers, 1896.

Mishkin, Bernard. *Rank and Warfare among the Plains Indians.* Lincoln: University of Nebraska Press, 1992.

Nabokov, Peter, ed. *Two Leggings: The Making of a Crow Warrior.* Lincoln: University of Nebraska Press, Bison Books, 1982.

Olson, James C. *Red Cloud and the Sioux Problem.* Lincoln: University of Nebraska Press, 1965; Bison Books, 1975.

Paul, R. Eli, ed. *The Nebraska Indian Wars Reader, 1865–1877.* Lincoln: University of Nebraska Press, Bison Books, 1998.

Peterson, John Alton. *Utah's Black Hawk War.* Salt Lake City: University of Utah Press, 1998.

Reedstrom, E. Lisle. *Apache Wars: An Illustrated Battle History.* New York: Sterling Publishing Co., 1990.

Rickey, Don. *Forty Miles a Day on Beans and Hay.* Norman: University of Oklahoma Press, 1963.

Smith, Rex Alan. *Moon of Popping Trees: The Tragedy at Wounded Knee and the End of the Indian Wars.* Lincoln: University of Nebraska Press, Bison Books, 1981.

Smith, Thomas T., ed. *A Dose of Frontier Soldiering: The Memoirs of Corporal E. A. Bode, Frontier Regular Infantry, 1877–1882.* Lincoln: University of Nebraska Press, 1994.

Stadius, Martin. *Dreamers: On the Trail of the Nez Percé.* Caldwell, ID: Caxton Press, 1999.

Stands In Timber, John and Margot Liberty. *Cheyenne Memories.* New Haven: Yale University Press, 1998.

Tibbles, Thomas Henry. Edited by Kay Graber. *Standing Bear and the Ponca Chiefs.* Lincoln: University of Nebraska Press, 1995. An account of Standing Bear's suit that resulted in Indians being recognized as persons.

Utley, Robert. *Frontiersman in Blue.* Lincoln: University of Nebraska Press, Bison Books, 1981; originally published New York: MacMillan, 1967.

———. *Frontier Regulars.* Lincoln: University of Nebraska Press, Bison Books, 1984; originally published New York: MacMillan, 1974.

———. *Indian Frontier of the American West, 1846–1890.* Albuquerque: University of New Mexico, 1984.

———, and Wilcom E. Washburn. *Indian Wars.* New York: American Heritage, 1965.

Walker, Dale L. *Bear Flag Rising.* New York: Forge Books, 1999.

White Bull, Joseph. Edited by James H. Howard. *Lakota Warrior.* Lincoln: University of Nebraska Press, Bison Books, 1998.

Wishart, David J. *An Unspeakable Sadness: The Dispossession of the Nebraska Indians.* Lincoln: University of Nebraska Press, 1994.

Indian Treaties

Anderson, George E., W. H. Ellison, and Robert F. Heizer. *Treaty Making and Treaty Rejection by the Federal Government in California, 1850–1852.* Socorro, NM: Ballena Press, 1978.

Brugge, David M., and J. Lee Correll. *The Story of the Navajo Treaties.* Window Rock, AZ: Research Section, Navajo Parks and Recreation Department, Navajo Tribe, 1971.

A Compilation of All the Treaties between the United States and the Indian Tribes Now in Force as Laws. Washington, DC: Government Printing Office, 1873.

Hill, Burton S. "The Great Indian Treaty Council of 1851." *Nebraska History* 47 (March 1966): 85–110.

Institute for the Development of Indian Law. *A Chronological List of Treaties and Agreements Made By Indian Tribes with the United States.* Washington, DC: Institute, 1973.

Jones, Douglas C. *The Treaty of Medicine Lodge: The Story of the Great Treaty Council As Told by Eyewitnesses.* Norman: University of Oklahoma Press, 1966.

Kappler, Charles J., comp. *Indian Affairs: Laws and Treaties, Vol. 2, Treaties.* Washington, DC: Government Printing Office, 1904. (Senate Document no. 319, 58th Congress, 2d session, serial 4624.)

Kickingbird, Kirke, and others. *Indian Treaties.* Washington, DC: Institute for the Development of Indian Law, 1980.

Kvasnicka, Robert M. "United States Indian Treaties and Agreements." *Handbook of North American Indians,* vol. 4, *History of Indian-White Relations,* ed. Wilcomb E. Washburn, pp. 195–201. Washington: Smithsonian Institution, 1988.

Prucha, Francis Paul. *American Indian Treaties: The History of a Political Anomaly.* Berkeley: University of California Press, 1994. This is an excellent reference and includes detail about many treaties as well as a complete timeline of ratified treaties.

———. *The Great Father: The United States Government and the American Indians, Unabridged Vols. 1 and 2, combined.* Lincoln: University of Nebraska Press, 1995. Detailed analysis of two centuries of federal Indian policy.

Trafzer, Clifford E., ed. *Indians, Superintendents, and Councils: Northwestern Indian Policy, 1850–1855.* Lanham, MD: University Press of America, 1986.

PART TWO

EVERYDAY LIFE

FAMILY LIFE

I ndian life revolved around one of two types of relationships. Either the tribe was patrilineal, meaning the kinship was determined based on the male line, or it was matrilineal, in which kinship was determined based on the female line.

For women, being in a matrilineal society meant they had greater influence. They owned the lodges, often the farm or garden plots, and they also had a role in tribal affairs. Among the matrilineal tribes were the Seneca, Cayuga, Mohawk, Onondaga and Oneida tribes in the Iroquois League and the Cherokee, Chickasaw, Choctaw and Creek tribes in the Southeast. In most of those cases, residence was matrilocal, meaning when a woman married, her husband lived with her family. In a patrilocal society, the woman would live with her husband's family upon marriage.

A clan was an organized group of people distinguished by a single blood family and including all siblings (thus it is called a *sib* by anthropologists). Someone belonged to a clan by right of birth. Any clan member was required to marry someone from a different clan, and that couple's offspring belonged to the clan of the family member that dominated in the tribe (the mother in a matrilineal tribe and the father in a patrilineal tribe). Because all members of a clan were considered blood relatives, to marry within the clan was tantamount to incest.

Clans had such names as elk, deer, beaver, bear, bison, corn, crayfish, puma, wolf and wind. These clan names came from a common ancestor or from a totemic symbol and date to the earliest days of tribal history. Clan totems were not objects of worship, but instead were guardian spirits. So, for example, to the bear clan, the bear was considered a spiritual companion, guide and protector, and as such it was taboo to the clan members. They could not eat it, kill it, or in some cases even look at or touch it. The bear was important in their traditional stories, and clan members mimicked its life as they sang and danced to honor it.

Tribes also had loose associations of clans (called *phratries* by anthropologists) and sometimes separated in two major divisions called *moieties*, where those with or without clan systems had separate names and traditions. Most tribes had moieties such as the Haidas with their eagles and ravens, the Creeks with the whites and the chiloki (or reds), and the Pueblo groups who had summer people and winter people (or squash people [soft/summer] and turquoise people [hard/winter]).

A number of other personal relationships existed as well:

Polyandry: where a woman has more than one husband—was rare, though men occasionally shared the same women in situations among Eskimo tribes and some Shoshonean tribes; for example, a man might offer his wife to another man, particularly to a guest.

Polygyny: where a man has more than one wife. (Both polyandry and polygyny are forms of polygamy.)

Levirate: an anthropological term for the situation when the place of a dead husband is immediately assumed by his brother (usually younger) or cousin.

Sororate: an anthropological term for the situation when the place of a dead wife is immediately assumed by her sister or cousin.

Indian women, often portrayed as being downtrodden, hardworking "slaves" to Indian men, actually had great individual freedom in most tribes. In matrilineal or matriarchal tribes Indian women owned the lodges and sometimes the land on which gardens were cultivated. They had the right to vote and wield influence in both family and sometimes tribal decisions. A woman had certain possessions that remained hers even after marriage (unlike the situation for white women during the same time period). And women alone determined when they would have children. They often abstained from sex while nursing or rearing a small child, so Indian births often occurred three to five years apart. In most cases Indian women were not forced to marry against their will, although families often arranged marriages. In most tribes women could easily terminate a marriage—often simply by placing their husband's belongings outside the lodge door.

Women almost always had autonomy within the home. They were responsible for building and moving lodges in tribes that had wandering lifestyles.

In most culture areas young boys and girls played together, though they were generally separated at about the time they reached puberty. Some Plains tribes instructed boys and girls separately from the time they were very young.

Among all tribes menstrual blood was a potent substance, compared with the power of warriors who performed certain rituals before heading into battle. Lakota people believed that when a girl began to menstruate, she was possessed by a *tonwan*, or spirit, and that it made her *wakan*, or powerful. Because of such power, a man coming near a girl during her first menstrual period might thereafter be plagued with madness or tremors. Therefore, young girls were required to follow certain rituals and be aware of taboos as well. Menstruating women couldn't touch any gun or other weapon or come into contact with a medicine bundle. To do so could mean warriors would have difficulties, their horses might go lame or their bullets or arrows wouldn't shoot straight. Women were almost always required to separate themselves from others in the tribe during their monthly menstrual period. They sometimes remained in a sealed-off portion of their own home and in most tribes spent the days in a special lodge or hut.

EDUCATION

Young children had little guidance or discipline prior to toddler stage, but from age three or four on they were subjected to continued education and often rigorous training. In certain tribes tattooing began at that age as well as special training to "toughen" children. Sometimes even infants were held under cold water to keep them from crying, and certainly older children (particularly boys) were required to plunge into icy water, to sting themselves with centipedes or ants and to participate in rigorous physical conditioning such as long-distance running in scorching or frigid temperatures.

Later in the period Indian children were often sent to boarding schools. After 1879 children from seventy-nine different tribes attended the Carlisle Indian School in Carlisle, Pennsylvania. There the boys cared for dairy cattle while girls sewed school uniforms, which were close-fitting, heavy garments with high collars and many buttons. Children were not allowed to speak their native languages at Carlisle or most other Indian schools of the era.

Edward R. Geary, superintendent of Indian Affairs, outlined the philosophy of the Indian reservation schools in the Pacific Northwest:

> The children educated at these institutions should, in most cases, be taken entirely from the control of their parents, and boarded under the care of a judicious matron, where habits of cleanliness, punctuality, and order should be carefully cultivated. The education of these schools should not only embrace letters, but the boys should be instructed in agriculture and trades; the girls in the use of the needle and the various branches of domestic economy. These schools should be governed and taught by persons of not only capacity, firmness, and amiability, but by those of decidedly religious character.

Indian schools were required to display the American flag, and they recognized—and taught their students to recognize—such holidays as Christmas, Washington's Birthday, Decoration Day (Memorial Day), the Fourth of July and Thanksgiving.

CRIME AND PUNISHMENT

In almost all cases except those of absolute rule, any decisions about punishment for crimes were made only after a group of elders—and in some cases all adults in the village—had an opportunity to comment and make recommendations. That group determined penalties for such crimes as murder, theft, insult, adultery, rape or assault. In the case of a murder, the perpetrator was often put to death (or if he or she fled, a member of his or her family or clan was killed instead). (Among the Creeks even murder could be absolved during the annual Green Corn Ceremony or Busk.) Other offenses might be penalized by payment of fines, flogging or otherwise causing injury to the perpetrator (perhaps by scratching him or her with sharp bones).

Karok people (California tribe) recognized no crimes against individuals or the community. Undesirable behavior involved transgressions against individuals or against the supernatural. In the first case the person would be required to pay for damages to families or individuals; in the latter the transgressor would have bad luck. In a murder, for instance, there was no criminal stigma, but the murderer was required to pay in some form of currency (dentalium shells or other valuables) for the person he or she had killed. If a murderer refused to pay, he or she in turn could be killed, and those people taking revenge then also had to make restitution, or they could be indemnified for their actions.

Among the Maidus (California) anyone who stole something of material value from a tribal member risked reprisals. Those thieves who were apprehended were required to make retribution, and if a thief failed to do so, the person who had been the victim of theft could kill the thief. Theft—or the killing—of a nontribal member had no punishment associated with it. In cases of murder, blood revenge most often occurred, where family or kin of the slain person killed the murderer (generally in the same way the initial killing occurred). To compensate for the murder of a woman, the village of the murderer often compensated the family of the murdered woman by giving up a woman from their own village. In that way blood revenge could sometimes be avoided. Blood revenge was less likely to occur in the 1800s than it had earlier.

In event of a killing among the Iroquois, the murderer forfeited his or her own life. The family of the victim could thus kill the murderer or a member of his or her clan or family. Sometimes adequate gifts could be exchanged to compensate for the death of the victim and therefore alleviate the revenge killing. If the person killed was from another tribe, war could result. However, fighting could be prevented by payment of gifts according to acceptable formulas. Generally the life of a man was worth ten strings of wampum, while a woman's life was worth twenty strings of wampum.

Among the Chiricahua Apaches, witchcraft and incest were the two greatest crimes. Anyone guilty of incest was almost always branded a witch. Witches generally were taken into custody, tortured, forced to confess and then executed if they failed to restore (or return to life) their victims.

GENERAL FAMILY LIFE

Arctic

Aleut men owned their hunting and fishing gear, kayaks and tools, which they passed down to their male relatives. Women owned items in the home and the house itself, passing them to an eldest daughter or other female relative upon death. Because women owned the homes, residence of a married couple was with the wife and her relatives.

Birth: After a birth, women were isolated for a period (forty days among the Eastern Aleuts). Pacific Eskimo women gave birth in a small temporary hut near their house and remained there for ten days. They generally nursed their children for about three years. To discipline a child, a parent used ridicule and scorn, not physical punishment. Bering Strait Eskimo women used ptarmigan feathers for diapers.

Puberty: Aleut girls were isolated, and women could not touch their husband's amulets or hunting gear during menstruation. Once an Eastern Eskimo girl had reached menarche, her chin was tattooed. At puberty boys generally lived with and were instructed by a male relative, usually an uncle, who taught them hunting and other skills. By age sixteen boys began hunting in their own kayaks. If parents wanted a child of the opposite sex, they might raise their daughter as a son or their son as a daughter. In such cases they gave girls masculine names and trained them in male traditions. More commonly males were trained as females; each male obtained a chin tattoo upon reaching puberty and continued in the female role throughout life.

Marriage: In puberty Aleut boys lived with and worked for their mother's brother (their maternal uncle), and when they wished to marry, they provided bride service for one to two years, generally to the uncle since the preferred marriage was between cross-cousins (the boy and his uncle's daughter). Girls could marry at age thirteen; boys generally were at least eighteen before they married. Aleuts practiced polyandry and polygyny (see page 83). It was permissible for a young unmarried brother to cohabit with his elder brother's wife, though unacceptable for an older brother to sleep with a younger brother's wife. The older brother was considered a substitute father to his younger brother and thus to the younger brother's wife, so to sleep with her was considered incest. Similar rules were in place for younger and older sisters and their spouses. A man often allowed an honored guest to have intercourse with his wife. Male transvestites were openly accepted among the Aleuts.

After marriage the couple generally lived with the wife's family until after the birth of their first child when they moved to the home of the husband's family. Occasionally after a birth they remained with the wife's family, particularly if the husband's family had other sons and the wife's father needed someone to help him. Men could divorce a wife by returning her to her family; women had a more difficult time divorcing a spouse.

Pacific Eskimo men provided valuable gifts in order to marry a woman. The marriage was consummated when a man began living with a woman. A woman could have two husbands, with the second having little status and being classed just above a slave.

Among the Bering Strait Eskimos, in the area around Cape Nome, good hunters and chiefs often had two wives. The older wife did the sewing and the younger wife handled household work. There was little formal ceremony to marriage; a man might give his wife something such as a parka. Girls often were betrothed at age ten to an older man and sexual intercourse prior to marriage had no stigma, though a woman could be punished if she was unfaithful to her husband.

Death: Aleuts had no fear of death and often wrapped a body and kept it in the family quarters (in a specially walled-off area). A woman mourned for forty days when her husband died. During mourning people ate no oil food and kept themselves physically clean. They abstained from sex. Some committed suicide; others gave away possessions. In the central Aleutian district, fasting by eating no oil food was common. When an infant died, a father fasted in mourning for ten days, and a mother fasted for twenty days. In that area spouses fasted sixty days in mourning unless a man died at sea, when the woman mourned for only thirty days. Sometimes Central Aleuts practiced mummification.

California

Men headed the families in most California tribes. They controlled the property and women lived with their husband's family. Land ownership also passed through the male line. Women, however, were in control of the household management, child rearing and food gathering and preparation. In almost every other way, men dominated the California tribes. Women walked several steps behind the men, and men and women often ate in different locations.

In the area of political leadership, however, occasionally women had a role. Among the Pomo Indians political leadership descended through the headman's eldest sister. A Miwok daughter could succeed her father as chief if he had no sons, or a Miwok mother could represent her son until he became old enough to take over the leadership role. California Indian women also could gain status and material wealth by becoming medical practitioners, and many of them blended natural medicines with supernatural practices, as they became adept at preparing and dispensing herbal remedies or working as medicine healers. They determined cures for diseases by dancing, singing and smoking, sometimes ritually removing disease by placing their mouth against the ill person and sucking it out.

Most California Indians lived their entire lives within a small region—often within an area that never extended more than a few miles from their birthplace.

Premarital sex often was a ritual and an expected part of courtship. If an Indian woman was raped, she might abort or kill a newborn child. Children generally were disciplined without use of physical force, although occasionally a disciplinary action would be implemented that would "shame" a child, like striking the child with a coyote tail. Generally anyone guilty of wrongdoing made restitution to victims. The death penalty was used only for serious offenses, such as the practice of witchcraft.

Some tribes were particularly fastidious about their cleanliness. As A.L. Kroeber wrote in his 1925 *Handbook of the Indians of California*, the routine of women in the Athapascan tribes involved little variation. Women rose early and at a nearby stream or river took a complete bath.

> She was expected to have finished her bath before the men were astir. . . . The men always bathed in the river on rising. . . . In the afternoon, the old men, and the religiously inclined young men, took a sweat in the sweat-house and sunned themselves. As they sat there they engaged in meditation and prayer. . . . In the evening the principal meal was served . . . A basket of water was passed after the meal that the men might wash their hands.

By 1820, California Indian tribes had already seen significant changes in their lifestyle, caused by the development of the missions under the Spanish and the Franciscans. The Franciscan friars developed twenty-one missions along the coast south of San Francisco, which became home to more than twenty thousand Indians. The native people were invited to the missions and encouraged to adopt Christianity, and those who did became neophytes, or new believers. Some friars enticed the native people to the missions by offering them items; for example, one friar said he would give children Spanish clothes if their parents had them baptized. Other missions served *pozole*, porridge made of beans and barley that the Indians particularly liked, and the opportunity to eat the meal served as an inducement to live at the mission. Clothing and glass beads also were traded to the Indians in exchange for their work and residency at the missions. One friar called the trade items "bait."

The Indians who lived at the missions were required to maintain structured routines as they performed the work necessary to the mission's existence: farming, harvesting, taking care of livestock and doing domestic chores. The work schedules and use of Spanish, rather than native, clothing created changes in Indian lifestyle, but even more predominant in changing Indian lives was the spread of disease, particularly venereal diseases. Syphilis was particularly widespread and women became sterile, had stillbirths, died in childbirth and passed the disease on to their newborns. One priest wrote that fully two-thirds of the infants born to mothers with syphilis died before they were two years old.

The missions each had a grouping of adobe buildings around an open courtyard. There were palisaded walls, which had only two entrances that remained closed at night to prohibit intruders from making their way inside. The buildings included kitchens, storage areas, workshops, priests' quarters, a church, and dormitories for unmarried girls. Indian people initially lived in traditionally built huts and later in adobe rooms.

One or more majordomos acted as overseers of all the Indians and the mission work, while the neophytes had supervisors chosen from their own ranks. The friars knew the supervisory men supported their own work, and therefore they would keep the Indians in line.

Besides requiring the Indians to participate in Christian worship, the missions also imposed other changes on their lifestyle. One revolved around the Indian custom of premarital sex. The California Indians for the most part believed premarital sex was a natural and necessary part of courting. But the missions forbade it, housing all single girls over age eight in special dormitories. The young men, however, found ways to enter the dormitories. The girls would tie silk shawls together, providing a "ladder" for the young men to climb and enter their rooms. The young men would visit for the night, leaving the girls' dormitory before morning.

To discipline recalcitrant Indians, the Friars adopted various—some vicious—means. Serious offenses by men like fornication, theft and insubordination resulted in flogging, imprisonment, hard labor or time in the stocks. Lesser violations could require the Indian worker to wear wooden shoes in the fields for several days or to be shackled to another worker. Women also could be placed in the stocks, and both men and women could be whipped.

Birth: California tribes had strict and precise rules related to pregnancy and birth that affected both men and women. Though the exact rules varied from tribe to tribe, in general women and men both were restricted from eating certain foods, and men could not hunt, fish or gamble at certain times (particularly immediately after the birth).

Upon learning of her pregnancy a woman in the Hupa Chilula and Whilkut tribes avoided eating fish and meat. Men were required to abstain from sexual intercourse. At the time of birth, women assumed a sitting position and held onto a leather strap suspended from the lodge roof beam. After birth, the baby was bathed then purified by being held over a steaming cooking basket filled with herbs and boiling water. Women remained in isolation following a birth, lying in a pit lined with heated stones and covered with sand or damp wormwood. For ten days following birth women ate no fresh fish or meat and drank no cold water; men could not gamble or hunt. Initially a child was fed a thin gruel of hazelnut meats or mashed pine nuts; after a few days the mother began nursing the baby, allowing it to eat whenever the child showed an interest in doing so. Babies were wrapped in deerskin and strapped into a basketry cradle ten days after birth, remaining in that sitting-type cradle except for cleaning and exercising until they learned to walk.

Among the Pomos, names were considered private property. Therefore, only a mother or father called a child by his or her name; others called the child by a nickname or a relationship term (brother, nephew, etc.) The Pomo man could not hunt, fish, gamble, make beads or dance for a month following the birth of his child; he could not even leave the house for eight days. Both Pomo men and women did not eat ground squirrels, bluejays, certain species of fish and some vegetables the entire time a child was nursing (about a year).

Puberty: There were few puberty ceremonies for boys, though sometimes they participated in vision quests. A public ceremony was held for girls upon reaching puberty. Girls and women were isolated during menstruation and required to abstain from certain foods (meat, fish and cold water) and activities. When not in their menstrual huts, girls covered themselves, particularly their heads, with deerskin or other cloaks.

Marriage: In all areas men paid a bride price to the family of the woman they married as compensation for her loss as a worker. In the central portion of California, a woman's family made contributions to the man's family that nearly equaled the bride price. The bride price was recognition of a woman's social worth. She did not become a slave to her husband, and he could not subsequently sell her to someone else. Though men could have plural wives, usually only chiefs engaged in polygamy. Women could not have more than one husband. After marriage the couple lived with the man's family or band of people except among the Pomos and Huchnoms, where residence was with the woman's family. Girls generally married at age fifteen or sixteen; boys at sixteen or seventeen.

Pomo and Huchnom people observed strict rules related to sexual intercourse, such as abstinence during pregnancy and prior to hunting or fishing trips. Men followed certain rules during their wives' menstrual periods: they could not hunt, fish or gamble. Men and women had separate sleeping quarters (they were restricted from sleeping together in their houses), and cohabitation generally happened only in the late summer and fall when the families camped together.

Among central California tribes, though premarital sex wasn't generally forbidden, if a child was conceived, the father needed to pay an indemnity in order to give the child legitimacy. If such an indemnity wasn't paid, the child was considered an outcast and could not attend the deerskin dance. Adultery was condemned and men could be denied access to the sweat house. Women who were unfaithful could be beaten or even killed by their husbands. Men who had sexual relations with another man's wife had to pay fines or they could be killed. If a killing occurred as a result of adultery, the husband still had to pay a fine to the family of the man he killed, as would occur in the case of any murder.

Men headed the family and women treated them with respect. A California woman never ate before her husband; often they dined apart. When traveling, the man always walked in the lead. If something was being moved, the woman carried it. In the areas of food gathering, child rearing and household management, women were in authority. Though either a man or a woman could end a marriage, men usually instigated divorce. For a woman to divorce in some tribes, such as the Tubatulabal or Yurok, her family had to refund the bride price, which wasn't always easy or possible to do.

Men owned the land property (in most cases) though usually communally with others in the band or tribe. Men or women owned individual property, such as clothing, tools and the like.

Death: Wiyots were left in their houses after death awaiting burial. The deceased was painted; ear and nose piercing was common in order to allow placing of dentalium in the piercings. When it was time for the burial, the body was taken out of the house on a plank or pole stretcher carried through the door. At the cemetery away from the village the deceased was placed in a plank-lined grave along with money and other valuable possessions. By contrast the Yuroks did not paint corpses, nor pierce them. They removed the corpse through the wall of the house and threw ashes after it. They had private family burial plots near their homes. In most cases relatives of the deceased cut their hair in mourning.

Among tribes such as the Hupa, Chilula and Whilkut, a widow was expected to marry her deceased husband's brother. It was an insult to speak the name of the deceased, and anyone doing so had to pay survivors. The only situation when the name of a dead person could be said was if it had been formally given to a new baby in the family. Among the Shasta River Shastans, a woman cut her hair in mourning while a man burned his slightly. Widows also painted their faces with pitch and charcoal, removing the black mixture only when they remarried.

Among Pomos, the deceased remained in the house four days; then the body was removed and cremated along with personal possessions and gifts that had been given at the time of death. The house was also burned. After 1850 cremation was not practiced, due to white objections.

Northeast

The five Iroquois nations and the Hurons lived in longhouses owned by a matrilineal lineage group, known as an *ohwachira*. Each ohwachira also owned interior furnishings, fields, tools and other resources, and the property was handed down from mother to daughter. The ohwachira determined use of burial grounds, when and what to plant, and controlled the stocks of both wampum and dried food, items that represented the public treasury. When a woman married, her husband joined her in the longhouse; if they divorced, he left. Any children remained with the mother and were cared for by women in the maternal line (grandmother, mother, sister or aunt). Iroquois men helped clear fields and killed game to provide meat, but otherwise they had little say or role in family life or domestic affairs. Instead they spent much of their time away from the longhouses on trading expeditions, hunting or fighting. During the 1800s many of the people in the Iroquois League began living in structures styled after those of Europeans.

Iroquois tribes had a Council of Clan Mothers, which included the heads of each household. That council nominated men to serve as sachems or chiefs on the League's Grand Council. The women established the agenda for League Council meetings, lobbied to influence the vote on important issues, and because they controlled food supplies, they could control every decision of the tribe, including whether or not to participate in a war.

In 1724 Jesuit missionary Fr. Joseph-Francois Lafitau wrote about the Iroquois women:

> It is of them that the nation really consists, and it is through them that the nobility of the blood, the genealogical tree, and the families are perpetuated. All real authority is vested in them. The land, the fields, and their harvest all belongs to them. They are the souls of the councils, the arbiters of peace and of war. They have charge of the public treasury. To them are given the slaves. They arrange marriages. Their children are their domain, and it is through their blood that the order of succession is transmitted. The men, on the other hand, are entirely isolated.

Other eastern tribal women also had considerable influence, including those from the Mohegan, Pequot, Montauk and Powhatan tribes. They arranged marriages, sponsored male political leaders and some became formal leaders themselves.

Each of the Iroquois tribes had clans that owned names, which were bestowed upon children and adults. Mohawk and Oneida clans were wolf, turtle and bear. Onondaga clans were wolf, turtle, snipe, beaver and ball in one moiety and bear, deer, eel and hawk in the other. Seneca clans were beaver, turtle, bear and wolf in one moiety and snipe, heron, deer and hawk in the other. Cayuga clans were deer, bear, turtle, ball, heron, wolf and snipe.

Birth: Birth took place in a birthing hut. A Delaware infant was rolled in the snow (if the birth occurred when there wasn't snow, then the rolling process was conducted the first time it snowed after the birth). Among the Hurons, soon after birth a mother pierced her child's ears with a fishbone or awl, subsequently inserting a feather quill or similar object to keep the hole open. Huron babies were swaddled, allowing an opening for a young boy's penis and placing a husk of corn so a baby girl would not wet herself; caregivers tucked cattail down around the infant's bottom as well. Once swaddled, the babies were placed on a wooden board, which mothers carried on their back or their breast by fastening it with a belt. The boards were generally decorated with paintings and strings of wampum beads.

Shawnee women gave birth to their children in a small hut located away from their family lodge, remaining in the birthing hut for ten days until the naming ceremony, held at a public feast hosted by the parents. In the early nineteenth century an elderly man from a different clan than the parents named the child. In the latter part of the century two middle-aged or elderly individuals (male or female) suggested names following prayer; the parents picked one of the two names.

Potawatomi women gave birth in a special bark house (after a woman had followed a restrictive diet in order to protect her unborn child from evil). The woman, assisted by other females, positioned herself on her knees or over a stretched cord as she gave birth. She remained in the hut for a month or longer before returning to her home with the infant. A child was named about one year after birth and might not be weaned for several years.

Puberty: Girls and women were isolated in menstrual huts both prior to and after marriage. Even after they'd been removed to Oklahoma, the Delaware women generally isolated themselves during menstrual periods, cooking and eating separately from other family members. Potawatomi girls were isolated during menstruation, and when the village was on the move, they were required to walk parallel to the main column, but some distance away.

Marriage: Women of some tribes within the Iroquois League had sex with many men, even participating in "trial marriages" before deciding whom to actually marry. When an Iroquois man wanted to marry, he approached the woman's parents and gave the intended bride gifts including a wampum necklace, earrings or bracelet. The couple then spent four nights together. Huron and Wyandot people had multiple partners and sex outside marriage. In those tribes a marriage was legitimate only when a child had been conceived.

Among the Shawnees, mothers of the couple arranged early marriages, which involved an exchange of gifts. After 1824 the couple cohabitated without arrangement by mothers or exchange of gifts. Divorce could be initiated by either spouse.

Death: Deceased people were placed in "dead clothes" and preparations made for a funeral. Mirrors and other reflecting items were covered so people (particularly children) did not see the ghost of the dead person. Food would be set out for the dead person, and at least two people remained with the body until the funeral. The night before burial friends and relatives held a wake and usually those attending played the moccasin game. (For details see "hidden ball game" on page 204). After the funeral, planning began for a ten-day feast where distribution of the deceased person's property occurred. A year after the death, another feast for the deceased was held, marking the end of mourning. The Senecas held a special ceremony known as Chanters for the Dead or Feast for the Dead either annually or semiannually, which included speeches, a tobacco invocation, singing and dancing. It concluded with sharing of food and gifts, particularly cloth items.

Death of an Iroquois League chief precipitated the Condolence Ceremony, held in the autumn or winter months. Each chief belonged to a certain group or moiety, and his death had to be mourned not by his moiety but by the opposite moiety. Therefore, if the deceased belonged to the Younger Brothers moiety then the Older Brothers were responsible for conducting the Condolence Ceremony. The ceremony began at a fire near the longhouse with a greeting called "At the Woods' Edge." Once completed the participants moved into the longhouse chanting the Roll Call of Chiefs. Inside the longhouse participants sang the Condoling Song, and they recited a Requickening Address before the man selected to take the deceased chief's place was announced and told what his responsibilities would be. Foods served at the subsequent feast were meat, bread and corn soup. The Iroquois exchanged wampum as condolence for a death.

Hurons believed life after death was not all that different from life on earth. They placed dead people on a mat in a flexed position so people from the deceased clan could view the individual one final time. During that time people would give speeches about the deceased. Three days after death the chief in charge of the ceremonies announced a feast where gifts were given to the bereaved and to those directing the funeral. The body was then placed on an eight- to ten-foot-high scaffold along with some grave goods. Anyone who drowned or who died in war was buried in the ground with a fenced shrine placed over the burial site. Infants up to age one month were buried in a path or another place where people often walked in the belief that the baby's spirit could pass into the womb of a woman. Mourning lasted about ten days except for a spouse, who mourned for a year, during which time he or she participated in no feasts and didn't remarry. Every eight to twelve years the Hurons gathered all of the individuals from single burials and re-interred them during the Feast of the Dead, where all remains were placed in a large common grave. The grave pit was lined with beaver robes and all bones of the deceased and some of their grave goods were then placed into the pit, which was subsequently covered with bark, mats, sand and logs before being surrounded by upright posts. Grave goods that were not placed in the pit were distributed to those in charge of the Feast of the Dead and to relatives of the deceased. Many of the items placed in the grave were broken, in order to release their souls (the Hurons believed all animate and inanimate objects had souls) to make the journey to the afterlife. Hurons believed each person had two souls. After the burial one soul went to the afterlife and the other was released to be reborn.

Among the Shawnees friends dressed and painted the deceased, and then they prepared a grave and carried the body to the cemetery. Possessions of the deceased were distributed among relatives and given to those who took care of the burial preparations and activities. The deceased was buried in new clothes, and tobacco was sprinkled in the grave to implore the body to not look back. Mourning lasted twelve days except for a spouse, who mourned for a year, not wearing paint, jewelry or changing clothing during the entire time.

Southeast

Southeastern tribes had many similar customs. All were matrilineal tribes with organized clans. They primarily lived in villages near rivers, and they had extensive trade relations, including trading centers or towns of their own people.

By the early 1800s, Southeastern Indians had cattle and hogs, which they branded to establish ownership. Men, who had traditionally spent much of their time hunting or on war parties, now participated almost exclusively in commercial hunting, providing meat for traders. The types of crops raised also shifted. Though the tribes still raised corn, squash and beans, they also began cultivating rice, wheat and fruit trees.

In 1794 the Cherokees approved the Hopewell Treaty, which limited some of their territory, leading to a shift in gender roles. Though traditionally only women cultivated fields, by the 1800s, men began working in fields, partially because so many of their hunting areas had been usurped by encroaching non-Indian people. Some Cherokee headmen became plantation owners, and they even had black slaves to do much of the work.

In May 1817 Cherokees debated whether to accept a federal government offer to relocate the entire tribe to a new region west of the Mississippi River. At the same time they adopted a constitution, similar to the U.S. Constitution, which ended the matriarchal clan system. The rift that resulted from the Cherokee constitution and a subsequent vote on removal permanently divided the tribe.

Birth: During pregnancy Cherokee women observed certain food taboos. For instance, they never ate speckled trout, believing the fish could cause skin blemishes on an unborn child. Once they felt the baby's movement, Cherokee women went to the river to participate in a prayer session. The woman drank an herb medicine made from slippery elm bark, pine cones and various other roots, believing that the slippery elm would ease the delivery while the pine ensured long life. After the birth a Cherokee man took the placenta in order to bury it, crossing one or more mountain ranges or ridges before doing so. When he buried the afterbirth, he prayed for another child. The Cherokees believed the next birth would occur the number of years later equivalent to the number of ridges the father had crossed to bury the placenta.

Puberty: Girls isolated themselves during menstruation.

Marriage: The Natchez as a tribe was virtually extinct by the 1800s, though some Natchez lived with other Southeastern tribes. The gifts given to a Natchez woman from a lover became a part of her dowry, so Natchez women had competitions to see which of them could attract the most men and receive the most gifts as a result.

Seminole people were matrilineal, and after marriage a couple lived in the house of the wife's mother. Children belonged to the same clan as their mother. Young boys were taught such skills as hunting, fishing and warfare by their maternal uncles. To obtain a divorce, a Seminole woman placed her husband's belongings outside the door of the house. Seminole men sometimes had two wives, but only if the first, or principal, wife approved his marriage to a second wife. Once divorced, a Seminole man would move in with his second wife or return to live with his mother.

Cherokees exchanged symbolic gifts at the time of marriage. Women cultivated fields and therefore might give an ear or two of corn, while men who hunted could give a piece of deer meat. Because homes belonged to the women, they could divorce by putting the man's possessions outside.

Among Southeastern Indians, marriage within a person's clan was considered incest and therefore not allowed—or severely punished (often by death) if it occurred. Men and women from different clans could marry by the exchange of gifts, and they divorced by removal of possessions from the residence. Infidelity was not condoned, and those who were found guilty could be punished (particularly if they were women). Punishment included whippings, head shavings, the cutting or clipping of an ear or nose, or even permanent exile. Among the Choctaws a man would take his unfaithful wife to the village public square and there allow any man who wanted to do so to have intercourse with her.

Some tribes allowed men to have more than one wife (generally sisters or maternal cousins of the first wife and almost certainly women from the same clan).

By the early to middle 1800s, many Southeastern Indian women began marrying outside their tribes and clans. They became the wives of white traders, in part to forge trade alliances and to enhance the status of their families. That shift caused a decline in the matrilineal kinship system as the women lived with their husbands (rather than the husband living with the woman and her clan), and a culture where women had been property owners also shifted because the property generally fell under the European practice whereby it was owned and controlled by the man.

Death: Creeks and Seminoles buried their dead in a round hole beneath the hut or cabin where death occurred, with the corpse wrapped in a blanket and then placed in a sitting position. The grave was then covered with canes and clay after which relatives mourned by howling. If the deceased had been a prominent man, the family built a new house to move into. Tribes in the Carolinas, including the Cherokees, used coffins for burial, placing the deceased in blankets or matchcoats and then positioning them with their head toward the east. Creeks in mourning smeared grease and wood ashes on their face.

The Choctaws built eighteen- to twenty-foot-high scaffolds for burial platforms. The corpse was placed on the scaffold then covered with a mantle. Friends and relatives routinely visited until the flesh decayed; then men and women known as bone pickers (who had particularly long fingernails) made their way to the corpse and carefully pulled all flesh from the bones, subsequently giving the bones to the relatives, who placed them in a coffin. The bone-pickers left the decayed flesh on the scaffold, which was burned, and then the relatives buried the coffin filled with bones in the bone house before holding a feast, presided over by the bone-picker who served the food prior to washing his or her hands.

Great Basin

The harsh climate of the Great Basin—hot in summer and cold in winter—affected all aspects of Indian lifestyle as the people spent most of their time and energy in finding food and shelter.

Birth: Shoshone women on the trail when they gave birth stopped by themselves, delivered their child, then usually caught up to the tribe within a few hours; though if birth occurred while they were in camp, they isolated themselves in their lodge for thirty days. Ute women spent more than a month recovering from childbirth, lying on a bed made from a pit filled with hot ashes. Even Ute men spent four days in "recovery" following the birth of a child. Ute children generally nursed until they were four or five years old. Fathers and mothers shared in the work associated with the birth of a Paiute child. Both fasted from all meat, and the father piled wood for twenty-five days and did his wife's household duties during that time. Every five days the child's basket was changed. Each of the five baskets during the first twenty-five days of life were retained, however, and at the end of the period all of them—the last one containing the child's navel string—was put into a tree while the child was placed into a new, ornamented basket.

Puberty: Paiute girls reaching puberty were taken by two friends to a wigwam just big enough for the three of them. There the girl entering puberty underwent twenty-five days of ritual.

> Every day, three times a day, she must gather, and pile up as high as she can, five stacks of wood. This makes fifteen stacks a day. At the end of every five days the attendants take her to a river to bathe. She fasts from all flesh-meat during these twenty-five days, and continues to do this for five days in every month all her life. At the end of twenty-five days she returns to the family lodge, and gives all her clothing to her attendants in payment for their care. Sometimes the wardrobe is quite extensive. It is thus publicly known that there is another marriageable woman, and any young man interested in her, or wishing to form an alliance, comes forward.—*Sarah Winnemucca Hopkins*

Uinta Ute warrior and his bride, northwest Utah. (John K. Hillers, 1874; National Archives, 57-PE-110)

Marriage: Young Ute men who had not accumulated wealth in order to impress and obtain a desirable young woman lived separately from the main band in a group known as the Dogs. They visited camps and considered it acceptable to carry off any girl who made fun of them. Young Shoshone men who didn't have wealth to pay for a wife also occasionally stole other men's wives or young unmarried women. A Paiute man entered the family lodge of the girl he wanted to marry. The girl slept next to her grandmother, and the young man would sit at the girl's feet. If the girl was not interested in him, she would get up and go sleep beside her mother. A Paiute girl would not be forced to marry against her will. When a girl made up her mind about which young man she wanted to marry, she told her grandmother, who in turn informed the girl's father. The father then contacted the young man and instructed both the man and his daughter on their duties should they marry.

> At the wedding feast, all the food is prepared in baskets. The young woman sits beside the young man, and hands him the basket of food prepared for him with her own hands. He does not take it with his right hand; but seizes her wrist and takes it with the left hand. This constitutes the marriage ceremony, and the father pronounces them man and wife.—*Sarah Winnemucca Hopkins*

Death: Shoshones buried the deceased in rock-covered graves, or sometimes they simply caved in the lodge of the deceased (which was constructed of poles and brush) and then moved to a different village location. Paiutes in mourning cut off their hair and also cut long gashes in their arms and legs. When a husband died, his widow was the first to cut her hair, taking what she cut and braiding it before placing it over her breast. Afterward the other relatives of the deceased also cut their hair. A widow was expected to remain unmarried until her hair had grown back to the same length as before. She was not to wash her face, use paint or engage in games or other lighthearted pursuits until given permission to do so by her father-in-law and mother-in-law. Though a widower mourned in the same way, he had greater liberties than did a widow.

Interior Plateau

Of all the cultural groups, Indians in the Interior Plateau were most amicable to each other. They commonly intermarried, visited each other's villages and had many similar practices related to their everyday lives.

Birth: Among the Spokanes, women adhered to dietary and behavioral taboos while they were pregnant. Upon birth a baby was plunged into cold water then rubbed vigorously. Spokanes considered the birth of twins a blessing, unlike some tribes that considered twins a curse. Several weeks after birth a Spokane baby was placed in a cradleboard. The cradleboard was often packed with moss that was used as an absorbent material in place of a diaper. Yakimas placed babies in cradleboards within five days of birth, keeping them thus confined for two or three years, though changing the size of the cradleboard as the baby grew.

Among some Plateau tribes, the heads of infants were flattened in the belief that it improved appearance. Such a practice was done by placing the baby in a cradleboard and putting a stiff pad on the head just above the eyes then tying it tightly to the cradleboard. The practice of head flattening generally disappeared in the 1840s.

Among the Wasco and Wishram tribes, children were named when they were six to eight months old. They subsequently received other names during their lives as they achieved higher rank or social position. Each time someone received a new name, he or she (or the family) sponsored a feast and distributed gifts and other valuables. Nicknames also were common.

Among the Nez Percés, children were routinely instructed in bathing. After bathing children were struck with switches or whips in a practice believed to make them strong. Aunts and uncles gave lectures on proper behavior.

Puberty: Girls were isolated in menstrual huts after they entered puberty, and both boys and girls sought guardian spirits during puberty. Among the Coeur d'Alenes adolescents used sweat houses and bathed in cold water every day. Yakima girls began the "time ball" or "counting the days ball" when they entered puberty. Like a diary, the ball helped them to remember important events in their lives. A young woman started with a piece of hemp string, tying a knot for each important event such as when she married or had a child. Sometimes a woman would add a bead or other object to the string ball as she tied the knots. This ball of life was continued until a woman died, when it would be buried with her.

Marriage: Among the Kutenai, a young man could sneak into the house and bed of a young woman. If she did not awaken her parents, she agreed that they would be married. Other Kutenai marriages could be encouraged by parents, which occurred so long as the parties involved "accepted" the marriage. Spokane marriages were arranged and took place when a young man was about eighteen and when a girl was between puberty and age twenty. Coeur d'Alenes practiced polygamy though other Plateau tribes were monogamous. Most Plateau tribes practiced levirate and sororate. Among the Wasco, Wishram and Cascades tribes, the man's family generally arranged the marriage.

Death: In the 1800s burials in the Interior Plateau generally involved interment in graves dug into the ground or under a rock shelf or outcrop which could be caved in to cover the body. The bodies were placed in a flexed or extended position, often wrapped in blankets and then positioned to face the east or the west. By late in the century Indians who had converted to Christianity were buried facing toward the west, while those who had not converted faced east. Cremation was often used, and multiple burials could be conducted for infants or children. Following a death some personal possessions might be buried with the deceased, others were distributed to friends and family members. A period of mourning always occurred ranging from a few days to a couple of years, during which time the name of the deceased would not be mentioned.

Among the Spokanes, bodies were flexed and wrapped in deerhide before burial. Mourning ended with a ceremonial feast hosted by the family. The Coeur d'Alenes left offerings such as roots, berries, horse skins or canoes at burial sites, hanging them from poles painted red and placed at the grave. Yakimas had elaborate burial ceremonies lasting five days and nights in which kin helped the deceased "along the way." After burial, additional ceremonies were held at the longhouse. Generally the name of the deceased was not spoken for about a year until a memorial ceremony was conducted. Then people who had been given items belonging to the deceased either wore them (if they were clothing items) or displayed them. At the memorial ceremony people who had inherited from the deceased distributed gifts as a way to honor the dead person. After the memorial ceremony the family of the deceased could again participate in tribal ceremonies. Wishram, Wasco and Cascade tribal members buried individuals by taking personal belongings along with the deceased to a family sepulcher, which was a structure on a bluff near the Columbia River or an island in the river.

Northwest Coast

The only region where native people recognized class status, the Northwest Coast also was the only area where the potlatch was common. A ceremonial feast, the potlatch was held for a variety of reasons: death, recognition of a girl reaching puberty, marriage or even the building of a new longhouse, was common though it was outlawed late in the century due to economic hardships it placed on families. There were three general class distinctions: hereditary nobility, commoners and captive slaves. Most tribes were patrilineal. Chiefs had clear authority.

Birth: Tlingits believed children were reincarnations of maternal relatives. Birth took place in a bark shelter where mother and child stayed for ten days. A Haida woman observed taboos during pregnancy to ensure the health of her child. Upon birth a Haida infant received a name from the parents and later additional names could be conferred upon a child. An infant had its ears pierced within a few days of birth. Tattoos were placed on an infant girl's arms and legs and an infant boy's arms, legs, back and chest. High-ranking Haida girls had their lower lip pierced during childhood to allow later wearing of a labret, an elliptical piece of wood, ivory or bone inserted into the lower lip that they generally received after puberty.

Puberty: Girls from all Northwest Coast tribes were isolated during puberty. A Tlingit girl was isolated for two years or so, the time dependent upon her rank and her father's wealth, in order to learn about clan traditions from a paternal aunt or sometimes from her mother or maternal grandmother. Upon completion of her isolation, the girl had a much-admired transparent complexion, but often was too weak to walk. A number of rituals were observed. The girl scratched herself only with a special scratcher, she wore a black feather cap and washed her hair in blueberry juice to help it maintain its color in old age. She fasted for eight days, with the exception of a drink of water on the fourth and eighth days. Throughout seclusion she didn't eat fresh fruit, fish or seaweed. She wore a large hood fringed with dentalia tassels to avoid seeing the sky, an act that could bring storms. Once she emerged, the girl was given new clothes and gifts and honored with a potlatch by her paternal aunts, at which time she was presented for marriage.

Marriage: Persons of equal rank were ideal marriage partners among the Tlingits so long as they were from differing moieties. The families exchanged gifts prior to the marriage. Men often married two or more sisters at the same time, and upon the death of a spouse a man could replace her with a younger sister or close kinswoman. Widows married their husband's brother or his maternal nephew. Some women of high rank had more than one husband simultaneously. Haida marriages were arranged, often in childhood and occasionally in infancy.

Death: Eight days of mourning generally were observed upon the death of a Tlingit man. Cremation was the preferred form of body disposal though heads and scalps of warriors and medicine healers might be preserved. After 1880 cremation was less common (due to missionary influence). Bodies of slaves were thrown onto the beach where they either washed out to sea or were eaten by scavengers.

Haidas cleaned and dressed a corpse, then allowed it to lie in state for several days before placing it in a coffin and removing it from the house through a hole in the wall. The body was then interred in a grave house behind the main dwelling. Later it could be transferred to a niche in a mortuary column. If relatives instead carved a memorial pole, the body remained in the grave house. Generally the grave houses and carved poles were reserved for high-ranking people. Haida slaves were thrown to the sea. As signs of mourning people cut their hair and blackened their faces.

Plains

By 1800 the Plains Indians had become a horse and bison culture, though some tribes also still engaged in farming. Those that relied on the bison were largely nomadic tribes, following the herds summer and winter. They became adept at moving villages (the work of women) and killing and processing large amounts of meat at one time. They considered territory particularly important, for it ensured them good hunting.

The Plains people divided into Northern Plains and Southern Plains tribes, though they had common beliefs. They learned how to adapt to the land, moving into areas where there was more grass for their horse herds and likewise greater likelihood of game. They formed alliances with each other, though some Plains tribes were bitter enemies. For Plains tribes warfare was a routine and regular part of their life. A young Plains boy could never expect to become a man—and therefore to marry—unless he engaged in warfare. In the first half of the century warfare primarily involved intertribal conflicts; in the second half it involved the U.S. military with occasional intertribal battles.

Plains tribal life was either matrilineal or patrilineal depending on the individual tribe. Chiefs for the most part served because they had earned respect, but for Plains Indians each person had the right to make individual choices, and no one could demand or require any particular action. When on the war trail, for example, if a warrior felt uncomfortable or uneasy about a coming engagement, he could leave his companions and return to the village with no loss of honor.

If a Crow man did not steal an enemy horse, his wife could not ride a horse at any tribal ceremony. When a Crow warrior saved another Crow warrior in battle, he then had the right to paint the face of one of his wives. Once a warrior had painted his wife's face, she could do so herself for special occasions such as a dance or big feast.

Mandan women were in a matrilineal society, therefore they controlled agricultural activities. The Mandan White Buffalo Society—a group of women who had already gone through menopause—each year performed buffalo-calling ceremonies to entice bison herds to move nearer the villages. The women in the Mandan Goose Society, meanwhile, had rainmaking ceremonies and other rituals associated with the annual spring and fall migration of geese.

Berdaches were Plains Indian men who acted and dressed like women. Among the Hidatsas males usually became berdaches as teenagers or later and only when the male involved had a series of dreams from the Holy Woman Above. Further, only brothers or sons of men who owned ceremonial rights to the Holy Woman or Woman Above bundles could become berdaches. Once a male had the required dreams, and if he was from the correct lineage, he could then begin wearing women's clothing and fulfill all the duties of a Hidatsa woman. The berdaches were considered to have mysterious spirit power.

Pawnee women—though in a matrilineal society—had less influence than those in most matrilineal societies because more of their subsistence came from hunting—which men did—rather than farming, which women did. Pawnee men lived with their wives' families only during planting and harvesting seasons when the tribal people stayed in earth-lodge villages. The remainder of the year the tribe followed game and lived in hide lodges, during which time the domestic situation switched and women lived with their husband's relatives. Most often Pawnee brothers joined together taking their families on hunting trips.

Other Plains tribes that relied primarily on hunting—such as the Arapahos, Cheyennes, Comanches and Sioux—also had relationships that primarily revolved around male lineage. The women supported their hunter/warrior husbands (fathers/brothers) and were responsible for moving the camp and taking care of meat and hides.

A skilled woman might be able to butcher three bison a day, but she could never keep up with all the work of butchering, processing meat and hides, moving camp, and cooking and dealing with children because her husband— once he had obtained horses—could easily kill more than three bison during a day of hunting. Therefore, she almost always had someone to help her. It could be a slave captured from an enemy tribe, a daughter, aunt, mother, grandmother or perhaps another wife of her husband, since many of the Plains tribes practiced polygamy.

Women struck the camp, packed lodges and household items onto travois and then moved from place to place as dictated by their husbands and tribal or band leaders. They also maintained a record of their accomplishments, keeping elkhorn tools onto which they carved dots, with each black mark representing a tanned robe.

As women shared labor they found they had skills to use in bartering. For example, one woman who was skilled at tanning hides might trade her labor for a cradleboard, which was generally as valuable as a horse.

By 1865 the Omaha tribe had been confined to reservations and their traditional lifestyle was virtually abandoned. After that time Omaha people lived in frame houses and Omaha men farmed, doing little hunting.

Birth: Most Plains Indian families were small with only one to three children, generally born from three to five years apart. During a Plains woman's pregnancy, usually the mother or grandmother of the child to be born made two objects. One represented a lizard, which had horsehair or breath feathers (the downy feathers of an eagle or other bird) attached to the legs. Upon the birth it would be used as a decoy to lure away any bad spirits. The other was a turtle into which the child's umbilical cord would be placed along with tobacco or herbs. When the child started walking, the turtle amulet would be attached to his or her clothing. Even later, young boys might attach their turtle to their shirt or to their headdress if they became successful warriors.

Babies were usually named soon after birth. A name could be a family, plant or animal name. It always had some connection to the child's clan, so the child of an Eagle clan mother might be Good Eagle or Soaring High. Later in life an individual might receive another name (particularly males).

A Crow child was named four days after birth, usually by his or her father, though sometimes by the mother or an elderly, respected individual. Girls generally kept the same name throughout their lives; boys often obtained new names.

Most Plains babies were carried on cradleboards. The Kiowas built their cradleboards with two sharply pointed sticks at the top. That way the child wouldn't be harmed if the cradleboard was dropped from a horse and landed head down. The Arikaras did not use cradleboards. Instead they wrapped the baby in a calf skin and then a heavy piece of bison skin. They stood the children thus wrapped in a narrow sack that they suspended from a roof timber.

Among the Otos, naming occurred within four days with four names selected by one of the old men in the tribe. The parents chose the child's name from among those selected by the elder.

Puberty: Children were disciplined in various ways but seldom, if ever, through whippings or by being struck. To keep a child from crying, it would either be cuddled, hugged, sung to, or in extreme cases, water might be poured into the child's nose until the child became uncomfortable enough to quit crying. Children were also threatened with the possibility that something bad might

A CROW BIRTH

When Crow Pretty-Shield was ready to give birth to her first child, she entered the birthing lodge. It had two stakes driven into the ground with robes rolled up and piled against them so when she knelt and took hold of the stakes her arms rested on the robes. As Pretty-Shield entered the birthing lodge, her helper took four coals from the fire and placed them on the ground in four different locations in the lodge. The helper put some grass on the coals and told Pretty-Shield to go around the lodge to her bed, moving in a clockwise motion and stepping over each of the coals. Pretty-Shield did as she was told and by the time she reached her bed (the two stakes and the rolled up buffalo robes), she knelt down, grabbed hold of the stakes and "my first child, Pine-fire, was there with us."

Once the baby was born, the helper placed a strip of tanned bison skin around Pretty-Shield's waist and rubbed the baby with a mixture of red paint and grease, powdered bison-chips (dried manure) and finely ground clay. Then the woman placed a layer of bison head hair around the child before wrapping the baby in a piece of soft buckskin and placing the child on a piece of stiff rawhide. Then she wrapped a piece of tanned calf skin around the rawhide and the child. The rawhide supported the baby's head. The dressing was removed each evening, and the baby was allowed to move freely for a while before being regreased and again covered with the bison chips, clay and bison hair. Newborn babies were never washed. Older children would be bathed with the women using warm water for girls and cold water for boys. Babies were placed in back cradles when they were about six months old; prior to that mothers carried them in their arms, even when riding horseback.

For a month after the birth, a Crow woman took only short steps and neither ate nor drank anything that was warm. When the village moved, new Crow mothers rode horses, but first they tied their legs together just above the knees, and they rode by sitting on flat packs with their legs straight out ahead of them, one leg to either side of the horse's neck.

happen to them if they disobeyed. Culture frighteners included medicine men, owls, and in the later period, white men.

Plains boys generally had their ears pierced soon after they were able to walk, with the piercing done with a sharp stick and usually during the Sun Dance ceremonies.

Older girls could care for baby girls in any way, but they could only feed or watch a boy baby, not minister to all needs. Children of both sexes were allowed to play together until they were about eleven years old, then a strict separation began.

Though most Plains Indian children did not attend "schools" until after the Reservation Period, they received intensive education. Little girls learned from their mothers, grandmothers, aunts and other women how to take care of a home and family, how to prepare hides and food and how to sew or gather plants. Little boys learned from their fathers, grandfathers, uncles and other men how to hunt and grow crops, how to fight and how to protect the tribe.

Among Plains tribes, young boys received their first small bow and arrows when they were about four years old. Training started soon after so they would learn how to hunt and fight. By the time a boy was ten years old, he would hunt with his playmates for rabbits and other small game. Boys learned how to imitate the calls of prairie animals such as wolves, coyotes, screech owls and hawks. This was a skill they would use throughout their lives in communicating with others while on war or hunting parties.

At age fourteen or fifteen, a young boy would be invited to join a Warrior Society. Soon he advanced to participation in raids, particularly in the effort to touch an enemy or "count coup." Only after a young man had counted coup could he marry, unless he had reached age twenty-five without touching an enemy.

Other essential skills included horseback riding and the study of animal habits and tracks in order to make clean kills. Tracking enemies also became important, and Indian boys learned how to "read sign" by noting bent grass or twigs and other natural elements that were out of place. Boys learned to endure cold, heat, thirst, fatigue and other hardships in preparation for the time when they would need those skills to survive. Other skills included dodging arrows by spinning around; shooting from horseback or a crouched position; riding horses and guiding them only with their knees, keeping their hands free for shooting a gun or bow and arrow; swinging shields to provide the smallest target for an enemy and throwing lances.

Marriage: Once youths reached puberty, males and females were strictly segregated. Most courting was done circumspectly. A young man might attract a girl's attention from a distance, and if she were interested in him, she would find a way to join him at his isolated location. A common meeting place for young people was at a watering hole when a young woman filled her water vessels, making such a meeting appear accidental. When a young couple wanted to marry, they informed their parents who had to agree.

Young Hidatsa men courted by playing eagle bone whistles or flutes. They paid for a bride only when necessary, and in such situations the married couple then lived with the woman's family; otherwise, the couple lived with the man's family. Some Hidatsa marriages were arranged without consent of those to be married. A man could divorce his wife for laziness or ill temper, and it was considered honorable for him to "throw away" a wife. If he took her back, however, he would be disgraced. A Hidatsa woman guilty of adultery might be beaten, but it was unlikely she would be mutilated by having her nose cut off as was done in many Plains tribes in cases of adultery.

The common present for betrothal among the Sioux was four to ten horses.

When courting, a Sioux man might exchange sweet grass (placed in deerskin bags) with a woman before abducting her from her lodge at night and taking her with him to his own lodge. Though such practice was a credit for men, it was not for women, who could be looked down upon for marrying without exchange of presents.

Comanches had no restrictions on whom they could marry, so long as it was not a blood relative. There was no ceremony.

Atsina (or Gros Ventre) men courted wearing bison robes, enticing women to go with them secretly. If a woman refused, then "negotiations" began between the families of the two individuals. Men had to prove themselves as warriors and hunters prior to marriage; therefore, few Atsina men married before they were thirty years old. Women generally married when in their late teens.

Men had multiple wives, and young men bragged about conquests of married women, though if a married woman had a lover, the men in her husband's "fraternity" or warrior society group could assault her. In many Plains tribes men cut off the noses of women who were unfaithful.

Among the Crows, men could not marry women from their own clan. A Crow man could marry when he had counted coup on an enemy or when he reached age twenty-five. If he had not counted coup by age twenty-five and he married, he could not paint his wife's face for ceremonies, though his wife could have her face painted by her uncle, if that man had counted coup.

Sex was a normal part of northern Plains hospitality. Men allowed visitors to have sex with their wives, sisters or daughters to show friendship and to forge trade or other relationships. Arikara matrilineal society did not place a high regard on exclusive sexual relations with male spouses. Sex was a commodity used for gain. For example, Arikara women wanted to obtain European goods, so they engaged in sex with the Europeans in order to get those goods, demanding and receiving high prices for their sexual services. Among the items Arikara women exchanged sex for were glass beads, ironware, paint and cloth.

The Mandans had a buffalo-calling ceremony, in which women slept with men who were believed to transfer spiritual power; generally the young women slept with older men, who had achieved status for their hunting practices. The Mandans believed that the women could then sleep with their own husbands, transferring the power from the older hunters to the younger men. In a similar way, Mandan women had sex with other individuals, such as white visitors, again believing they could transfer power from the visitor to their husband.

The Mandans often shared their wives, sisters or daughters, giving them to a visitor or guest in camp for the evening as a token of friendship. When Meriwether Lewis and William Clark spent the winter of 1804–5 with the Mandans, they and their men had many offers from Mandan men to spend time with the Mandan women. The men particularly wanted their wives to sleep with York, Clark's black slave, believing the black man had special powers that would be transferred from him to the women and ultimately to the Mandan warriors through sexual encounters. Most of the men with Lewis and Clark slept with the Indian women, and as a result venereal disease was a commonly treated ailment.

A Crow man could not speak directly to a sister-in-law who was married or to his mother-in-law. He could not even sit together with his mother-in-law in the same lodge. Crow men demanded as wives the unmarried sisters of a first wife. When a Crow man wanted to marry a woman, he would first visit the woman's father (or older brother if her father was deceased), sometimes taking a gift of horses. The father and the woman's clan relatives would discuss the marriage, and if they agreed to it, would announce the match. There would be a feast and a new lodge set up for the couple, even if the man had additional wives and children living in other lodges. The man's family gave presents such as clothing and horses to the bride.

When fur traders and hide buyers sought large numbers of pelts and hides, Indian men often took more wives in order to keep up with demand. It took more than one woman to process the pelts and hides a single man could kill. In 1787, for example, the maximum number of wives for a Blackfeet man was six, but by 1840 that number rose to an astounding twenty or thirty wives for some men. Each wife was purchased through an exchange of horses, so that animal obviously had great value.

Divorce was common, effected when someone else attracted either spouse.

Among the Otos, couples who eloped were severely punished. An Oto wedding consisted of the bride's family hosting a feast during which an older family member spoke of the responsibilities of marriage and child rearing. The formal feast was the wedding. Families were also involved in divorce. The couple asked their parents for permission to divorce, and if everyone agreed, the woman returned to her family. Though such separation was no disgrace, adultery was severely punished. An Oto man accused of adultery would be brought before his soldier society members (in part to prevent his being killed by the husband of an adulterous wife). If found guilty, the man was whipped and the woman declared an outcast with whom nobody should associate. In such cases the woman often became a prostitute. Should the husband take action prior to the soldier society, the adulterous man was often killed, the woman beaten and the end of her nose might be cut off.

Death: Crow people never spoke the names of the dead. Old people were often left to die. Old women would be abandoned when the tribe moved. They would sit in their lodges and survive until their food ran out or their fire died. Old men would dress in their finest clothes and would then seek an enemy to attack so they could die in battle.

John Ordway, who traveled with Lewis and Clark in 1804–6 wrote of Mandan burial practices: "The form of these savages burying their dead is after they have deceased they fix a Scaffel on raised 4 forks about 8 to 10 feet from the ground." The Mandans located the burial grounds outside villages and wrapped corpses in bison robes before placing them upon the burial scaffolds. "When any of them loose a particklor friend or relation they morn and cry for some time after," Ordway added.

Primarily scaffold burials were for prominent men, while other Mandans might be interred or placed in rock cairns with only their face showing. Mourning for the Mandans involved slashing of the legs (women), cutting off fingertips or the ends of hair braids (men) and wailing and fasting (both sexes).

Wichita tribal members buried the dead in an elevated place, which was then covered with slabs of stone or logs piled in a conical formation. The body was extended with the head toward the east. Mourning lasted four days as individuals purified themselves by bathing four times a day for four days.

Tree burial of the Oglala Sioux near Fort Laramie, Wyoming. (Photographer/date unknown; National Archives, 111-SC-87740)

The Sioux dressed the deceased in his or her finest clothes, painted the body red and placed a packet of food and implements near the head, before wrapping it in a buffalo robe or blanket. Once prepared, the body was either placed on an elevated platform or in a tree, with the head toward the north. Anyone who touched the body was purified with cedar smoke and sweating, and the lodge of the deceased also was purified by burning cedar and offering prayers.

Arikaras dressed and painted deceased members, then interred them with the head placed toward the east. Four days later they placed water and food near the grave. Cheyennes disposed of the dead in a variety of ways. Once they had been dressed and painted, a deceased person could be placed in an earth grave, lashed onto a scaffold or in a tree, put in a cave that was walled up or put in an ordinary lodge. The Cheyennes usually saddled then killed a favorite horse of the deceased, leaving it along with weapons beside the burial.

Arapahos buried the deceased in the ground, also killing a favorite horse of the deceased. In mourning, both sexes cut their hair, refrained from adornment or painting themselves, ate little and wore old clothing.

For most Plains tribes mourning called for women to slash their legs, men to cut their hair and both to wail and fast.

Prairies and Woodlands

The region around the Great Lakes, particularly to the west and south, was a transitional zone for tribes who were often heavily influenced by their neighbors. Some tribes had customs similar to the Northeastern tribes, while others were more closely aligned with Plains tribes. The Prairie and Woodland tribes engaged in both hunting and fishing, and also harvested native plants in addition to cultivating garden plots.

Ojibwa/Chippewa women controlled their homes and the family's property, such as wild rice beds, garden plots and maple sugar groves. They participated in all types of activities, ranging from taking care of children and homes, to hunting, processing and butchering game and gathering food or planting crops. Upon completion of an intense apprenticeship some women became involved in the Midewiwin, or Grand Medicine Society. Ojibwa/Chippewa women were in charge within the home, deciding all activities including where people put their belongings and where each individual slept.

Birth: Fox women gave birth in a separate birthing hut; ten days later the woman returned to her own lodge, but she continued to eat in the birthing hut until resumption of menstruation.

Soon after birth Ojibwa/Chippewa infants were placed on cradleboards made of cedar with a hickory hoop at the top to protect the child's head, and they remained on the cradleboards for about a year, being removed only for cleaning and exercise. When on the board they were in a bedding of sphagnum moss and tied with two layers of cloth or buckskin, which was almost always beaded by the mother in intricate floral patterns. A baby's moccasins had holes in them to remind any spirit that might want the child to return to the land of the dead that the infant wasn't prepared to make such a journey. A naming ceremony took place at a gathering of relatives and friends, and the individual selected to name the child held the baby on his or her lap when doing so.

Puberty: Fox discipline of children involved requiring them to fast. Fox girls were isolated in a separate lodge prior to their first menstrual period; subsequently Fox women spent time each month in the menstrual lodge. Most other Prairie and Woodland tribes practiced similar isolation for menstruating females.

At puberty Fox boys participated in vision quests. (See information about vision quests on page 224). When an Ojibwa/Chippewa boy neared puberty, he also participated in a vision quest. He would arise in the morning and when offered food or charcoal would select the charcoal, which he used to paint his face to indicate his participation in a vision quest. Then the boy left and built a shelter—sometimes accompanied by his father who could help the youth build a shelter and who might even take him water or food. Most vision quests lasted four days.

Marriage: Courting among the Fox began before age twenty. A young man entered the lodge of a girl in which he was interested. He carried a piece of burning bark, and the couple spoke near her bedside. If they agreed to marry, he stayed with her until morning. Sometimes a Fox suitor would approach the girl's brother instead of the girl. A Fox man could play a courting flute only if the woman had been previously married. Similar practices occurred among the Sauk and the Kickapoos. The Illinois male told his family the identity of a woman he wanted to marry. Then usually while he was away with a war party (it being necessary for a male to go into battle before he could marry), his family would gather together a variety of gifts, which his sisters would present to the girl's family. If the girl's family accepted the gifts, then the marriage could take place.

An Ojibwa/Chippewa boy could play the courting flute for a girl he admired, but she could not leave the lodge (where she was closely watched, usually by her grandmother). After a young man brought game to the girl's family he would be allowed to stay and eat the meal, ultimately also being allowed more freedom in visiting the girl. Eventually the two were married though there was no formal ceremony. Instead they simply moved out of the family lodge for a short period or established a new lodge of their own. Though a man might have two wives (or rarely three), most marriages were monogamous. Divorce was effected by the woman returning to her family's lodge.

Death: The Fox people had an all-night mourning ceremony and burial in graves grouped by clan. The feet of the deceased were placed facing west, and the corpse was dressed in the finest clothes then wrapped in mats or bark. Grave goods including water and food were buried with the body. Mourning lasted six months and sometimes up to a year, during which period the people in mourning took little care with their appearance. They avoided dancing, amusements and laughter and always wore moccasins, believing that if their bare feet touched the earth it would cause a drought. Mourning ended when the family adopted someone from the tribe, though the adoptee would not change his or her name, nor leave his or her household. The adoption included an exchange of gifts and ensured that the deceased wouldn't roam as a malevolent spirit.

Death practices (including later adoption) among the Sauk and the Kickapoo tribes were similar to those of the Fox tribe. Generally among the Kickapoos grave goods included a wooden spoon belonging to the deceased because they believed anyone buried without a spoon would eat foam into eternity.

The Illinois buried dead based on sex with women burying women and men taking care of other men. In both cases they painted the hair and body of the deceased red and dressed the corpse in fine clothes before burial along with grave goods such as tobacco, pots, calumets, kettles or bows. Two forked sticks were placed at each end of the grave. A number of ceremonies took place after the burial to assist the deceased in reaching the land of the dead. Those ceremonies included participation in events the deceased had enjoyed, ranging from dances to gambling, races or lacrosse. Widows and widowers generally mourned for a year. A woman was released from mourning when the dead man's sister combed the widow's hair and invited her to attend dances again.

The Miamis recognized different types of burial including interment of the body in an extended or seated position. Some Miamis had scaffold burials.

The Ojibwas/Chippewas had ceremonies for the dead, then removed the corpse through a wall in the lodge (never the doorway, so the soul of the deceased wouldn't be enticed to return some day). The body was wrapped in birchbark and buried in a shallow grave. Four days after the burial a fire was lit at the gravesite. Eventually a grave marker was placed in front of the grave house, which was constructed over the interred body.

Southwest

Apache male-female roles were sharply defined. Men hunted, fought battles and raided other tribes. Women cared for children, tended house and obtained food for the family. The women prayed for the men as they went off to battles or raids, taking responsibility for spiritual support of the warriors.

However, because the area where they lived was a harsh environment, and due to the ever-present possibility of a raid by hostile forces (either Indian or white), Chiricahua girls learned early in their lives to keep spare rations and weapons nearby, so if they had to flee the village, they could protect themselves and survive. Older girls learned tracking, use of camouflage and horse handling. They also learned to fight using a bow and arrow or a knife and rifle.

The Hopis had certain routines associated with each of the months. In January they hunted, bred sheep and participated in pottery making and construction of other objects. In February they cleared fields so they could prepare seed and begin planting corn in March and April. By May they planted melons, squash, beans, sunflowers and more corn. In June they planted late crops, irrigated, went on rabbit or turtle hunts, made pottery and kachinas and built houses. In July they weeded and hoed crops, began harvest of the early crops, killed eagles, made pottery and did weaving. In August they picked early peaches, hunted deer, antelope or mountain sheep and made pottery. In September and October they harvested fruits and vegetables and made trading and salt trips to Zuni. In November they finished harvest, wove, and made moccasins, tools and pottery. In December they spent time playing games.

The Hopi clans included sparrow hawk, parrot, bow, bear, badger, kachina, spider, snake, lizard, corn, bluebird, snow, coyote and squash.

Hopi women owned their homes, household goods and furnishings and gardens, while Hopi men were expected to work for the benefit of their wives' families. A Hopi woman made baskets and pottery and had the difficult task of providing water for the household, a chore that often required many trips a day from springs to their mesa-top villages. Because the women ultimately owned the property, Hopi people placed a higher value on girls than on boys. Before marriage a Hopi woman had to demonstrate that she would be a good wife. Therefore, she spent four days grinding corn at the home of her husband-to-be, in order to prove her qualifications.

Navajo gender roles were more flexible. Though Navajo women owned property, including their hogans, and tended the sheep and goats, they sometimes helped men in the fields, while men occasionally herded the livestock. But the "head mother" or family matriarch was in charge of the small camps, which were comprised of extended family members. The individual women were responsible for their own hogans, but the "head mother" had responsibility for the entire camp, and she was the ultimate authority in all family matters.

There are two major divisions of Pueblo people, the Eastern Pueblos of the Rio Grande and the Western Pueblos of the mesa and canyon country. Generally the Western Pueblos are matrilineal, while the Eastern Pueblos are patrilineal, though not all tribes fit within those parameters.

Birth: Both Walapai men and women adhered to numerous taboos during pregnancy. Women weren't to laugh at strange animals or jokes, and they were to avoid fatty or salty foods. Women avoided some other foods in the belief eating them could cause twins. At the baby's birth the father and three other women assisted.

Chiricahua infants had their ears pierced shortly after birth so they would obey and hear appropriate things. A child was placed in a cradleboard usually four days after birth and donned clothes at the time it could walk, in a ceremony known as "putting on moccasins." At that time the child walked toward the east through a trail of pollen, in a prayer for a successful and long life journey.

Puberty: Boys and girls among the Walapais learned certain skills as youngsters, and at puberty girls were involved in a simple ceremony that involved their mothers washing their bodies with yucca soap. Apache girls participated in elaborate puberty ceremonies, for which their families spent considerable time preparing. Among the Mescaleros, the rite continued four days and nights ending on the fifth day. It involved singing and dancing, feasting, visiting and other social activities. Apaches put great stock in virginity, and fathers could publicly whip young girls who did not maintain their virginity.

Marriage: Walapais and Yavapais exchanged gifts to signify a marriage, and divorce was common, caused by adultery, jealousy and compatibility problems, though divorce was less common before the reservation era among the Yavapais. Mohaves married by simply living together, and divorce was equally simple with the couple discontinuing cohabitation. The primary residence group of the Navajos revolved around a head mother and included a land area, agricultural lands and a sheep herd—all of which were termed "mother." Though there were individual owners of sheep, the animals were collectively herded and nearly everyone, from child through adult, had animals in the herd, making it to everyone's advantage to protect and care for the animals.

Pueblo people often expected young couples who were planning to marry to first sleep together. There was no stigma for an illegitimately born child. Instead an unmarried mother would be supported in the same way as a widow who had young children.

Death: Traditionally Walapais and Yavapais were cremated, but after the Ghost Dance (see page 241) began in 1889, people were buried in cairns and rock slides, which was a method more likely to allow ancestors to return to life. When a death appeared likely, Mohaves gathered together to sing and wail. Upon death the deceased was placed in a funeral pyre made of cottonwood or willow logs (later mesquite) along with all his or her possessions and cremation then occurred. As part of the ceremony, speeches and songs were shared and people often placed some of their own belongings upon the funeral pyre. The burning was believed to help the soul to reach the land of the dead. The granary and home of the deceased also were burned. After death the person's name was not mentioned; to do so was a great insult. The Mohaves believed that the deceased went to the land of the dead, unless they had not been tattooed, then they went down a rat hole. A further mourning ceremony included a mock battle.

Apaches went into mourning immediately upon learning of a death. Men and women cut the ends of their hair and put on old clothing. Apache women wailed; men wept. An Apache burial occurred as soon as possible in the daytime, with the deceased placed on his favorite horse along with as many personal possessions as could be carried. Then the deceased was taken to a hill or mountain far from where the people lived where burial occurred in a rocky crevice, if one could be located. The corpse and possessions were placed in the crevice and covered. The horse was killed. Any items that wouldn't fit into the grave were broken and left at the site. The burial party then returned home taking a different route than the one used on the way to the site, careful not to look back. After burning their clothes and washing themselves, they burned juniper, sage or another pungent plant as a "ghost medicine" in which they could "bathe" or purify themselves with the smoke. They also spread ashes over themselves and the camp to discourage the ghost of the deceased from returning. Generally all other possessions of the deceased were destroyed and the camp then moved to a new site, so the ghost couldn't return.

When a ghost made an appearance, it often was in the form of a coyote or owl. Indications that a ghost was nearby included the hoot of an owl or evidence that a coyote was roaming around the camp. People with "ghost sickness" had bad dreams, heart palpitations, seizures, hysteria, fainting spells, insanity or paralysis of the face or upper body. In such cases cures were effected through ceremonies of the Mescalero or Chiricahua Apaches or in the Navajo Enemy-way rite.

Navajos, Kiowa-Apaches and Western Apaches took corpses from a building through a hole in the wall, rather than through the doorway to prevent the soul of the deceased from returning. Kiowa-Apaches, Lipans and Navajos feared the dead and sought outsiders—often slaves—to remove and bury bodies. After establishment of trading posts to serve the Navajos, traders often undertook the responsibility of burying Indian people.

ADDITIONAL READING

Axtell, James, ed. *The Indian Peoples of Eastern America: A Documentary History of the Sexes.* Oxford: Oxford University Press, 1981. Firsthand and contemporary accounts related to life cycles of Eastern Indians in the 1800s.

Bettelyoun, Susan Bordeaux and Josephine Waggoner. Edited by Emily Levine. *With My Own Eyes: A Lakota Woman Tells Her People's History.* Lincoln: University of Nebraska Press, 1998.

Blair, Helen. *The Indian Tribes of the Upper Mississippi Valley and Region of the Great Lakes.* Lincoln: University of Nebraska Press, 1996.

Bowers, Alfred W. *Hidatsa Social and Ceremonial Organization.* Lincoln: University of Nebraska Press, 1992.

Burch, Ernest S. Jr. *The Eskimos.* Norman: University of Oklahoma Press, 2000.

Carlson, Paul H. *The Plains Indians.* College Station: Texas A&M University Press, 1998.

Carson, James Taylor. *Searching for the Bright Path.* Lincoln: University of Nebraska Press, 1999. History of the Mississippi Choctaws from prehistory through Removal.

Carter, Cecile Elkins. *Caddo Indians: Where We Come From.* Norman: University of Oklahoma Press, 1995.

Catlin, George. *Letters and Notes on the Manners, Customs, and Conditions of North American Indians.* 2 vols. New York: Dover Publications, 1973, originally published in London, 1841.

Corless, Hank. *The Weiser Indians: Shoshoni Peacemakers.* Caldwell, ID: Caxton Printers Ltd., 1996.

Gibson, Arrell M. *The Chickasaws.* Norman: University of Oklahoma, 1981.

Grinnell, George Bird. *The Cheyenne Indians.* 2 vols. Lincoln: University of Nebraska Press, Bison Books, 1972; originally published by Yale University Press, 1923.

Haines, Francis. *The Nez Percés: Tribesmen of the Columbia Plateau.* Norman: University of Oklahoma Press, 1955.

Hassrick, Royal B. *The Sioux: Life and Customs of a Warrior Society.* Norman: University of Oklahoma Press, 1964.

Hopkins, Sarah Winnemucca. *Life among the Piutes.* Reno: University of Nevada Press, 1994; originally published by G. P. Putnam and Sons, New York, 1883.

Howard, James H. *The Ponca Tribe.* Lincoln: University of Nebraska Press, 1995.

Hyde, George. *Indians of the High Plains.* Norman: University of Oklahoma Press, 1959.

———. *Indians of the Woodlands.* Norman: University of Oklahoma Press, 1962.

———. *The Pawnee Indians.* Norman: University of Oklahoma Press, 1974; paperback, 1988; originally published by University of Denver Press, 1951.

———. *Red Cloud's Folk: A History of the Oglala Sioux Indians.* Norman: University of Oklahoma Press, 1937.

Kavanagh, Thomas W. *The Comanches: A History 1706–1875.* Lincoln: University of Nebraska Press, 1996; reprinted by Bison Books, 1999. An excellent reference to Comanche lifestyle.

Kilpatrick, Jack Frederick, and Anna Gritts Kilpatrick. *Walk In Your Soul: Love Incantations of the Oklahoma Cherokees.* Dallas: Southern Methodist University, 1965. Incantations related to attraction, loneliness, retaining affection, separation and other matters of the heart.

Krause, Aurel. Translated by Erna Gunther. *The Tlingit Indians.* Seattle: University of Washington Press, 1956. A good reference.

Landes, Ruth. *The Ojibwa Woman.* Lincoln: University of Nebraska Press, Bison Books, 1997; originally published by Columbia University Press, New York, 1938.

Linderman, Frank B. *Pretty-shield: Medicine Woman of the Crows.* Lincoln: University of Nebraska Press, Bison Books, 1974. Originally published under the title *Red Mother,* 1932. An excellent reference to Crow women.

Lockwood, Frank C. *The Apache Indians.* Lincoln: University of Nebraska Press, 1987.

Lowie, Robert H. *The Crow Indians.* Lincoln: University of Nebraska Press, 1983.

Mathews, John Joseph. *The Osages: Children of the Middle Waters.* Norman: University of Oklahoma Press, 1961.

Mayhall, Mildred P. *The Kiowas.* Norman: University of Oklahoma Press, 1962.

McClintock, Walter. *The Old North Trail: Life, Legend & Religion of the Blackfeet Indians.* Lincoln: University of Nebraska Press, Bison Books, 1992; originally published by Macmillan and Co., London, 1910.

Morgan, Lewis Henry. *Systems of Consanguinity and Affinity of the Human Family.* Lincoln: University of Nebraska Press, 1997. Detail about the kinship systems of more than 100 cultures.

Oswalt, Wendell H. *Eskimos & Explorers.* 2d ed. Lincoln: University of Nebraska Press, Bison Books, 1999. Originally published Novato, CA: Chandler & Sharp Publishers, 1979.

Perdue, Theda. *Cherokee Women: Gender and Culture Change, 1700–1835.* Lincoln: University of Nebraska Press, 1998.

Phillips, Joyce B., and Paul Gary Phillips, eds. *The Brainerd Journal, A Mission to the Cherokees, 1817–1823*. Lincoln: University of Nebraska Press, 1998.

Radin, Paul. *The Winnebago Tribe*. Lincoln: University of Nebraska Press, 1990.

Riney, Scott. *The Rapid City Indian School, 1898–1933*. Norman: University of Oklahoma Press, 1999.

Taylor, Colin F. *The Plains Indians*. New York: Crescent Books, 1994; reprint, New York: Random House Value Publishing, 1994.

Thornton, Russell. *The Cherokees*. Lincoln: University of Nebraska Press, 1990.

Trenholm, Virginia Cole. *The Arapahoes, Our People*. Norman: University of Oklahoma Press, 1970.

Trenholm, Virginia Cole, and Maurine Carley. *The Shoshonis: Sentinels of the Rockies*. Norman: University of Oklahoma Press, 1964.

Underhill, Ruth M. *The Navajos*. Norman: University of Oklahoma Press, 1956.

Walker, James R. *Lakota Society*. Lincoln: University of Nebraska Press, 1982.

Wallace, Ernest, and E. Adamson Hoebel. *The Comanches: Lords of the South Plains*. Norman: University of Oklahoma Press, 1952.

Warde, Mary Jane. *George Washington Grayson and the Creek Nation 1843–1920*. Norman: University of Oklahoma Press, 1999.

Wilson, B. D. *The Indians of Southern California in 1852*. Lincoln: University of Nebraska Press, Bison Books, 1995.

Woodward, Grace Steele. *The Cherokees*. Norman: University of Oklahoma Press, 1963.

Wright, J. Leitch Jr. *Creeks and Seminoles*. Lincoln: University of Nebraska Press, 1986.

Yarrow, H.C. *North American Indian Burial Customs*. Ogden, UT: Eagle's View Publishing, 1988. An excellent resource particularly because it includes numerous accounts of Indian burials that were written in the 1800s; there are also many detailed line drawings.

CHAPTER FIVE

FOOD

T he most important food for American Indians was maize, also known as Indian corn, which was planted and harvested throughout most of North America. The three major types of corn were flour corn in the Southwest, flint corn that flourished in the Northeast and on the Plains and dent corn primarily grown in the Southeast. Other commonly raised plants used as food sources for Indians were beans and squash including pumpkin and summer squash.

Though Indians had dogs, they generally ate them only on ceremonial occasions; some tribes never ate dog meat. Indians ate horses when they first obtained the animals, but when the animals' use to obtain other types of food became clear, few Indians ate horsemeat.

Salt is an essential item in any diet, and Indians generally received the nutrient from the meat of animals. Even so, Indians—particularly those with limited amounts of meat in their diet and those who lived in hot climates—processed salt by evaporating salt water. In the Great Basin, the Southwest and California, Indians gathered salt from dry lake beds or by evaporating salt water. Because not every area had such sources, salt became an important trade item.

After the 1850s many Indian people obtained food from government rations which included beef, sugar, wheat flour and coffee. Those government-supplied products replaced bison, deer, wild honey and cornmeal. The government supplies—or annuities—were part of treaty agreements.

OBTAINING FOOD

Throughout North America hunting, fishing and farming were the three primary ways Indians obtained food. Some tribes depended largely on hunting and gathering their food supply, while others primarily raised it in farm fields and garden plots.

Hunting

In the early portion of the 1800s, most hunting was accomplished with a bow and arrows; Indians used guns in the latter portion. Some hunters also used a lance to kill animals. In bison hunting, for example, a hunter would ride his horse alongside the bison and then stab it with the lance. In earlier periods hunters used spear-throwing devices for hunting, but those were seldom, if ever, used in the 1800s.

Hunters also participated in cooperative drives. Prior to obtaining horses, people would drive bison over cliffs, causing the animals to either die or be injured in the fall. In the Arctic and Subarctic, people sometimes drove land animals such as moose and caribou into water where they could be killed. In the Prairies, Plains, Great Basin and Southwest, people used techniques to surround animals, particularly small animals such as rabbits, which could then be killed. Though the earliest surround technique involved people on foot, after Indians obtained horses, they often surrounded game while riding.

In surround situations, Indians forced animals into an enclosure formed by a fence or net. The nets sometimes were used to capture deer and antelope, but were most often used in rabbit drives.

Some hunters also used pits into which they forced animals to fall, or they set snares and traps using deadfalls, which were triggered by the animal falling or stepping onto them. The animal was either killed or injured and held until the hunter could arrive to harvest it.

Indians routinely burned dead grasses in the spring. That encouraged new grass growth and enticed animals onto the range.

In most areas, Indians made sounds that lured animals into traps or areas where they could be killed. Antlers rubbed together sounded like deer fighting, water poured into a stream mimicked the sound of a female moose urinating, rocks struck together replicated the clash of mountain sheep horns. Each of those sounds attracted other animals of the species to investigate.

Men did most of the hunting in all culture areas, though women sometimes harvested small game and birds, and they almost always assisted in butchering game.

Indians in all culture areas had strong beliefs about animal souls. There were many taboos related to hunting including a widespread belief that menstruating women should have nothing to do with it. In California, Indian hunters removed boards from the walls of their homes to take meat in rather than entering through the door, fearing that a woman might have dripped menstrual fluid in the entrance. Often a hunter whose wife was menstruating would not hunt at all, and usually men abstained from sexual intercourse for a day or two prior to going on a hunt.

Likewise, anyone suffering from an illness could affect hunting luck and was often prohibited from eating meat. Such restrictions also applied to menstruating women, medicine healers who were practicing their craft, anyone in mourning and warriors who had recently killed an enemy.

In the Arctic, Eskimos would not hunt for several days after someone in the community died. Otherwise, men hunted whales from two-person kayaks, maneuvering close to the animal and then striking the whale with a spear tipped with a piece of slate twelve inches long. In secret whaling rites the men smeared aconitine poison on the spear tip. The whale would die from the poison or the saltwater. Usually the animal then floated into a bay, where it could be processed. When hunting other sea mammals, such as sea otters, Arctic people often surrounded them and struck them with a harpoon or darts. Aleuts and Eskimos harvested sea otters on shore by clubbing them. Eskimos carved helmets to look like seals, which they donned to use as a decoy in order to approach the seals closely enough to club them to death. Traditionally Eskimos hunted fur seals from February to April; sea otter from April to June; harbor seals, sea lions and porpoises from April through October; sea lions and whales in June and July; and salmon from May through September.

In almost all culture areas, hunters and fishermen shared their kills with others in the tribe.

Fishing

In most areas Indians ate fish, though some tribes would not eat them. Where fish were a part of the diet, they were obtained through use of harpoons, gaffs and dip nets. Indians also shot them with bows, snared fish, used rakes to catch them in streams and even poisoned the fish enough to stun them and allow harvest. Though they used hooks, Indians found fishing was more effective using weirs, traps and nets. The nets they used included gill nets, made from twine tied to form a mesh through which a fish stuck its head and then became entangled, or a seine, which was similar but more effective in shallow water. A reef net, used by Indians seeking sockeye salmon, was anchored to the sea bottom and then tied between two canoes. The salmon were "funneled" into the big net, and then a smaller net was used to actually catch them and put them into the canoes.

Chumash Indians of California regularly trolled for tuna, while Arctic people used a hook and line to seek char through the ice in winter. Men did most of the fishing, though more women were likely to fish than to hunt.

Plant Gathering/Farming

Farming was widespread in most areas, though in the Arctic the climate made it impossible to raise crops. Most farms were plots assigned to a family or individual, though the land itself belonged to the larger cultural group rather than to an individual. The individual responsible for actually cultivating the fields varied depending upon the tribe.

Women did almost all wild plant gathering and most of the farming. In the Prairie-Woodlands area, Ojibwa men did the farming as did a few tribes in upper New England. In the Southeast, men planted and cultivated "town fields" while women maintained individual garden plots. In the Pueblos of the Southwest, men did all the planting and cultivating. However, women did the farming among other Southwestern tribes such as the Apaches.

Tribes that raised crops used hand tools including a straight, pointed digging stick (also called a dibble stick) effective for both planting and harvesting. The stick could be used to make a hole in which to place seeds for such crops as corn, beans or squash. Often a digging stick had a fork on it, which could be stepped on to make a deeper hole in areas of dry soil. Some tribes had a tool that looked and worked like a shovel or spade. The blade could be made of a variety of products, most often the shoulder blade of an animal. Some hoes of shell, stone or fish bones were used in the East.

In the Southwest, Indians developed irrigation systems for crops. There Indians planted crops at the foot of mesas, where natural runoff from winter snows or spring, summer and fall rains would flow and provide moisture.

In most cases, Indians prepared the land for crops by removing grass, brush and trees, either through pulling or cutting those plants or more likely by burning the area. The fires not only removed vegetation, they also provided residue that fertilized the soil. Sometimes Indians girdled trees so they would die. Indians routinely allowed cleared areas to be in production for a few years, then to grow up with trees and other plants in order to restore nutrients. They also recognized that planting beans along with squash and corn affected nitrogen in the soil, making all three crops grow better. Fish heads and ground shells as well as horseshoe crabs were used as fertilizer for crops, particularly for corn in New England and Virginia.

Missouri River tribes developed a rake made of wood or antler that could be used to clear brush or eliminate weeds. The Hopis in the Southwest had similar tools.

Wild plants harvested by Indians varied depending on location. Some of the common plants used by Indian people included dandelions, milkweed, pokeweed, lamb's quarters, mustard, dock and watercress, which were parboiled and served with meat. Wild rice was a food staple for the people living near the Great Lakes, known as *manoomin* or "good seed" by the Ojibwas. Harvested in the fall with a gathering stick (called a hoop) and a knife, the green grain was dried, threshed and winnowed before being ground into a meal and used to make bread. Some Indians even popped wild rice, as they did corn. Other common plants eaten by Indians included domesticated sunflowers, a tuber that resembled a radish but which is known as a Jerusalem artichoke, giant ragweed, maygrass, sumpweed and goosefoot. Like other plants, they were boiled and then cooked with meat in soups and stews.

Food Annuities/Rations

Once Indians were living on reservations, they were forced to rely on federal government annuities for their food. The food was distributed, generally weekly, by the Indian agent, and each person had a ration card, which allowed him or her to obtain supplies. The ration cards were often kept in small decorated pouches made just for that purpose. The ration card pouches were kept around the person's neck. In 1881 each Indian was allowed a pound and a half of beef a day.

Each ration was considered the amount of food for one person for one day. A family of ten people, obtaining food for a ten-day period would have received the following amounts of food in March 1881:

Bacon, 10 lbs.
Beans, 3 lbs.
Beef, 150 lbs.
Coffee, 4 lbs.
Corn, 50 lbs.
Flour, 50 lbs.
Salt, 1 lb.
Soda, 1 lb.
Sugar, 8 lbs.
Tobacco ½ lb.

GENERAL FOOD DETAILS

Arctic

Arctic people depended primarily on sea mammals including seals (first choice) and whales for their food supply. Caribou provided meat and other products, including hides with hair that provided good insulation, sinew that could be made into thread, and antlers to be used for weapons and a variety of implements.

Arctic people ate most meat raw, including fat and internal organs. The Arctic people also ate the partially digested mosses and lichens found in a caribou's stomach—providing them with a source of vegetable nutrition. In many cases, caribou hunting involved creating a trap area, where the animals could be forced to fall to their death or to enter a corral built of sod or walls of ice, snow or rocks, where hunters could then kill them. Prior to any hunt, the hunters abstained from sexual activities for four days and participated in primarily ceremonial activities.

The bowhead whale provided meat and blubber. Though hunted primarily for food, whales also had other uses including oil for light and heat and baleen—a flexible, fernlike growth in the whale's mouth that could be used for fishing lines, nets and other equipment. Whalebones were used for framework for boats, storage racks, sleds, housing frames and even gravemarkers.

In the Subarctic, people depended on caribou and moose, though they occasionally ate bear, beaver, deer, porcupine and rabbit.

People hunted sea mammals with harpoons that had detachable heads. When the head struck the animal, the hunter allowed a line to release or "play out" that kept the animal hooked but able to move. Eventually the animal tired and could be killed. Seals were hunted using hand-held lines. Hunters wore mittens or gloves to protect their hands. When hunting larger sea animals, such as whales, an inflated float was attached to the line that made it possible for the hunter to track the animal.

Another food source, polar bear, was particularly dangerous to hunt. The bears spent time on the ice, making it necessary for hunters to venture there as well. When a bear was spotted, hunters turned loose their dogs, who would attack the bear, diverting its attention while the hunter used a harpoon or lance to kill it (striking near the rib cage). Polar bear hunters attempted to remain between the bear and its place of refuge—the open sea. Sometimes more than one hunter was involved in the kill. Generally they shared the meat, with the hunter making the fatal stab earning the right to at least half of the bearskin.

Besides the danger associated with hunting the bear itself, Eskimo hunters also faced danger from the sea. Sometimes the ice broke away forming an island and making it impossible for them to cross the open water to return to their homes. In such cases, hunters tried to sustain themselves by harvesting seals, hoping their ice island would eventually merge with solid ice. Women of stranded hunters also did their part to help their husbands return home. They wore parkas indoors, in the belief it would keep the man warm. A woman would hang up a pair of boots, studying the way they hung in an effort to determine where the man was. A woman would not abandon hope that her husband would return until the next summer hunting season began; then she would accept the fact that he had not survived. Arctic women believed the *inyusuq* or "personal soul" of their husband would return home, so if a woman heard or saw the *inyusuq* enter the house, she then knew her husband had died.

Though men did most of the hunting and fishing, the fall salmon harvest for people along Alaska's Kobuk River saw women doing the work, primarily because men were involved in the annual caribou hunt at the same time.

To harvest birds, Arctic people used nets, snares, bows and arrows, multipronged darts propelled from a throwing stick and traps. They also used a bola, which was a length of braided sinew to which several weights were tied. Hunters whirled the bola above their heads and threw it at a bird. When the sinew and weights struck the bird, it fell to the ground where it could be killed.

California

Acorns were the primary food item among California Indians. The people harvested acorns in the fall, and Indians kept an eye on the oak trees to deter-

Salmon drying, Aleut village, Old Harbor, Alaska. (N.B. Miller, 1889; National Archives, 22-FA-264)

mine exactly when to begin the process. When the acorns were ripe and ready for harvest, a three-day observance took place to give thanks for the crop and to conduct ceremonies that would limit rainfall, which could ruin a crop if it occurred just prior to harvest. For the harvest, boys and young men climbed trees, shaking the limbs or striking them with a long pole to force the acorns to fall to the ground, where women, children and elderly people gathered them. The work started at sunup and lasted all day. During the night tribal members engaged in dancing, feasting, trading, gambling and courting.

After harvest, the nuts were stored in basket granaries that were suspended on stilts. The granaries were lined with herbs such as mugwort and bay leaves, which repelled insects and kept the nuts from molding. Some of the woven willow-twig granaries held up to one thousand pounds of acorns. Some California Indians, such as the Shasta tribe in northern California, stored acorns in subterranean caches lined with leaves and sealed with a pine-bark covering. The Maidus and the Hupas stored acorns in baskets on shelves in their homes. When properly stored acorns would keep for a year.

The nuts were mashed or ground into a meal and soaked in water to remove the tannic acid. In some cases, tribal members buried the acorns for a year in streambeds or in mud near swamps. That prolonged immersion helped leach the tannic acid from the nuts, and after the tannic acid was removed, Indians ground the nuts into a meal. Acorn meal was made into a mush, soup or baked into an unleavened bread. The Indians flavored the mush or soup with crushed berries, mushrooms, cedar bark, herbs, meat, greens or dried fish.

The Sierra Miwok women cracked the acorn shells and removed the kernel. They then rubbed the kernel in a flat winnowing basket to remove the red skin surrounding it before putting the acorns into bedrock mortars where they ground the acorn meat with heavy stone pestles. Such bedrock mortars were common in the foothills and an example of them is at Grinding Rock State Historical Park in California.

California Indians also ate other seeds and plants, as well as rodents, birds and invertebrates such as caterpillars, earthworms and grasshoppers. Those Indians living near the seacoast ate clams, mussels and fish. The seabeds of kelp had tuna, yellowtail, sea bass and bonito, which attracted pelicans, otters, sea lions and seals that the hunters also could harvest. The Indians snared rabbits and harvested piñon nuts, dates, cactus, wild plums, wild strawberries and apricots. They raised dogs particularly for meat.

To harvest reptiles and rabbits, desert-dwelling California Indians used a macana, a war club made of very hard wood shaped like a boomerang. When flung it could slice a rattlesnake in two or fell small game. These Indians also harvested tule, a rush similar to cattail. They ate the seeds and green shoots, but used the tule primarily as a building material. Young girls and women harvested the small round bulbs of wild hyacinth (called brodiaea), cooking and eating them like small baked potatoes. Hunters used basket traps or snares made from woven human hair to catch squirrels, quail or rabbits.

Northeast and Southeast

Wild plant foods, particularly nuts, as well as crops such as corn, squash and beans provided most of the food in the diet. Much of the food was raised in town fields, which were worked by men and women. In Cherokee and Iroquois cultures the women controlled planting operations and fields.

Among the plants raised by Indians in the East were beans, Jerusalem artichoke, maize, marsh elder, pigweed, ragweed and sunflower. The three primary domesticated crops, corn, beans and squash, became known to the Iroquois as "three sisters." The Mohawk women planted corn in holes poked with their digging sticks. After the corn sprouted, they piled earth around the base of the corn plant. Later they often planted beans near the corn, so the beans could "climb" the cornstalks. And they planted squash near the base of the plants so the broad leaves of the squash plant could provide shade and preserve soil moisture. Generally the Iroquois cooked beans and corn together, believing the spirits of the "sisters" should remain together.

Dogs were raised for eating, though usually only in ceremonial occasions and certainly not in every tribe. For instance the Iroquois ate dog in ceremonial situations, but Cherokees never did.

Those tribes whose lands were near the sea or rivers turned to the water for food sources, ranging from herring, smelt, sturgeon, salmon and shad to other seafoods including oysters and clams. Occasionally a whale was washed ashore and harvested by the nearby people for the meat, oil and bone. Creeks had many ways to snag fish ranging from bass, sunfish, perch and shad to sturgeon eight feet long and one hundred-pound catfish. The Creeks used traps, weirs, dams, nets, lines with turkey bone hooks, and spears that used the tails of horseshoe crabs as sharp points. When seeking the huge sturgeon, they sometimes literally roped the fish and then hung on until they could force it to shore. Creeks also used a powder made from the roots of *Tephrosia virginiana*, commonly known as devil's horseshoe, which they spread into creeks and streams. The poison powder paralyzed the fish so they could be harvested, but it did not affect the meat.

The Creeks ate walnuts and also used them to make a formula for babies. The Indian women mixed ground nuts with water and cornmeal. The Powhatans served milk of walnuts, considered a delicacy by adults, to any guest of honor.

The Algonquians in the Hudson River area became known as "bark eaters" because they included the inner bark of conifers in their regular diet. From tree sap women also made syrup. The wild plants on the menu included yellow pond lily (served boiled and roasted), tuckahoe (a starchy root), marsh marigold and fiddle fern. Among the wild herbs used to season foods were rose hips, wild leeks and milkweed flower. Cattails served a variety of purposes. In spring the young shoots became part of the meal, as did the flowers and seeds produced in summer and fall. Mature plants were pounded into a meal or flour or boiled into syrup.

Among the berries used by Eastern Indians were cranberries, currants, shadberries, elderberries, thimbleberries, blackberries, blueberries, strawberries and raspberries. The most common and popular item was the strawberry, which Algonquians called grassberry. Some people living farther to the south used the name heartberry for strawberries.

Various types of game were harvested for food including deer, raccoon, bear, fox, otter, mink, rabbit, elk, porcupine and in some areas, moose.

Shellfish were prepared by heating rocks, then placing clams, fish and green corn onto the hot rocks and covering them with seaweed to maintain the heat as the food cooked.

Like other tribes, the Creeks relied on corn as a primary food source. One of their corn products, "sofke," is a broth made using a bit of lye. Creek legend says the sofke was sent to earth—and to the Creek people—through a tear in the sky.

Iroquois women planted and harvested the crops, believing that female fertility was essential to crop growth. They also supported the concept that a woman walking over the fields dragging her clothes could actually enrich the soil.

The Creeks drank a tea made of holly leaves and twigs that they called "white drink," but which became known as "black drink" because of its color. To make the ritual tea, Creeks roasted the dried leaves and twigs then boiled them until the liquid turned dark brown. Occasionally medicine men would blow into the tea through a straw to invoke sacred powers. As soon as the drink was no longer scalding, people drank it, most often from a conch shell. It was a stimulant and a diuretic (due to the high levels of caffeine). When consumed ceremonially, the Creeks vomited the tea in order to purify themselves.

The Seminoles made a bread out of coontie root.

Great Basin

A variety of seeds provided food for people living in the Great Basin, but the most common was the piñon pine nut. Indians in this area used digging sticks to find and harvest roots. They also ate rodents, reptiles and insects. They had communal hunts for rabbits, which were a primary food source. The Utes hunted antelope and deer and used cords of sage or juniper bark to catch birds and rabbits. They utilized fish when near streams and made a pemmican cake by mixing berries with crickets and grasshoppers.

Interior Plateau

The people of the Plateau area had diets based upon their region. For example, those nearer to the Northwest Coast, often relied on fishing and other techniques for gathering food similar to those of Northwest Coast tribes. Likewise, those living near the Subarctic zone, relied on hunting large animals such as moose or bears. In most areas, the Plateau people relied on gathering wild plants, particularly the camas roots, which they collected and then dried. When a Spokane girl dug her first camas root, she ritually cleaned it and placed it in a hide bag she wore around her neck whenever digging roots. Plateau people also ate moss, particularly that harvested from the Tamarack trees because it was less bitter than moss collected from other tree species. Chewing gum came from the ponderosa pine, white fir, subalpine fir and western larch trees.

Once they had obtained horses, people from Interior Plateau tribes, such as the Nez Percé and Kutenais, could make periodic journeys across the mountains to the plains in order to harvest bison.

For most of the tribes, fishing served as a major way to obtain food. The Sanpoil and Nespelem harvested salmon while standing on platforms over the river or sometimes on the riverbank itself. They used single-pronged harpoons to spear the fish. At night they used canoes to pursue fish, using a trident leister to spear the fish. They seldom used nets, though they often used willow baskets, which they hung near a waterfall. Other tribes used seines, conical falls traps, hook and set lines, dams and impoundments, spears and torchlights. Some even shot fish or caught them with a noose, while others "tickled" fish by running a hand up along the fish body until it could be grasped by the gills and tossed to the bank of the stream or river. When fishing with a hook and line, the Kalispels used a variety of bait including grubs, grasshoppers and fish entrails, particularly the gizzard.

Once the Indians along the Columbia harvested salmon, they dried the fish

Paiute woman grinding seeds in doorway of thatched hut. (John K. Hillers, 1872; National Archives, 57-PE-7)

and then packed the meat into reed baskets so it could be transported easily to areas where it was used as a primary trade item.

By 1800 European ships had made their way to the Northwest Coast and brought with them iron and steel tools. Many of those items—through trade practices—made it to the Plateau where they were fashioned into fishhooks and particularly into cutting implements used for processing fish. Plateau tribes also obtained knives and iron fishhooks from the Hudson's Bay Company.

On his travels in 1811, explorer Wilson Price Hunt noted that when he reached the village of Wishram, the great fishing ground of the Columbia, large platforms used to dry fish lined both sides of the river.

In hunting, the Indians used traps, snares and deadfalls. The Spokanes hunted black bear, using the fat for a burn medicine, lubricant or soap. They ate the meat except in late May when bears fed on skunk cabbage and in July when bears fed on red ant nests because those food sources tainted the taste of the bear meat. Most Plateau tribes did not hunt grizzly bears for food.

Plateau people ate a variety of other foods. They gathered wild waterfowl (particularly duck) eggs and harvested waterfowl including quail, sage hen, pheasant, chuckers, geese and duck. They used bone marrow to strengthen young children and as hair oil.

Northwest Coast

The primary food in this region was salmon. People also used sea plants (dried and pressed into cakes), salal berries, blueberries and camas roots. Northwest Coast Indians roasted salmon in a latticework frame made of cedar splints. They obtained oil from seals and whales harvested off the coast.

Plains Indians

Hunting was a primary way Plains Indians obtained food, and all tribes relied on it to a certain extent. The Mandans believed they could appease the spirits of animals, so they made offerings to skulls prior to beginning a hunt.

Plains Indian people seldom ate wild turkeys; they believed those who ate

Arapaho camp with buffalo meat drying near Fort Dodge, Kansas. (William S. Soule, 1870; National Archives, 75-BAE-48c)

turkeys would become cowards and flee from enemies. Primary meat included bison, elk, deer, antelope and small game. The hump meat of bison provided fat as did bears. Without question, the most important item in the Plains Indian diet was bison, and virtually every portion of the animal was consumed or used in some manner. People ate the liver, kidney, heart, tongue, eyes and testicles, as well as portions of the intestine, marrow from bones, and certainly the various cuts of meat. Though much of the meat was dried and preserved for future use, some was eaten when fresh—either cooked or often raw and just after the kill. For the Sun Dance (see page 225), Lakota women boiled bison tongues.

Crow women made pemmican by cutting meat into strips and drying it somewhat, then roasting it until it turned brown. The dried/roasted meat then was pounded with stone hammers. After soaking chokecherries in water, the women crushed the meat bones and boiled them with chokecherry juice. After the bone mixture had cooled, they skimmed the grease from the top and mixed it with the pounded meat. They poured the mixture into bags made from the skin of the bison heart and allowed it to solidify. Pemmican made in this manner would last for many weeks or months and was easy to carry on trips.

Old people were given meat stripped of all sinew. It would be dried and then pounded and mixed with bone marrow. Old men received their serving in a bowl while old women were served on a square of rawhide.

To dry meat, Crow women cut it off the animal and split it into sections, then spread it on racks in the sun. They turned the meat pieces regularly and at night took it from the racks and piled it on the ground before covering it with a bison robe. The women then stomped on the pile of meat to squeeze out any remaining blood and other juices before again hanging it on the drying racks. To avoid spoilage, they did not let the meat touch the racks in the same places it had the previous day.

The bison provided more than meat for the Plains Indians—it was a virtual pantry and general store. The hide was used to make lodge covers, moccasins, dresses, shirts, breechclouts, robes, bedding, mittens, caps, pouches, containers, shields, drums, rattles, saddles, bridles and other tack, bull boats and snowshoe lacings. The horns became spoons, cups, ladles, powder flasks, fire carriers, rattles, headdresses and toys, while bones could be used for shovels, hoes, sled runners, saddle trees, war clubs, awls, scrapers, paintbrushes, arrowheads and knives. Other products made from the bison included padding, ropes, halters, glue, cooking vessels, buckets, cups, thread and bowstrings. Even waste such as bison dung was used as a fuel and for ceremonial smoking, while the brain was a valuable item needed to tan the hides.

The buffalo provided almost everything needed for survival on the plains. As the Crow woman Pretty-Shield put it: "When the buffalo went away the hearts of my people fell to the ground, and they could not lift them up again."

Dogs were raised for eating on special ceremonial occasions. Many hunting groups of the Plains Indian tribes forbade the eating of fish. The Arikaras ate fish and used hooks and weirs to catch channel catfish in the Missouri River.

The Arikaras also grew a variety of crops including watermelon, pumpkin, squash, corn and tobacco. They had hoes or digging sticks made from the shoulder blades of deer or bison and used a rake made from binding reeds onto a pole or handle. Most of the farming was done by the Arikara women.

Fruits used by Plains Indians included wild currant, gooseberry, serviceberry, highbush cranberry, buffalo berry, chokecherry, wild plum and grapes and persimmon. They ate a variety of nuts including black walnut, hickory, hazelnut and pecan. To obtain Vitamin C, they used the roots of tipsin, known as Indian turnip, which also had a high protein content.

Some Plains tribes relied more on horticulture than did others. For example the Mandans and Santees obtained most of their diet from crops they grew such as corn, squash, beans and pumpkins. Hidatsa women planted several varieties of corn. Women planted sunflowers around the edges of cornfields and placed beans near corn so they could climb the cornstalks. Women guarded their fields to protect them from rabbits, deer, birds, horses and other animals.

PLAINS EATING

A typical Plains Indian meal included soup or stew cooked in one pot and eaten directly from the pot (most often with the person's fingers) and bread made from ground meal and water and cooked on a hot flat stone. The bread could be dipped into the soup or stew pot. Food was available constantly throughout the day when Plains Indians were in their home camps.

Prairies and Woodlands

About half the diet of Prairie and Woodland tribes came from crops such as maize, beans and squash. People also ate wild rice, particularly in the region around the Great Lakes, and they raised sunflowers for the seeds and oils, beans, Jerusalem artichokes, maize, pigweed and ragweed.

Ojibwas had small winter camps involving just a few families, so hunters would not have to range so far to find prey. Although they raised some crops (corn, beans and squash), tribes living near the Great Lakes had short growing seasons with which to contend, so they relied primarily on hunting, fishing and gathering wild plants for their food supply.

The wild rice fields harvested by the Menominees and the Ojibwas were divided into different sections, or plots, so each family had an area from which to collect rice. Traditionally the people allowed some rice grains to fall into the water as an offering for future harvests. To harvest the rice, men handled the canoes while another worker, generally a woman or young girl, pulled the rice stalks over the edge of the canoe striking them with a stick to knock the ripe rice kernels into the boat. (Sometimes women handled the canoes.) Once the rice was knocked from the stalks, it was placed on a birch bark mat and allowed to dry in the sun or suspended over a slow burning fire to cure. Once the rice was dried, it was then put into a pan where it could be roasted or parched. That process loosened the hull so it could be discarded; that kept the rice from sprouting. In some cases the rice was hulled using a mortar and pestle. When the hull was separated from the rice, it was placed in a birch bark container called a *nooshkaachinaaganan*, and the hulls or "chaff" were then winnowed from the parched rice by tossing it up into the air. The rice was stored in bags or baskets made from the inner bark of birch or cedar trees until needed.

Navajo hogan and cornfield. (F.A. Ames, 1889; National Archives, 106-FAA-54)

Southwest

The primary diet in this region involved crops raised in farm and garden plots. Little meat was eaten early in the period, though by the middle of the period the Navajos raised sheep, eating the meat as well as using the fleece for clothing and other products. Throughout the century the primary meat source was rabbit.

Among the crops raised or gathered by Southwest Indians were amaranth, barnyard grass, several varieties of beans, Jerusalem artichoke, maize, marsh elder, panic grass, peanuts, ragweed and sunflowers. They also raised corn, summer squash and pumpkins, bottle gourds and potatoes. By the nineteenth century, many tribes raised a variety of fruits including peaches, figs and apricots. Most of their food was dried for winter use.

Southwest Indians raised turkeys, but did not use them for food. Instead they used the feathers for making sacred costumes and other ceremonial objects.

Among the Hopis, corn was the most important food, followed closely by beans. The corn came in varieties: yellow, blue, red, white, black and sweet; the beans also were colored: blue, red, yellow, white, black and speckled. These colors corresponded to the traditional directions of the Hopis. For Hopis corn was their "mother," and it represented about 90 percent of their diet.

WILD PLANT FOODS
GATHERED BY THE YAVAPAIS

Spring	*Summer and Fall*		*Winter*
Amaranth	Acorn	Mulberry	Wild garlic
Chenopod	Banana yucca	Palo verde	Wild onion
Thistle	Cactus fruit	Piñon	Wild potatoes
Wild spinach	Cedar	Squawberry	
	Goldeneye	Sunflower	
	Juniper	Walnuts	
	Manzanita	Wild grapes	
	Mesquite	Wild grasses	

Among the Apaches men did the hunting, and it was considered inappropriate for women to be involved in any way in hunting parties. Chiricahuas would not eat several types of animals, including bear, peccary and turkey, or fish. A primary food item was the agave or mescal. Tender shoots would be roasted while the crown was dug, trimmed and then baked in an underground oven or sun-dried. Other foods included juniper and sumac berries, mesquite beans, tule rootstocks, locust blossoms, potatoes, onions, sunflower seeds, acorns, piñon and pine nuts, prickly pear and other cactus fruits, berries, grapes and a variety of grass seeds. The Chiricahuas scraped the inner bark of pine or the stalks of yucca, agave or sotol to use as a sweetener, and they also harvested honey from wild bee nests found in ground hives. Occasionally the women made a weak corn beer, called tiswin.

FOOD PREPARATION

In general, women did the cooking and they also processed most of the food supply. In most areas, Indians prepared at least a portion of their food by boiling it in a vessel filled with liquid and placed near a fire or by heating stones and then putting the hot stones into the liquid in a pot causing it to boil. In regions where stone pots were used, such as the East, Prairie and Southwest, most boiling was done by placing the vessel filled with liquid directly over the fire. In regions such as the Northwest Coast, Plateau and California, where pots were primarily made of wood, bark, hide and basket techniques, stone boiling was more common. Later in the period most Indians had access to iron pots and kettles, which could be exposed directly to heat.

In 1811 explorer Wilson Price Hunt visited various Plateau tribes and noted that they used kettles and copper pots, and axes and stone hammers to pound roots, cherries, fruit and fish. Though some of the Plateau Indians continued to use water containers made of willow as cooking vessels, using the hot stone method for boiling, most preferred the copper pots.

At least some tribes in all culture areas except the Arctic used earth ovens, or fireless cookers, which were simply holes in the ground. The hole was filled with hot stones and food, then covered with dirt to allow the heat and steam to cook the meal. Usually Indians wrapped the food being cooked in bark, leaves or other plant materials to insulate it from the dirt. Though all types of food were cooked in such earth ovens, most of the time they were used to prepare plant foods. For example, the Nez Percé Indians prepared camas roots in earth-based ovens.

Most meat was prepared by broiling or roasting, although Indians also dried or smoked a considerable amount of meat. Indians of the Arctic had little firewood and used oil lamps for cooking, so if they cooked their meat at all it was boiled. In other areas Indians often placed meat on a stick and then wedged the stick into the ground so the meat hung over the fire. Sometimes they roasted meat on hot stones placed near the fire.

Though the term "jerky" (from the Quechua word *charqui*) is applied to meat preserved by drying it over a low fire, actually most meat used by Indians was simply air dried. They dried fish in the sun and air, and also sometimes put fish into pits allowing it to partially decay. Though some Indians smoked fish, that method of food preservation was less often used with fish than with other meat.

To prepare both animal and vegetable foods, Indians often used a variety of implements—such as stone mortars—to grind or pulverize it. They shelled or hulled seeds and ground meat to tenderize it. Indians soaked corn in water mixed with wood ashes (forming lye) to turn the corn into a product known as hominy and sometimes called lye corn. Indians ate the hominy cooked, dried or ground into a product that came to be known as grits.

Both fish and meat were sometimes pulverized and then mixed with berries and fat to form a nutrient-rich, easy-to-carry food source. If it contained meat, this mixture was known as pemmican, and it was often stored in a hide bag known as a parfleche.

Many vegetables were dried. Indians parched corn (known as *pinole*) and they also popped corn, though that was not employed as a preservation technique. Indians ate corn on the cob, as succotash and stewed, and they ground it for grits, bread or tortillas. They also mixed cornmeal with milk or buttermilk, then cooked it by dropping spoonfuls into hot bear fat, making the food known as "hush puppies." They fried bread and ate it with honey, sugar or maple syrup.

Choctaw cooks first used sassafras to flavor foods.

FOOD STORAGE

All tribes preserved food and stored it for future use. Indians in the Midwest and West stored food in underground pits called caches.

Among Algonquians, cornhusks were stripped from ripe corn and allowed to dry for later use in soups and stews. The corn itself was boiled on the ear, shelled and allowed to dry. When prepared in this manner it would keep for an indefinite time. Some corn was stored still on the cob in woven grass baskets or placed into logs that had been hollowed for the purpose. The baskets or logs were then placed in a grain barn or cache and covered with mats and a layer of sand.

The Mandans had underground bell-shaped food caches into which they placed preserved corn, sunflower seeds, squash and corn.

GENERAL

Tobacco

Though not a food, tobacco was an important product used by Indians. Most Indians mixed tobacco with other plants to improve its flavor, to dilute the strength of the wild tobacco plant and to make it last longer. Most Indians smoked tobacco, though on the Northwest Coast they crushed tobacco leaves in a stone mortar with water and lime and chewed it. Southwest tribes ate tobacco with lime from mollusk shells and smoked cigarettes made by rolling tobacco in corn husks.

Use of tobacco was both secular and religious. The Creek tribe used tobacco to make the "black drink," which was a ceremonial beverage. The drink caused vomiting and served as a ritual purifier before war expeditions, before important council meetings and during sacred ceremonies. Medicine bundles commonly had a pipe and tobacco in them. In such instances the pipe stem and the pipe bowl were only put together when the pipe was actually in use. The pipe became known as a calumet on the prairies. It was used for a variety of purposes: to greet visitors; to support requests for favorable weather or rain; to ratify alliances, treaties or contracts between various tribes or with governmental representatives; and in ceremonies designed to placate enemies. One important use was in peace ceremonies, where both sides of a dispute smoked the pipe while other ceremonies such as dancing and singing took place. In almost all instances tobacco was considered sacred. (See more about tobacco on page 226.)

Alcoholic Beverages

Southwestern Indians made wide use of agave and also beverages made from the fruit of cactus plants such as pitahaya, nopal and saguaro. Pima and Papago tribal members made cactus wine once each year. It was an important item in the rainmaking ceremony, the most important ritual of the year for those tribes. Everyone drank the wine on the tribe's New Year's Day, in the belief that if they drenched themselves in wine, the ground would subsequently be drenched in rain.

Other alcoholic beverages were made from mesquite and screwbeans, and some Indians made wine from persimmons.

Sweeteners

A variety of products were used including wild honey, fresh or dried fruit and maple sugar or syrup.

Narcotics

Indians used a variety of narcotics, some for medicinal purposes and others for religious reasons.

Peyote: The most well-known Indian narcotic is peyote, a member of the cactus family. It has no spines and is shaped either long and angular like a carrot or more rounded like a turnip. The rounded top of the plant, which is above ground, forms the peyote "button," which is cut off of the plant and dried before being eaten or used to make tea. When ingested, the peyote button produces hallucinations. Indians used it to reduce hunger or thirst, to help them find stolen or misplaced articles and to predict the outcome of a battle or even the weather. Some people wore peyote buttons to ward off disease and other dangers, and this is probably the way peyote was most often used. Plains Indians who used peyote were men in special groups with restricted membership who held meetings throughout the year. Northern Mexican tribal members all participated in peyote ceremonies. The greatest use of peyote by Plains tribes occurred after 1890.

Jimsonweed: Used extensively in California, Indians pounded the leaves, stems and roots of the plant then soaked them in water and drank the liquid. Jimsonweed produced visions and dreams, so many Indians used it when seeking a spirit helper. It was most often used by young people at the age of puberty. Southwest Indians used jimsonweed for many reasons including to find success in hunting, to help the user make prophesies and to control dizziness or vomiting.

Mescal bean: In western Texas and southern New Mexico, organized cults used the mescal bean in group rituals. Mescal was used before peyote became popular.

FOOD CEREMONIES

Food ceremonies included those held for the first crops of the season. Some of the ceremonies were these:

Anirsaak (Polar Bear Dance) Ceremony: Celebrated in the Arctic to honor an individual who successfully killed a polar bear.

Appanaug: A traditional feast of the Mashpee Wampanoag tribe. The feast included lobsters, clams and other shellfish, along with corn and other vegetables. The foods were placed in an oven formed by heating rocks. Cooks then laid the foods on top of the hot rocks and covered them with a type of seaweed commonly called rockweed. The rockweed insulated the food so the heat from the rocks cooked it.

Blessing of the Corn Ceremony: Celebrated by the Arikaras to ensure an abundant harvest. The three-day celebration included establishment of an altar in the lodge of the principal chief of the village. The altar was decorated with green branches, dried meat, large gourds, and arrows decorated to look like cornstalks. Hoes and empty baskets placed before the altar symbolized hope for a bountiful crop, while crowns of plaited straw were left to ward off insects. In order to have good weather, the Arikaras also left green branches as offerings to the moon and stars. Women wearing their finest clothes sat near the center posts in the lodge because the women had an important role in Arikara agriculture.

Busk or Cherokee Green Corn Ceremony: Celebrated in a four- to eight-day ceremony, this was the most important religious event each year and provided an opportunity to give thanks to the Great Corn Mother and the Sun Father. Women cleaned public buildings in the town as well as their homes, throwing away broken pottery or tools. They put out all fires, later lighting new fires from embers taken from a sacred fire in the center of the square. The men drank black drink, fasted and resolved grudges; then they participated in ritual scratching, their blood flowing as a means of purification. During the ceremonies unhappy marriages might be dissolved, and couples who had eloped could be welcomed into the community. At the culminating feast, the people ate the first corn of the season.

California Indian Acorn Harvest or "First Fruit" Ceremony: Conducted throughout California prior to harvesting the annual acorn crop. Except for a ritual purpose, it was a serious offense to eat or gather any acorns prior to the ceremony.

Hopi Niman Kachina Ceremony: Celebrated in June to recognize that the Kachina spirits who have been with the tribe through the winter depart to go to the San Francisco Mountains, where the spirits plant their own crops.

Iroquois Green Corn Ceremony: Celebrated in early spring to mark the first ears of corn. As part of the ceremony, Indians used immature "milk" corn to make puddings.

Iroquois Strawberry Ceremony: Celebrated the new strawberry plants.

ADDITIONAL READING

See references listed under chapter four Additional Reading.

Cox, Beverly. *Spirit of the Harvest: North American Indian Cooking.* Stewart Tabori & Chang; distributed in U.S. by Workman Publications. 1991. Traditional recipes and food lore.

Ebeling, Walter. *Handbook of Indian Foods and Fibers of Arid America.* Berkeley: University Press of California, 1986.

Erdosh, George. *Food & Recipes of the Native Americans (Cooking Throughout American History).* New York: PowerKids Press, 1997.

Hudson, Charles. *Black Drink: A Native American Tea.* Athens: University of Georgia Press, 1979.

Kavasch, E. Barrie. *Native Harvests: American Indian Wild Foods & Recipes.* Washington, CT: Birdstone Publishers, Institute for American Indians Studies, 1998.

Kuhnlein, Harriet V., and Nancy J. Turner. *Traditional Plant Foods of Canadian Indigenous Peoples.* Philadephia: Gordon & Breach Science Publications, 1991.

Mitchell, Patricia B. *The Good Land: Native American & Early Colonial Food.* Chatham, VA: Patricia B. Mitchell Foodways Publications, 1992.

Neithammer, Carolyn. *American Indian Food & Lore.* New York: Macmillan, 1974.

Penner, Lucille Recht. *A Native American Feast.* New York: Simon & Schuster for Young Readers, 1994.

Turner, Nancy J. *Food Plants of Coastal First Peoples.* Vancouver: University of British Columbia, Royal British Columbia Museum, 1995.

———. *Food Plants of Interior First Peoples.* Vancouver: University of British Columbia, Royal British Columbia Museum, 1979. Tells about how people harvested, prepared and preserved native foods.

Vennum, Thomas Jr. *Wild Rice and the Ojibway People.* St. Paul: Minnesota Historical Society Press, 1988.

Williamson, Darcy, and Lisa Railsback. *Cooking With Spirit: North American Indian Food & Fact.* Bend, OR: Maverick Publications, 1988.

CHAPTER SIX

CLOTHING AND ACCESSORIES

Women made traditional clothing from readily available materials including hides, furs and plant materials variously laced, sewn or woven together. Though individuals often wore at least some traditional clothing and accessories throughout the 1800s, the availability of different materials including trade cloth, known as stroud, certainly had an impact. In regions where white settlement had already spread (such as the Northeast and Southeast), Indian people wore some clothing patterned after European styles in the very early 1800s. To learn more about these styles see other books in the Writer's Digest Books Everyday Life series; including *Everyday Life in the 1800s, The Writer's Guide to Everyday Life in Colonial America 1607–1783* and *The Writer's Guide to Everyday Life in the Wild West.*

By the latter half of the century almost all Indian people had access to such styles of clothing, so calico shirts often replaced buckskin shirts, and women wore dresses of calico rather than those made from two or three skins. Most of the clothing styles outlined in this chapter are traditional garments, in use at least to some extent throughout the century, and usually worn for ceremonies and major tribal gatherings or in combination with clothing influenced by European styles. By late in the century few Indian people wore solely traditional clothing; most had adopted certain garments from other cultures.

American Indians decorated their clothing with porcupine quills, beads or wampum. The earliest trade beads, known as big beads, were about twice as large as the seed beads used by Indians in the late nineteenth century. The trade beads came from European manufacturers, including those in Italy. They

One-Called-From-A-Distance (Midwewinind), a Chippewa from White Earth Reservation, showing beadwork sash and vest, 1894. (National Archives, 106-INE-1)

were distributed through companies in New York working with trading firms throughout the country.

The early beads had such names as padre bead, sun bead or chevron bead. After 1750 the pony bead was the most popular, named for the traders who carried the beads on their ponies. The pony beads, which were up to a quarter inch in diameter, were primarily used in necklaces. After 1800 the tiny seed beads became more popular because they could be closely aligned and sewn onto articles in a variety of patterns, such as quills had been earlier. Eventually the tiny seed beads replaced most quillwork or feather embroidery. The two most popular bead colors after 1830 were blue and white.

People attached beads to garments and articles by various methods. Plains and Plateau tribes used a lazy stitch (several beads on a string attached in a single stitch). The Iroquois attached beads by padding and embossing them. Tribes in California and the Basin used netting and open-work sewing. Southern Prairie tribes plaited the beads into strings, and the northern Prairie tribes including the Winnebagos and Ojibwas/Chippewas wove them on small handlooms.

The wives of white traders introduced seed beads and floral designs among the Blackfeet. They also introduced commercial dyes to use in coloring porcupine quills, commercial paints for use on parfleches, as well as changes in clothing styles, so the clothing worn by Indian women resembled that of white women. The influence of trader wives also included changes in hairstyle to involve more braiding of women's hair and use of trade cloth for clothing.

Tribes most likely to use quillwork to decorate articles were the Huron, Ottawa, Iroquois, Ojibwa, Winnebago, Sioux, Cheyenne and Arapaho. Individual workers soaked the quills until they were supple, then folded, wrapped or wove them around other materials.

Some tribes used hair (human or animal such as horse, moose, bison or dog) for sewing, stringing and binding beads or quills.

By 1800 the Northeast tribes made their own ornaments of metal including copper or an alloy of nickel, zinc and copper. As trade improved they purchased German silver and later sterling silver to make combs, gorgets, bracelets, brooches, buttons, earrings, pendants or anklets. Plains tribes transferred such items to Southwestern tribes, who perfected techniques, particularly in working with silver and turquoise.

Concho belts and silver bracelets were first worn by Plains Indians but later adopted by the Southwestern tribes, and now they are most often identified as Navajo. Among the design elements used by the Southwestern tribes were the squash-blossom fastenings that resembled the inverted good luck piece Spanish conquistadors placed on the necks of their horses.

Materials ranging from vegetable fiber to human or animal hair and wool were woven using a variety of methods such as hand or finger weaving and simple loom weaving; only in the Southwest did Indians use the true loom. Other techniques were twining, looping, netting, plaiting and methods similar

Navajo silversmith with samples of his work and tools. (Ben Wittick, 1880; National Archives, 75-BAE-2421B-6)

to knitting and crocheting.

All tribes practiced some tattooing, though face painting was far more popular. Indians created a tattoo by pulling a thread blackened by soot just under the skin.

Arctic and Subarctic

Men and Women's Dress: Men and women wore similar clothing in the Arctic. In the summer both sexes wore a tunic or shirt made of sealskin (fur

Hopi man weaving a blanket, showing use of true loom. (John K. Hillers, 1879; National Archives, 106-IN-2435b)

side in toward the person's body). Arctic women's tunics were larger at the top, allowing room for a baby to be carried underneath (either on the woman's back, or in front if she was nursing). Some wore sealskin trousers tied below the knees and tucked into boots. Women's trousers had feet in them, though they were meant to be worn with shoes. The Pacific Eskimos did not wear trousers or boots. In the winter they switched to caribou skin, which was warmer (the hollow hairs trapped air adding to the insulation value of the garment). While indoors, people wore little, perhaps only a garment made of caribou calfskin or of fabrics imported to the region. All Arctic region people wore an *anorak*, or what we know as a parka, as the Russians first named the coat. Pulled over the head, it had a hood and tails in front and back. Parkas were generally made of caribou for heavy winter use and of sealskin for summer use. Sometimes men had parkas made from bird skins such as cormorant or puffin, and they also had waterproof parkas sewn from the intestines of walrus or seals. These were closely fitted around the waist and wrists to make them truly waterproof, particularly important when men were hunting in sea kayaks. Both men and women also had lighter-weight parkas made of rabbit or ground squirrel skins.

Eskimo mother and child in furs, Nome, Alaska. (H.G. Kaiser, 1915; National Archives, 126-ARA-2-235)

Hairstyles: Arctic men cut their hair short with bangs, leaving the hair just long enough to cover their ears. Women left their hair long and braided it or piled it on top of their head using a bone to hold it in place.

Accessories and Jewelry: Arctic people wore mittens, snow goggles and belts to hold up their trousers and hold in their parkas. Little jewelry was worn, though some people placed labrets on their face. Occasionally they wore an ear pendant or a necklace of shell, carved ivory, bone or amber. Eskimo men carried amulets carved of ivory, bone or stone, which were believed to bring success in hunting. In the summer and throughout the central Arctic, people wore slippers; otherwise, everyone wore boots made of sealskin uppers. The "mukluk" style had a large sole, crimped and sewn into a vamp. Fur placed in geometric shapes decorated boots. To absorb moisture people stuffed the soles of their boots with moss or dried grass; sometimes they added bone or ivory "hobnails" on the bottom to improve traction. People in the region that became Alaska wore socks made of woven grass. In the Arctic there was really very little snow, but in regions of the Subarctic where snowfall was heavy, people made small, round snowshoes with webbing over the frame.

Facial and Other Aesthetics: Tattooing was common among the Arctic people, though face painting was rare. Women had more tattoos than did the men, though the latter kept a tally of successes in the form of short bars tattooed on their faces.

In the Subarctic women pegged a hide on the ground to remove flesh from it and held it over a log to shave the hairs from it. Among the West Main Cree women tanned hides of seals and white (beluga) whales in a mixture of brains from the animals themselves. Then they stretched the hides and allowed them to dry before they smoked them and used them to make garments. Preparing such hides was much more difficult than dealing with the furs of hares, which were cut into strips and sewn into garments and other items. West Main Cree and Northern Ojibwa men wore a breechclout and, depending on the weather, a short coat of dressed hide or hareskin strips, a belt, leggings with garters, moccasins and possibly a warmer coat, fur robe, mittens and cap. Women wore a long dress or smock along with a coat, leggings and moccasins, and if weather dictated, mittens, caps and a fur robe or heavy coat. They wore a breechclout during menstruation and sometimes in winter for warmth.

Traditionally the Northern Ojibwas clothed themselves in caribou and moose hides, but after the arrival of fur traders they had access to European cloth and Hudson's Bay blankets. The Indians made snowshoes of solid wood, and later in the period they laced them with moose and caribou materials called *babiche*. The laced snowshoes were designed in two styles: long and pointed or short and round.

California

When white people started entering the region (primarily after 1849 though in some areas after missions were established in the 1820s), the California

Indians quickly abandoned their traditional clothing and began wearing European dress.

Men's Dress: Traditionally men often went naked, donning clothing only for dances and colder weather. They wore a kilt of buckskin and a breechclout of leather held in place with a belt but there were no flaps in either the front or back. Men wore leggings only in winter when there was snow. Those in the northern areas sometimes wore a poncho made of fur or skins. Men also wore regalia such as cloaks and headdresses made of feathers. A headdress might involve a cluster of brown pelican wing feathers or magpie tail feathers gathered into a topknot. Cloaks were made of raven feathers or of the skin and feathers of the California condor. One condor, with its nearly ten-foot wingspan provided enough feathers for an entire outfit for a man. Pelicans were particularly sought for their feathers, which were used on ceremonial garments.

Women's Dress: California women wore beaded skirts and aprons carefully woven and decorated in patterns with different colored beads. Shells were used on ceremonial aprons and as general ornaments on clothing. Beads, seeds, shells and similar objects were attached to fiber strands or buckskin fringes and carefully tied to hang so that a horizontal pattern emerged. Women generally wore nothing above the waist. After missionaries arrived women wore tops to conform to social mores.

Hairstyles: Both men and women wore their hair long and loose, though men sometimes piled it on top of their head and used hairpins or hair nets to hold it in place. Both sexes had bangs.

Accessories and Jewelry: Bags made of finger-woven fibers and belts made of leather straps were among the few accessories used by California Indians. Jewelry included necklaces made of bone, stone, beads, shells, pine nuts, seeds, pine cones and even twisted or braided straw. The people wore abalone gorgets and earrings made of small bones, feathers, loops of beads, or rings and sticks, which were pushed through pierced ears or noses.

Facial and Other Aesthetics: Most California tribes practiced facial tattooing, especially among women. People also painted their faces, usually black, red or white, though such face painting was generally reserved for rituals.

Northeast

By the 1800s most Northeastern Indians had adopted use of English or European-style clothing items, though they also occasionally wore some traditional items.

Both men's and women's dress could be decorated with porcupine quillwork, moose hair embroidery and European glass beads. Blue and white beads were the most popular colors, and designs generally were floral patterns that often covered the entire garment. Silk ribbons obtained from traders were placed on garments in an appliqué style. Stroud, a coarse woolen trade cloth made in England, became popular. The cloth came in red, green and blue and was used for breechclouts, dresses and blankets. Women used both calico and broadcloth for skirts, blouses and dresses, and to make men's shirts and leggings. Throughout the 1800s many women purchased ready-made clothing, though most continued to wear moccasins.

Mohave men in loincloths. (Timothy O'Sullivan, 1871; National Archives, 106-WA-151)

Men's Dress: Traditionally men wore fitted breechclouts with flaps in the front and back or those styled as kilts or aprons. The apron-style breechclout often had embroidery or quill decorations. Men also wore fitted thigh-length leggings or knee-length leggings held in place with garters made from pieces of hide tied together at various intervals and generally adorned with fringe. Their robes were of animal skins like bear, beaver or deer. They wore one-piece, ankle-high moccasins, though for winter their moccasins and leggings were often one piece. Some men also wore "hock boots" made from a piece of an animal's hind leg, or hock. The boots had a natural bend and were lined with deer hair or cattail fluff for insulation in the winter months. Snowshoes made of ash bent and tied into a somewhat circular shape and then laced with a web of rawhide strips, made walking easier in the winter months. As trade goods became available, men obtained military greatcoats and vests.

Women's Dress: Prior to 1800 women wore a knee-length wraparound skirt held together with a belt. In the warm weather they wore no top, but as it became cooler, they wore a poncho-type shirt. By 1800 women generally wore a two-piece dress made of skins. Known as a "strap-and-sleeve" dress, it had two straps that fit over the shoulders, was seamed down the sides and reached to the knees or beyond, depending upon the preference of the wearer and the size of the skin used. When necessary in cooler weather, women added sleeves held together at the back of the neck and in the front with buckskin strings that sometimes tied around the waist. The sleeves had no underarm seams, though they were gathered at the wrists. The women also wore knee-length leggings held in place with garters, cloaks made of rabbit skins, and moccasins similar to the men's. As the century passed the women adopted more English/European clothing.

Hairstyles: Men braided their hair occasionally into two braids, but most often wore a roach, which they called a Mohawk. Men sometimes wore artificial roaches made of the white hairs of a porcupine or of deer hair dyed red. They held such pieces in place with a "roach spreader" made of bone that could be tied to the scalp lock. As part of their ornamentation, men wore a single eagle feather. Women usually wore their hair in braids or long and flowing. They "clubbed" it for special occasions, gathering it into a knot at the back resembling a beaver's tail then adding quillwork ornaments. Both men and women used bear grease to keep their hair smooth and shining. Potawatami men let their hair hang long in time of peace, but they roached it when they were on the war trail. Most women in the tribes braided their hair.

Accessories and Jewelry: Men carried pouches or bags with a single strap over the shoulder, which were usually made of deerskin and decorated with embroidery or quillwork. They had small bags made of fibers or basswood hanging from their belts, and both men and women wore sashes woven of plant fibers and featuring geometric patterns. Both men and women wore woven headbands into which either could add feathers, though generally only the men used the feathers of turkeys, cranes or herons in their headbands. Men sometimes wore an entire skin of a fox or other animal on their head or body, particularly when hunting. Women usually wore nothing other than a headband on their head except in winter when they covered it with a hood or cap. Both sexes wore strings of wampum as jewelry, such as necklaces, headbands, caps, bracelets and belts. They also wore gorgets (breast ornaments), rings, earrings and necklaces made of bone, wood, rolled copper or shells. Men often fashioned silver armbands, and after they obtained European money, they turned coins into necklaces or brooches, sometimes in the shape of crosses.

Facial and Other Aesthetics: Fish oil rubbed on the skin kept faces smooth, and both men and women painted their faces and bodies, often using red on the cheeks and forehead.

Southeast

By the early 1800s, most Southeastern Indians no longer wore full traditional clothing. Though they wore some traditional items, they were just as likely to have cotton or wool matchcoats (similar to a mantle or cape), ruffled shirts and calico skirts. Headgear included cloth turbans, occasionally decorated with imported ostrich feathers. Chickasaw men wore turbans and sashes, while the women dressed their hair in elaborate curls high on their heads. War paint came not from natural sources but from suppliers in Europe.

Men's Dress: Traditionally men at all times wore breechclouts made of softly tanned deerskin. In the southernmost areas, the breechclouts were made of woven plant fibers. Generally when traveling men wore knee-length leggings that were often held tight by a tied fringe or band of woven cloth. A woven sash tied around the waist usually completed the outfit. In winter, men might add a skin garment, similar to a poncho or a mantle, that they referred to as a matchcoat, made of marten, raccoon, deer, various types of wildcats such as panthers or bobcats, bear, elk, or in areas to the west, even of bison. They also made robes from the woven bark of mulberry trees or feathers. Some men wore feathered headdresses, but only for ceremonial occasions. In certain tribes men wore caps or hats. Tanned skins were dyed a variety of colors: red, blue, black, yellow and green. Woven sashes had geometric designs, particularly featuring a W or V pattern in the eastern areas and circular shapes in the western areas.

By the 1830s men wore cloth coats over white shirts with black cravats. Sometimes they wore silver bands around their head, adding an ostrich or other bird plume for decoration; at other times they wrapped their heads in cloth turbans, adding a bird plume. Traditional shell gorgets gave way to silver gorgets. They continued to wear moccasins or occasionally boots.

Women's Dress: Women wore shawls wrapped around their shoulders or a cape and wraparound skirts that extended below the knees. Both shawls and skirts were made of softly tanned skins or woven plant fibers, and they often had fringe along the edges. They used leather belts to hold their skirt in place and sometimes wore knee-length leggings held up with garters. Women wore mantles similar to those used by men, and made of similar materials, but women did not wear feather capes. By the 1830s Southeastern Indian women wore full, flounced skirts and blouses with long, full sleeves and large collars made of such materials as calico, gingham or plain-colored cotton. They often had ribbons hanging from their hair at the back of their head, and they usually wore multiple strings of bead necklaces as well as earrings. They also started wearing European shoes.

Hairstyles: Men usually wore their hair in a roach, shaving the sides and leaving an upstanding fringe at the top with a scalp lock to the back. Occasionally they shaved only one side of their head and had the scalp lock at the side, twisted and decorated with such items as pieces of fur, feathers and even small rocks. Women generally wore their hair long and loose, except in times of mourning when it was cut short. They decorated it with shells, stones or flowers. They seldom wore feathers in their hair or on their clothing. Both men and women put bear grease and red ocher in their hair, believing that it kept them warmer in winter and cooler in summer.

Accessories and Jewelry: Men and women wore sashes made from mulberry tree bark, and men wore snakeskin belts. Men had pouches they hung from their belts in which to carry pipes, tobacco and fire-making materials. Men and women pierced their ears and wore a variety of earrings made of bird claws, buttons or strings of pearls. Necklaces and bracelets were made of copper, beads or pearls. Gorgets to hang around the neck were made of large shells carved with intricate designs.

Facial and Other Aesthetics: Both men and women tattooed their faces, though men had more tattoos than women. Men also used face paint, particularly for war and games, that most commonly was red, black, yellow or russet, with white used only at the end of a festival. Some tribes flattened a child's skull by applying pressure with a bag of sand or a buckskin-wrapped block of wood.

Great Basin

Men's Dress: Men wore nothing during the summer, and in winter they wore a kilt or breechclout and leggings made of tanned deerskin, when available. Many of their garments were made of woven grass or shredded bark, and men also wore hip-length tunics made of rabbit skin. The Great Basin is a region of contrasts, with extremely hot, dry weather in the summer and cold weather in the winter. So people who wore nothing in the summer, bundled into bison robes or rabbit skin robes in the winter. It took about one hundred rabbit pelts to make one robe. Other robes were made of skins from beaver and even ducks or small animals, including the meadow mouse.

Women's Dress: In the summer women wore an apron made of buckskin, strips of sagebrush, juniper bark or yucca held in place with a braided cord or

The Arrow Maker and his daughter, Kaivavit Paiutes, in front of their home. (Clement Powell, 4 October 1872; National Archives, 57-PE-1)

belt. In colder weather, they wore two aprons and a tunic or poncho. If they had buckskin, women used it to make dresses with fringe at the hem and sleeves. They wore robes made from skins of rabbits or other animals or woven from plant materials.

Hairstyles: Women pulled their long hair forward and tied it with cords. Those from tribes in the eastern part of the region sometimes braided their hair. Men wore their hair long, usually hanging loose, except in the eastern areas where they braided it and wrapped the braids with otter fur.

Accessories and Jewelry: The people in the Great Basin had few accessories, occasionally a belt or sash and sometimes a buckskin pouch added to their clothing. They had little ornamentation, though in the nineteenth century the Utes and Shoshones began adding beadwork to their garments. Great Basin people made earrings and necklaces of shells, seeds, feathers and bones. Though they often went barefoot, sometimes Great Basin people wore sandals woven from yucca leaves, twisted sagebrush bark or other plant fibers. They occasionally wore "hock shoes" or moccasins made from the rear leg or hock of an animal, particularly a bison. Thongs tied around them kept the moccasins in place. They also wore moccasins, made from three pieces of leather, known as Fremont moccasins. The dewclaws of the animal were left on the leather and provided traction when walking. Another style of moccasin was made from one piece of leather with cuffs that could be pulled up as leggings. Snowshoes were made by forming a round or oval frame and covering it with a net made of woven fibers. In winter the people had crude fur caps, and in the summer some wore basket-style caps or hats, though most went bareheaded.

Facial and Other Aesthetics: The people engaged in limited facial tattooing. They used red, black, yellow and white face paint for ceremonial gatherings. When going to war, Shoshones painted their faces black.

In 1811 Wilson Price Hunt, exploring in the West, noted that in a camp of Snake Indians the "women were poorly clothed, the children even more shabbily, though each one had a robe of buffalo skin, or of rabbit, badger, fox, wolf, or possibly some skins of ducks sewn together."

Interior Plateau

Men's Dress: Men didn't wear many clothes, even in the northern, colder areas, restricting their dress generally to a buckskin breechclout with front and back flaps, a pair of moccasins and a robe. The men also sometimes used leggings made of cloth or deerskin, held in with a garter at the knee. The leggings were thigh-high and usually had fringe along the edges as well as large buckskin flaps. Some men also wore short, poncho-style shirts made of deerskin. Though some shirts extended to the waist, others fell just below the shoulders. Later shirts were longer and had seams at the side as well as short sleeves and long fringes hanging from the shoulders. Wealthy men had buckskin capes, often painted with yellow, red and white designs depicting the man's dreams. Men started wearing European dress by about 1875, including dark, heavily beaded vests, trousers, cotton shirts, neck scarves, gauntlets that were also heavily beaded and "ranger" hats (those with flat brims).

Women's Dress: Women wore a wraparound skirt and poncho top. By the early 1800s they also wore ankle-length dresses made from elk, deer and mountain goat skins. The typical two-skin dress had seams across the top and along the sides with a fold-down yoke decorated with deer tails in both the front and back. Generally the side seams were left open to about the waist (making it easier to nurse children). Besides the deer tails hanging at the yoke, women embellished the yokes of their dresses with quill- and beadwork. When they could obtain it, women made dresses of stroud cloth, usually a plain or striped fabric made into a T-shaped garment with the seams of the arms left unsewn. Contrasting colored ribbons or materials were added to the edges of the seams, and a leather belt or sash held in the stroud cloth dresses at the waist. Women often wore a separate blouse under their dress. In the region along the Columbia River, women used bark capes and skirts.

Both men and women wore moccasins made of deerskin with the hair left on and worn to the inside. They were often decorated with quillwork. Other clothing items were decorated with elk teeth, stone and shell beads, painting, bear claws, burned-in designs and feathers. Both men and women had robes of bison or buckskin, and they also used rabbitskin robes. In the latter part of the 1800s, Pendleton blankets (made in Pendleton, Oregon) replaced bison robes.

Hairstyles: Both men and women wore their hair in long braids or loose. Sometimes the men adopted Plains styles such as pompadours or a coiled knot of hair above the forehead. Men often wrapped their braids in otter skins, especially for special occasions. To remove facial hair, men plucked it out with tweezers of hardwood or joined mussel shells.

Accessories and Jewelry: Plateau Indians carried "friendship bags" made of twined cornhusk woven into complex geometric shapes. In the later portion of the 1800s the bags might be decorated with beads or yarn. The Plateau people also carried small buckskin bags, and they wore armbands and belts made of strips of fur or leather covered with quillwork or floral beadwork. Necklaces of copper tubes, shells and bones as well as three-strand chokers were popular. Men wore loop necklaces with up to fourteen strands of disk-type beads. Earrings were made of abalone shell. Many Plateau Indian people fashioned ornaments of shellfish. People living closer to the plains wore visors or sunshades to protect their eyes, and the men often wore warbonnets made of upright feathers with strips of ermine hanging at the sides. Women wore basket-styled hats.

Facial and Other Aesthetics: Plateau Indians painted their faces. They particularly liked red, but also used yellow, black and green. In the first half of the 1800s some tribes in the region practiced head flattening, though they generally abandoned the practice by about 1850.

Northwest Coast

Men's Dress: Men often did not wear anything, though after arrival of Europeans in the early 1800s, they began trading for clothes. They particularly liked the Hudson's Bay Company blankets, which by about 1850 replaced

Flathead delegation and an interpreter. Note their blanket coats. (C.M. Bell, 1884; National Archives, 106-INE-31)

the traditional Chilkat blanket. They made coats or "button blankets" of dark blue or black stroud or lightweight blanket cloth like the Chilkat or Hudson's Bay blankets. The button blanket coats had a border and central appliqué of red cloth, often felt or flannel, and rows of white buttons. In winter men wore tunics made of woven cedar bark trimmed with rabbit or other furs. The knee-length tunics were rectangular shapes folded over and under the left arm and fastened on the right shoulder. They had a tie or girdle at the waist. The only tribes to use leggings were those in the north as they traveled into the interior.

Women's Dress: Women wore cedar bark aprons made by attaching the bark to a waistband and tying it at the back. Over the apron they sometimes wore a knee-length skirt, which was made of deerskin by northern tribes, of woven cedar bark by the central tribes and of shredded or split cedar fibers by southern tribes. When not wearing a skirt, the women sometimes had a tunic fashioned like those of the men made of cedar bark and edged in fur. Capes of shredded cedar bark were used in winter and to protect against rain. Likewise, cedar bark blankets were generally waterproof. These blankets were rectangular and decorated with painted designs, patterned edgings or a fringe of bark. When combined with a basketry hat, the capes or blankets worked well as rain gear.

Northwest Coast Indians wore fur robes, particularly sea otter, marten, marmot, fur seal, bear, raccoon and bobcat. Some robes also were made from duck or loon skins. A thong or blanket pin of bone or wood held the robe together in the front. The most popular robes were those made by the Coast Salish and the Chilkat people, and they were widely traded. The Chilkat robes were popular until about 1850, when Hudson's Bay blankets essentially replaced them. For the most part people went barefoot, though when traveling into the interior and during winter they might use moccasins and snowshoes made in simple round or oval forms of rawhide rope and woven netting.

MAKING A CEDAR BARK GARMENT

Women stripped the fibrous inner layer of bark from a red or yellow cedar tree, allowing it to dry before they split it lengthwise. Once stripped, the lengths of bark were placed over a sharp edge and pounded with a shredder to separate them into fine fibers or strands. The shredder was made from the nasal bone of a whale, a piece of yew wood or from some other piece of bone. Once the strands of bark had been separated, the women wove them on a two-bar loom using a twining technique. The primary garments made of cedar bark included women's aprons, a conical cape, blankets and some basketry hats.

Hairstyles: Men coiled their hair into a bun on the top of their head or wore it long and loose. Women wore their hair in braids down their back.

Accessories and Jewelry: Almost all people had pouches of cedar bark decorated with porcupine quillwork and used to carry dentalium shells (currency). They attached them to belts made of bark fiber strips or leather and decorated them with shells, claws and teeth. The kind and amount of jewelry worn by

Northwest Coast Indians depended on the status of the wearer. Women sometimes put carved wood or shell pendants in their braids. They wore bracelets of copper, mountain goat horn or iron. Some women pierced their nose and inserted a dentalium shell, piece of abalone or a silver ring. Men also pierced their noses. Young girls and women inserted a labret (an elliptical piece of wood, ivory or bone) into the lower lip. Necklaces and chokers were made of olivella shells, abalone shells, animal teeth, thin copper rolled into tubular beads, or pieces of bone, antler and animal claws. Earrings were most often made of dentalium shells, either a single shell or a cluster of shells.

Facial and Other Aesthetics: Men often had goatees or full mustaches. People painted their faces for ceremonial reasons and for warmth and protection against the sun and wind. Black, white and red were the most popular colors. At puberty, Northwest Coast girls received their first tattoo, a small mark on their hand. Some tattoos were elaborate and involved inherited designs only the owners were allowed to use. Little new tattooing occurred in the 1800s. Northwest Coast tribes also practiced head flattening, considering it a sign of aristocracy. Sometimes they attached a board to the infant's head in the cradle, causing the head to flatten or become pointed. Other times, as among the Kwakiutl and Nootka, the people used a wrapping or "bandage" to shape the head into a "sugar loaf."

Plains

Men's Dress: Men seldom wore a shirt during the early part of the period, though by the latter half of the century they sometimes wore calico shirts. They almost always wore a breechclout made of buckskin or later of trade cloth, called stroud cloth, and wore thigh-length leggings made of buckskin that were tied together at the sides or sewed with sinew. The breechclout could be decorated with quillwork, and the sides of the leggings sometimes had quillwork bands attached. Leggings were generally fringed or left tattered at the bottom. Though deer was the preferred type of skin used in garments, elk or antelope could be used. Men used buffalo robes for warmth in winter and as ceremonial garments year-round. The robes were decorated in many ways.

By the 1800s they also used Hudson's Bay blankets, which they sometimes had fashioned into capotes, the long hooded coats of the French *voyageurs*, held in place with a long sash. In winter, men might wear a cap; otherwise, they went bareheaded except for their ceremonial headgear such as feathered warbonnets. Very late in the 1800s they also began wearing flat-brimmed, black felt hats known as the "Indian hat."

The people of Plains tribes also used bird feathers for ornamentation. They particularly liked the feathers of the Great Horned Owl. Golden and bald eagle feathers had symbolic meaning. Plains Indians called the golden eagle "War Eagle." They made whistles out of the hollow bones of the eagles and prayed to the eagles.

Women's Dress: In the early part of the period, women wore a simple wrap-around skirt, with a poncho or cape used in periods of cold weather. Later they used strap-and-sleeve dresses or side-fold dresses. The former had straps over the shoulders, and sleeves could be added if necessary by tying them in the front and back. The latter was made of a single hide folded around the body with one side left open and the top bent down producing a large flap. A strap went over the right shoulder. Subsequently two-skin dresses were made by sewing the skins together at the top and sides, leaving openings for the head and arms. Three-skin dresses were further refined with two skins sewn together at the sides and a third skin fashioned into a yoke. Women wore knee-length leggings held in place with garters of otter fur or thongs. They made their dresses of deer, elk or antelope skins and decorated them with quillwork, rows of elk teeth, shells, fringe or animal tails. Women wore buffalo robes for warmth and ceremonial occasions. Later they used Hudson's Bay blankets. By late in the 1800s, women added tin cones, called "tinklers," to their dresses so they jingled as they walked.

Plains boys and girls often went naked. When they were seven years old, they were required to wear clothing, though the amount of it depended on the number of older children in the family and their sex.

Hairstyles: Men in the northern plains usually braided their hair into two braids, sometimes wrapping them in otter fur or later with red cloth. Those living in the southern plains often let their hair hang loose down their back. Sometimes men had a forelock hanging forward over their nose, or they cut their hair shorter in the front and then smeared it with clay to make it stand up into a pompadour. Usually only medicine men cut their hair into a roach. All men had a scalp lock, which they braided and decorated with ornaments. Women on the northern plains braided their hair, rubbed bear grease on it to make it shine, and sometimes added red ocher in the part, particularly to express great joy. Married women let their braids hang forward in front of their shoulders, while single women had their braids hanging down their back. Women of the Southern Plains usually let their hair hang loose. Hair combs were made from the tail of a porcupine. Crow men not only took care of their own hair, they also did their women's hair. After about 1855, Cheyennes of both sexes braided their hair into two braids, though the men left a scalp lock at the crown.

Accessories and Jewelry: Generally men had two belts, one that held their leggings and breechclout in place and another outer belt onto which they attached tools, weapons, pouches and bags. Medicine bags included important ceremonial or spiritual items; "strike-a-light" bags held the materials needed to start a fire. Men also carried fans, often of eagle feathers, and after 1850 men wore breastplates made of two- to five-inch-long hair pipes that tied around their necks and waist and which were decorated with brass beads, trade ribbons, shells and quillwork or beadwork. Both men and women wore a variety

Curley, Crow scout for Custer at Little Bighorn, 1876. (David F. Barry, 1876; National Archives, 165-AI-4)

of jewelry including chokers made of fur strips; otter skins rolled, stuffed and decorated with quillwork; hair pipes (see page 160), and dentalium shells (traded from the Pacific Coast Indians). Necklaces made of shell beads, animal claws, antlers, horns, teeth (especially elk teeth), seeds and grass were popular as were shell gorgets. Hair bows made from rawhide in an hourglass shape with shells and beads as ornamentation were popular, as were armbands and bracelets, which were often made from strips of quillwork. Chiefs often wore peace medals given to them by government representatives. The peace medals featured an image of the United States president on one side and usually an eagle on the other side.

Plains Warbonnets: The flaring feathered headdress most often associated with North American Indian tribes was, in fact, used by few of them. The Crows may have invented the flaring headdress, which was adopted by other tribes, particularly in the Upper Missouri region. The flaring headdress had feathers laced to a buckskin skull cap. The feathers maintained their spacing by a second buckskin lace strung through the feather quill part way up its length.

Blackfeet adopted the flaring headdress late in the nineteenth century, but traditionally they used a straight-up headdress, which had important sacred meaning. It is the simplest of all feathered headdresses. Made from a piece of rawhide or heavy leather folded lengthwise and used as a headband, the feathers were then carefully placed along the headband and sewn rigidly into place with sinew or buckskin lacing. The straight-up headdress of the Blackfeet was usually ornamented with multiple rows of ermine tails (which had spiritual powers and provided sacred protection) and sometimes with brass studs or tacks across the headband.

Feathers were an important symbol for most Plains tribes, often having meaning depending on how they were worn. The meaning varied by tribe. In

Oglala Sioux Red Cloud delegation, from left Big Dog, Little Wound, John Bridgeman (interpreter), Red Cloud, American Horse and Red Shirt. Note the different styles of wearing feathers in the photo taken prior to 1876. (Photographer/date unknown; National Archives, 106-IN-200).

some tribes feathers pointed toward the right signified the number of scalps taken, feathers facing left were worn by war leaders who had achieved great power and control in battle. Sometimes feathers worn by scouts who were particularly skilled would be stripped nearly to the top with only a fringe of the black tip left to flutter in the wind. Among the Sioux a feather with a *V* slash on one side represented an act in which the Sioux warrior cut the throat and then scalped his enemy. The man who first struck—or counted coup on— an enemy earned the right to wear an upright golden eagle feather. The second man counting coup tilted his eagle feather to the left, while the third placed an eagle feather horizontally. Finally, the fourth warrior to count coup wore a buzzard feather that hung vertically.

Feathers each represented a man, and before they were attached to a warbonnet, a ceremony was held to recognize war honors associated with the individual feather. When feathers had a piece of scalp lock attached to the tip, that indicated a separate honor.

In certain cases individual warriors presented the feathers they had earned in war honors to a respected individual or chief, thus creating the full-length warbonnets that trailed to the ground.

Cheyenne warbonnets usually had a pair of bison horns, which distinguished men of high rank and which provided sacred protection during battle. After the 1870s the Cheyennes often attached the bison horns to flaring style bonnets subsequently making the wearer believe he was bulletproof.

Ornaments

Three common types of ornaments were the beaded choker, hair-pipe hair ornament and the beaded hair bow. Men wore chokers made of hair pipes or of a buckskin material stuffed with soft materials and decorated with blue and white trade beads.

Beaded Chokers: Made by stringing beads together, often interspersed with hair pipes, these chokers were worn by both men and women, tied snugly around the neck.

Hair Bows: Hair bows were of various materials, including long strips of rawhide, sometimes decorated with trade beads or brass tubes, and sometimes having a feather or other ornament attached such as dentalium shells or large trade beads. These hair bows were most popular among the Mandans, and in fact may be an ornament first designed by those tribal members that was later copied by other tribes.

Hair Pipes: Cylindrical tubes known as hair pipes were made of Bahama conch shells by wampum makers primarily in Bergen County, New Jersey. The conch shells were cut and then shaped into tube-like shells before they were drilled by hand. They were provided by Canadian and American traders in Montreal and St. Louis. Lewis and Clark took two dozen hair pipes on their journey west in 1804, purchasing them from St. Louis's leading trader, Auguste Chouteau. The American Fur Company in New York sold wampum hair pipes to Pratte, Chouteau and Company of St. Louis in the 1830s, and the hair pipes were then used in trading farther west.

> We want 3250 inches Wampum Hair Pipes, none less than 5 inches long, and not many of them over 6 inches—You must have them here by the first day of February next, or say 4 weeks from this time, and we shall pay you the same price as last season—some of those you furnished last winter were not bored entire through— This will not do. . . .
> —*American Fur Company order sent to Samuel Campbell, Franklin, Bergen County, New Jersey, 1834.*

Facial and Other Aesthetics: Plains Indians painted their faces and bodies for ornamentation and spiritual power. Both men and women painted for war with a woman's face generally having streaks down the cheeks, nose and across the forehead. Men painted their entire face and body, and often that of their horse as well, as a talisman for protection in battle. Some colors and symbols depicted secret military societies. Paint was also used as a protective way to shield a person from sun, wind, snow and insects. In those cases the people first rubbed bear grease onto themselves and then covered the grease with paint.

Paint was made from a variety of natural products, such as berries or plants that could be boiled or crushed to create color, and certain types of soil and mineral pigments, such as red, black or yellow ocher. Pigments were mixed with grease or bone marrow.

Crows made paint hold color by using the gum (or pitch) from chokecherry trees or the hooves of bison. They would boil the hooves until they formed a jelly, which would be mixed with paint and allowed to dry. Once dry, the paint mixture could be cut into squares. When mixed with water or grease the color would revive and could be used on faces, bodies, animals or material objects such as parfleches or tipis.

Wichitas elaborately tattooed their faces and earned the name "Raccoon Eyes" as a result. Men tattooed arms and chests with war deeds.

In 1904, George A. Dorsey of the Field Columbian Museum in Chicago described Wichita tattooing of women:

> Among the women, the most complete and most common (tattoo) is a single line which passes down the nasal ridge and is carried to the end of the upper lip, from which a line passes in each direction to the corners of the mouth where each joins a short line passing downward and terminating in another line directed toward the center of the lower lip. Before these lines meet, they turn downward to the chin. The space between these two lines is occupied by two short parallel lines and all four terminate in a line which

passes entirely around the jaw from ear to ear, and which is surmounted by a row of solid triangles. Similar rows of triangles pass across the neck and down the upper part of the breast.

Down each arm are two series of four parallel zigzags, while four long lines pass down the middle of the breast. Above each of the breasts are three pairs of lines, each pair crossing at a wide angle, the open space at each end being occupied by V-shaped connecting lines. The nipple is also tattooed, and around it are three concentric circles. . . . The whole tattooed design is said to have been derived from the buffalo.

Prairies and Woodlands

Men's Dress: Ojibwa (Canada) and Chippewa (United States) men wore breechclouts with long flaps in both the front and back as well as close-fitting leggings with garters below the knee. Sometimes they wore a kilt and a buckskin poncho. Their moccasins were fitted and had a puckered seam up the front and where the skin met the vamp (shoe upper). Moccasins were decorated in floral patterns with moosehair embroidery or quillwork, and in the winter they were lined with muskrat or rabbit skins. Fox men dressed similarly, with thigh-length leggings and a shirt made of tanned elk or deerskin.

Miami men wore only a red-painted breechclout, deerskin shirt and moccasins in winter, usually leaving off the shirt in the summer. For special occasions they donned leggings that reached just above the knees or were thigh-length. In the 1800s the men in these tribes generally wore at least some European clothes made of stroud cloth, and they particularly liked Hudson's Bay blankets, which they fashioned into capotes (long, hooded coats with a sash to tie the waist).

Women's Dress: Women wore strap-and-sleeve dresses (see Northeast women's dress for details, pg. 148) or wraparound skirts. They often added knee-length buckskin leggings. Most traditional clothing was made from elk- or deerskins. The clothing was decorated with quillwork in geometric designs (among the Fox, for example) and with ribbons attached to shawls, leggings, moccasins and dresses. By the mid-nineteenth century, Sauk women wore wraparound skirts made of blue, red or black broadcloth and decorated with ribbon bands at the hemline. They also wore calico blouses.

Hairstyles: Prairie and Woodland Indians used a variety of hairstyles. The Chippewa and Ojibwa men and women wore their hair loose or sometimes braided. Fox, Sauk, Ottawa and Miami men had a roach, shaving both sides of their head and allowing the remainder of their hair to stand up in the middle. Menominee men either roached their hair or let it hang loose.

Accessories and Jewelry: People used many accessories ranging from sashes, collars, fans and medicine bags to pouches and envelope-style bags, all of which were embellished with paint and quillwork or, later, beadwork. Both men and women wore many necklaces made of shells, grizzly bear claws (which were especially prized), copper and beads. Both men and women wore earrings made of beads, shells, feathers and other materials.

Facial and Other Aesthetics: Most people painted both their faces and bodies. Chippewas liked red, black, green and yellow paints. Upon achieving adulthood Fox Indians painted their faces red, and for special occasions the women painted the center part of their hair red as well. Menominee men painted parallel black bars across their face and added red designs on their cheeks. Sometimes they painted just a part of the face black. Menominee women painted red spots on their cheeks. Miami men also used red paint on their faces, sometimes adding a bit of black; the Miami women tattooed parallel lines on their chins and cheeks. Ottawa men also tattooed lizards, geometrical figures and snakes onto themselves, sometimes covering their entire body. They painted their faces red, black, green or brown. Sauk men and women painted their faces, most commonly black and white, often putting a red circle around the eyes.

Southwest

Men's Dress: Men wore cloth breechclouts in either the apron style—with flaps hanging down in front and back and tied at the waist—or those which were fitted, passing through the crotch and held in place by a belt. Men sometimes wore a kilt over the breechclout. They also wore a skin poncho, which gave way to woven cotton shirts made from a rectangular piece of material that had a hole for the head and square-cut sleeves tied together under the arms and at the wrist. Leggings were made of skins or woven plant fibers such as yucca, or even human hair. In areas where there was cactus, men wore heavy hide leggings. By late in the period, Pueblo men wore loose cotton pants similar to what Mexican peons wore. For footwear, men wore either square- or round-toed sandals woven from yucca or Indian hemp. Indians living in the eastern part of the region, whom Plains Indians influenced, sometimes wore sandals made of leather or moccasins. Generally men who were good hunters could supply the buckskin needed for moccasins, while those who were less skilled relied on plant fibers for sandals. They sometimes wore socks made of yucca fibers, cotton or mountain sheep wool.

Women's Dress: Women wore aprons made from weaving fibers, such as yucca, dogbane, Indian hemp or juniper bark, fur, feathers and human hair or mountain sheep wool. In eastern areas of the region and near the mountains, women wore skirts made of tanned leather and added a poncho over their shoulders. Residents in the northern areas of the region wore wraparound robes of tanned deerskin, and other Indians in the region wore rabbit skin robes or those made of twill-weave cotton blankets. They raised their own cotton. Those living in the southern part of the region wore feather mantles, often made of turkey feathers stripped to the shaft of the feather and then woven together. By late in the period, women (and a few men) wore Indian robes that resembled Mexican serapes, and their shawls were like the Spanish rebozo (scarf). Women wore sandals made of yucca and other plant materials or moccasins. Women's sandals had flaps that resembled moccasins, and those in the eastern part of the region wore buckskin moccasins. They sometimes wore socks made of yucca fibers, cotton or mountain sheep wool. After 1864 (when they spent time at Bosque Redondo), Navajo women began wearing dresses based on patterns of white women's dresses, particularly those with wide skirts.

Hairstyles: Many women cut their hair short, subsequently using the hair for a material woven into various garments. Men wore their hair long, often tied into three separate portions. In some tribes the women wore bangs. The Mohaves prided themselves on their shiny hair, cleaning it with a mixture of boiled mesquite bark and mud. Mohave women let their hair hang loose, while the men coiled theirs into twenty to thirty ropelike strands that hung

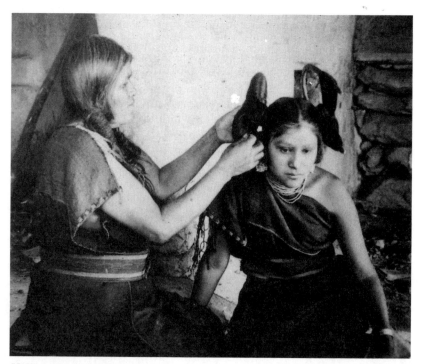

Hopi woman dressing hair of unmarried girl. (Henry Peabody, 1990; National Archives, 79-HPS-6-3274)

down their backs (similar to dredlocks). Other men, particularly in the southern part of the region, also wore their hair in twisted ropes or braids.

Accessories and Jewelry: Southwest Indians wore braided or twined sashes around their waists. The sashes were from six to nine feet long and between three and six inches wide, with geometric patterns made from variously colored fibers and shells hanging from fringes at the ends. Belts or tumplines (burden straps) were made of yucca and painted various colors. Necklaces and earrings of stones or shell beads were popular. Head coverings included headbands made from turkey feathers and caps made with basketweaving techniques. In the south elaborate headdresses were made from macaw feathers imported from Mexico.

Facial and Other Aesthetics: Most Southwest Indians did not paint or tattoo their faces. The Walapais and Yavapais painted their faces and created tattoos using cactus needles. Mohaves also tattooed their faces and believed anyone who had not received a tattoo prior to death would descend down a rat hole rather than proceed to the land of the dead.

ADDITIONAL READING

See references listed under chapter four Additional Reading.

Hartman, Sheryl. *Indian Clothing of the Great Lakes.* Ogden, UT: Eagle's View Publishing, 1988.

Hofsinde, Robert. *Indian Costumes.* New York: W. Morrow, 1968.

Koch, Ronald P. *Dress Clothing of the Plains Indians.* Norman: University of Oklahoma Press, 1977.

Mails, Thomas E. *Creators of the Plains.* Tulsa, OK: Council Oaks Books, 1997. An excellent volume including details about beadwork, quillwork, shields and other types of gear/equipment.

Mason, Bernard S. *The Book of Indian Crafts and Costumes.* New York: A. S. Barnes & Company, 1946.

Parker, Arthur C. *The Indian How Book.* New York: Dover Publications, 1975, reprint of 1927 edition.

Paterek, Josephine. *Encyclopedia of American Indian Costume.* New York: W.W. Norton & Co., 1994. This is an essential reference book about Indian clothing, with general information about tribal groups and specific details about most tribes.

Reedstrom, Ernest Lisle. *Historic Dress of The Old West.* New York: Blandford Press, 1986.

Wilbur, C. Keith. *The New England Indians: An Illustrated Sourcebook of Authentic Details of Everyday Indian Life.* Old Saybrook, CT: Globe Pequot Press, 1978; 2d ed. 1996.

CHAPTER SEVEN

SHELTER

All Indians built some type of dwelling, ranging from simple brush-covered wickiups to elaborate pueblo-style homes, and from hide-covered lodges to snow-covered, domed igloos. In every instance the dwelling was made from materials readily available in the area. In the early portion of the period, the dwellings were generally smaller and more crudely constructed than those of the latter part of the century. An example of this change can be seen when comparing the tipis or lodges of Plains Indians of 1800—which were small, often made of three or four bison hides—to those of the 1870s, when fifteen or more hides might be used for one family lodge. A major reason the lodge size increased so dramatically was the acquisition of the horse. Though most tribes had horses by 1800, they almost all had *more horses* by 1870. The additional horses made it easier to move camps, and possible to have more personal possessions than previously, which consequently required larger lodges.

Not all Indian people lived in hide-covered lodges. The people of the Arctic and Subarctic lived in domed structures covered with dirt and ice or snow at least during a portion of the year; when temperatures rose above freezing, their snow lodges melted and were replaced with structures of other materials, such as earth or animal products. Southwestern people lived in adobe structures, and Southeastern tribal members often had log or frame houses, much like those of people of European ancestry.

The ownership of the home also varied. In patrilineal tribes men owned the homes, and in matrilineal tribes women did. Almost always, women owned the materials in the home, such as cooking pots, baskets and the like.

MAJOR TYPES OF INDIAN HOUSING

Earth lodge: Often semisubterranean, large, dome-shaped structures used in many culture areas, but particularly near the Upper Missouri River. The dome was formed by bending flexible poles, and the framework was then covered with earth.

Hogan: Used by Navajos and usually made of brush or wood frames covered with mud or sometimes stone and formed in a hexagonal, octagonal or conical style facing toward the east.

Lodge or Tipi: A cone-shaped mobile structure made from a framework of poles covered with skins, primarily, and occasionally with bark or canvas if available. Indians prefer use of the word "lodge." These structures were commonly used by Plains tribes, but also by those in the Southeast, Arctic, Subarctic and Southwest.

Longhouse: A large structure which often had a domed roof, walls and sometimes a latticed porch. Woven mats or slabs of bark covered the structure. Some longhouses were used as dwellings, but most were ceremonial or meeting houses. They were used in the Northeast cultural area, specifically by the Iroquois and Huron tribes.

Plankhouse: Used along the Northwest Coast and made of a log frame covered with split planks.

Pueblo: A structure in the Southwest built of adobe bricks with a roof entrance, small windows and thick walls.

Wickiup: A primitive, small structure of grass, brush or rushes placed over a framework of sticks or poles. Most common among Great Basin, Southwest and California tribes. It was sometimes used by other groups as temporary housing.

Wigwam: A structure similar to a tipi made of a pole or stick framework, but having a rounded top and covered with woven mats or birch bark rather than skins. It was generally rather small. These were used by Northeast tribes, particularly the Algonquins.

In almost every style of shelter people kindled a fire in the center of the structure to provide heat, light and a place for cooking or for gathering for storytelling and other activities. Furnishings were generally sparse, with space limited to sleeping areas made from blankets, furs or hides, an area for cooking utensils and food and a place for sacred objects such as medicine bundles. Some structures, because they were more substantial and therefore more permanent, had built-in, elevated sleeping and storage platforms, but many simply had spaces for people to work, visit or sleep on the floor. Though some structures had planks for flooring, most had the earth as a floor, which was occasionally covered with mats of woven grasses, rushes or bark. One common furniture item, used by people of many different tribes, was a backrest made of woven

Kickapoo wickiup, Sac and Fox Agency, Indian Territory, 1880. (Photographer unknown; National Archives, 75-IP-3-4)

materials and supported with a tripod-like series of sticks. Most were decorated with quillwork or beadwork. They could be rolled into a small parcel for easy movement.

Arctic and Subarctic

The most common dwelling in the Arctic, and much of the Subarctic, was the domed house, often made of wood or whale rib frames and covered with dirt, rocks, sod, and sometimes in winter with blocks of snow.

A low passageway—through which people crawled on their hands and knees—provided entry to the dwelling. Between the passageway and the main lodge, hung a double hide door, serving to keep the cold air out and the warm air in. Some entrances were through center holes at the top of the structure, with a ladder to provide access.

Inside, platforms were built along the sides and back of the domed house. The family slept on the back platform, using hides as bedding. Other activities, such as food preparation, took place along the side platforms or more commonly in the central area where the fire was located. Sometimes a single family lived in snow houses (which were temporary because they melted in spring and summer), but most larger structures served more than one family.

In some Arctic dwellings constructed using whale rib bones as the basic structure, stones and earth were piled and stacked to a certain point, and then more whale bones were used to bridge the cap and form the roof. These dwellings were generally constructed along the same basic plan as the true snow house, with a long narrow entry way, in an oval or near-oval shape and with side and rear platforms inside.

Alaskan Eskimos and Athapaskans built permanent Arctic houses called winter houses. Usually three families shared a permanent house. They were shallow pit homes made from a rectangular log framework covered with earth. Raised log platforms inside provided seating during the day and sleeping areas at night. There was a roof hole under which was the fireplace, necessary for heat, light and cooking. Though some fires were fueled with wood, in many areas that was a scarce item so seal oil was used as an alternative heating and cooking fuel.

Aleuts had large houses—called *barabaras*—with stall-like living areas along the sides of the interior. Many families lived in a single house with a common area in the center of the structure. A roof hole provided light and a way to enter the structure (by climbing down a log-notch ladder). The barabaras were semisubterranean, often excavated three to four feet into the earth with walls made of drift logs or whale ribs. Other wood formed rafters with an outer covering of skins, grass or sod. People sat on mats and used them as curtains around personal spaces. After Russian influences spread through the region, planks were added to floors, and a side door served as an entrance.

Pacific Eskimos had similarly constructed houses, in which up to twenty people lived. The common area at the center was used as a place to cook and serve meals, as a workshop where men made such items as kayaks, spear throwers, bows, quivers, arrows, harpoons and darts, and where women made baskets or sewed clothing. It also served as a place for ceremonies and gatherings, particularly in villages with no hall, or Kashim. The Eskimos heated their private rooms in the house with hot rocks. They also used the heated rocks to create steam baths taken by both sexes for purification and relaxation.

Most Subarctic tribes utilized crude conical-shaped tipis covered with hides or even bark. The Subarctic hide coverings were not sewn together like Plains Indian lodges, but were simply placed over the pole framework with additional poles laid on top of the hides to hold them in place. If hides weren't available, bark was placed over the frame with other poles holding it in place. Arctic people also used conical tents of caribou, seal or walrus as temporary shelters, particularly when traveling or hunting. Fires kindled in the structures provided heat and a way to cook.

In western areas of the Subarctic, people built double lean-tos with pole frames covered with bark, brush or hide. Such structures served a single family and had no interior platforms or other furnishings.

California

The earliest types of houses used by California Indians were pit houses excavated into the earth then framed with timber and covered with a layer of dirt that served as insulation. The layer of dirt formed a mound above ground covered with grass. There was a hatch at the top with a ladder to descend into the pit house itself. Indians including the Achumawi and Modoc in the northeast and the Pomo, Miwok, and Patwin and their neighbors in the central part of California used the same type of pit house. Many California Indians also had similar structures to use as general meeting or assembly lodges and as sweat lodges.

Tribes in the northwest, such as the Hupa, Karok, Yurok and their neighbors, made gabled plank houses from locally available cedar and redwood. They split the redwood with wedges made from elk antlers. The houses were often large, up to thirty-five feet by twenty-five feet.

Indians living in warmer areas made houses that were lightweight and constructed of reeds, grass or branches. Tule rushes were particularly popular as housing materials. The tule was woven into mats, which could then be placed against pole-and-brush frameworks to build a home or other structure that was fairly water- and wind-resistant. Some of the multifamily dwellings were thirty-five feet long and twelve feet wide, made when builders put mats of tule over bent sapling frames.

Black Beaver, a Delaware born in Illinois in 1808, photographed 1872. (Alexander Gardner; National Archives, 75-ID-118A)

Northeast

The Iroquois Indians built the largest of all Indian dwellings—the longhouses—which averaged sixty to eighty feet long, and eighteen to twenty-five feet wide. A single longhouse provided living space for several families along with storage areas. There were elevated benches for seating and sleeping to avoid damp ground.

By the 1800s, Indians in the extreme eastern portion of the region seldom lived in traditional houses. They had instead acculturated to living in English-style homes or in log cabins. After the Delawares relocated farther west (to Kansas and Oklahoma), they lived in frame houses, but built small dome-shaped structures for sweat houses. Though the Delawares lived in frame houses, the interior was structured similarly to traditional housing, with raised sleeping and sitting platforms located around the inside of the building. Babies slept in hammocks made from a blanket tied with two ropes and hung from the ceiling.

Southeast

The houses of the Seminoles, called chickees, were open-sided with a platform inside located about thirty inches off the ground, where people could keep their possessions out of the mud and rain. The roofs were made of thatched grasses or palmetto leaves placed over a pole framework.

Cherokee winter council houses or *tcokofa* were twenty-five feet in diameter and had a domed ceiling extending about twenty-five feet high at the center. The interior had benches lining the sides that were generally about seven feet square and covered with mats. Some towns had large tcokofas with two or three levels of benches. A smoke hole in the roof above the fire and the low entryway provided the only ventilation and light, so the council houses were dark and often musty.

A Cherokee summer council house consisted of a grouping of rectangular shedlike structures. Each was about thirty feet long and made with wattle-and-daub walls, open fronts and a roof canopy made of brush and leaves woven together. The sheds faced each other in a square pattern, leaving room for an open area, or central plaza, where the sacred fire burned. Like the winter council house, each of the sheds had benches. Usually the different sheds were separated so each clan had its own space, which could be decorated with clan symbols and ritual objects such as herbs, eagle feathers or war clubs.

Cherokee homes surrounded the central plaza. Each family had a cluster of buildings including a winter house, a summer house and storage sheds. The round winter house had a floor excavated into the earth. A single L-shaped entryway allowed access, and the winter house was insulated with Spanish moss, dried grass or clay. Surrounding the room were sleeping platforms. The only light came from the doorway, candles made from dried canes or torches and the central fire. Because of the insulation, the Cherokee winter houses were easy to heat and often "hot as a vapor bath," according to French missionary Fr. Jacques Gravier.

Cherokee summer homes sat on frameworks of notched posts. The single rectangular room might be two stories high and had a gabled roof shingled with cypress or pine bark held in place by logs. To provide for cooling breezes, the gable ends of the roof often were left open.

Early in the 1800s, Cherokees still used the traditional housing, but as the century passed, they adapted so their homes were smaller, often resembling the log cabins of white settlers. Their homes also generally clustered around the trading post, rather than the council house.

Great Basin

Wickiups made with grass or brush covering served as shelters for the Great Basin tribes, who had little in the way of material wealth. Later in the period some of the tribes like the Shoshones had hide lodges similar to those of the Plains tribes.

Family of Bannocks in front of grass tent. (William H. Jackson, 1872; National Archives, 57-HS-996)

Interior Plateau

People of the Interior Plateau commonly lived in three types of settlements: winter villages, seasonal sites and temporary camps.

Typical dwellings for Plateau Indians were semisubterranean pit houses, plank houses and mat lodges. Almost all tribes also had sweat houses and menstrual houses (constructed with a bent willow frame covered with mats and earth) for each extended family.

The semisubterranean houses were generally constructed over four- to five-foot deep circular—or sometimes oblong—pits with a pyramidal or conical roof supported by posts placed near the center of the pit. The center of the roof was left open. It served as a smoke hole and also as the entrance/exit of the dwelling with access provided by using a notched log ladder. One or more families occupied such dwellings. The structures had bed platforms as well as scaffolds to hold supplies. Winter structures were generally sturdier and covered or insulated with bark or tule; summer and temporary structures were made of tule mats.

Among the Spokanes, each March some tule mats were rolled up and stored in trees near the winter village sites, while others were taken by tribal members as they journeyed to summer locations. In the summer Kalispels used lean-tos as lodging. Flatheads and Pend d'Orielles used conical-shaped tipis or lodges covered with branches or grass mats and, late in the century, with canvas or skin covers.

Coeur d'Alenes lived in lodges made of mats of tule, but they were not semisubterranean like those of most other Plateau tribes. They used a double lean-to in the summer, which served two families and had a central fire. The double lean-tos also served as training areas and gathering places for young men. When it was available, the Coeur d'Alenes covered their structures with cedar bark. Sometimes the tribe constructed palisades or stockades made of either horizontal or vertical posts. When they built a stockade, they made a zigzag entryway that could be closed with wooden bars, and they sometimes excavated underground tunnels that provided access routes.

Among the Wasco, Cascades and Wishram tribes, the winter houses had characteristics of both the Plateau and Northwest Coast dwellings. They were partially subterranean as in the Plateau area, but they had vertical plank walls as did those along the Northwest Coast. Strips or slabs of bark were used for roofs.

Typical Nez Percé structures were double lean-tos—some of them up to one hundred feet long—covered with mats. When traveling, the Nez Percés used conical lodges covered with mats or bison hides. As trade made it available, canvas was used to cover the structures.

Klamaths and Modocs used semisubterranean earth lodges, mat lodges and a small wickiup, which was also covered with mats.

Northwest Coast

A framework of logs covered by rough planks of yellow or red cedar provided the basic dwelling of Northwest Coast Indians. It was occupied by several individual families, who were part of a large extended family. The planks might be attached to the log frame either horizontally or vertically, and the dwelling was generally fifteen to twenty feet wide and from fifty to sixty feet long. It had a gabled end with an oval doorway that faced the sea. Each individual family was allotted a certain amount of space in the house. Platforms made of poles and planks lined the interior walls for use as sitting and sleeping areas. Sometimes the platforms were made by excavating the center of the floor, placing the soil to the sides and forming a sort of terrace. Planks also covered the floors and terraces.

The Haida, Tlingit and Tsimshian tribesmen were skilled woodworkers who cut tongues and grooves then steamed the planks so they fit tightly together. Bark served as roof shingles, and each of the houses had partitions intricately carved and painted with totems. Outside the houses stood carved totem poles that depicted the history of the clan or family. The thirty-foot-high totem poles often could be seen from the sea and therefore served as landmarks for travelers.

Some people in the region constructed houses that had a one-pitch or shed-style roof, and a few tribes in northwest California built houses that had three pitches to the roof.

Kit Carson recalled an attack on a Klamath village of fifty lodges (1846):

> Their houses were built of flag [a lakeshore plant with sword-shaped leaves], beautifully woven. They had been fishing and had in their houses some ten wagon loads of fish they had caught. All their fishing tackle, camp equipage, etc., was there. I wished to do them as much damage as I could, so I directed their houses be set on fire. The flag being dry, it was a beautiful sight.

Plains

The bison-hide-covered conical tipi or lodge served most Plains people. A fire pit was constructed in the center of the lodge with beds arranged around the edges of the interior of the structure, except near the door. Early lodges were small and made of just a few hides, but during the 1800s the size enlarged, so some of them were twelve to fifteen feet in diameter and covered with between fifteen and twenty hides. Women dismantled and erected lodges whenever the tribe moved its camp, and they also prepared the hides and sewed them together. Men often obtained the straight poles used as the framework.

When setting up a lodge the women lashed the main poles together and then raised them in a triangular shape. Additional poles were set in place, and the hide covering, in the shape of a half moon, was hoisted up and laced together with sinew. The women staked the lower edge of the covering with

Little Big Mouth, a medicine man, seated in front of his lodge near Fort Sill, Indian Territory; medicine bag behind tent. (William S. Soule, 1869–70; National Archives, 75-BAE-1448D)

wooden pegs in periods of colder weather, adding an interior liner during the winter to serve as insulation. In the summer and in warmer weather, the lower sides of the tipi could be rolled up allowing for better air circulation. Smoke from the central fire rose in the cone-shaped lodge to exit through the top opening, which could be controlled by shifting the exterior poles of the smoke flap to provide better drafting and directional control. Lodges could be left plain or decorated with paintings and symbols as determined by the lodge owner.

Capt. Meriwether Lewis provided this description of a plains lodge:

> This tent is in the Indian stile, formed of a number of dressed Buffaloe skins in such manner that when foalded double it forms the quarter of a circle, and is left open at one side. Here it may be attatched or loosened at pleasure by strings which are sewed to its sides for the purpose. To erect this tent, a parsel of ten or twelve poles are provided, fore and five of which are attatched together at one end, they are then elivated and their lower extremities are spread in a circular manner to a width proportionate to the demention of the lodge; in the same position other poles are leant against those, and the leather is then thrown over them forming a conic figure.

The two flaps at the top of the tipi used to control the smoke hole are called "ears" by the Crows. Northern Plains women burned sweet grass in their lodges to make them smell good. Crow women did not paint lodges; that was a job for medicine men. The women did sew the lodge-skins, but only certain women were allowed to become "lodge-cutters" and to have lodges with a distinctive mark. If a lodge skin fit over lodge poles particularly well, it was said to "fit like a leaf-tepee." Little girls often had lodges of their own, which were smaller versions of family lodges. The girls would play in their lodges, and sometimes even stay in them.

If a man wanted to visit another man, he would go to the lodge door and inquire whether the person he wanted to see was in. If the man in the lodge wished to see his visitor, he would invite him into the lodge and place some meat before his visitor. If a woman wished to visit another woman, she would lift the lodge door and look inside. She would only enter if asked to do so by the woman in the lodge.

Arikara-style housing was described by Patrick Gass of the Lewis & Clark Corps of Discovery in his 1807 account of the trip:

> In a circle of a size suited to the dimensions of the intended lodge, they set up 16 forked posts five or six feet high, and lay poles from one fork to another. Against these poles they lean other poles, slanting from the ground, and extending about four inches above the cross poles: these are to receive the ends of the upper poles, that support the roof. They next set up four large forks, fifteen feet high, and about ten feet apart, in the middle of the area; and poles or beams between these. The roof poles are then laid on extending from the lower poles across the beams which rest on the middle forks, of such a length as to leave a hole at the top for a chimney. The whole is then covered with willow branches, except the chimney and hole below to pass through. On the willow branches they lay grass and lastly clay. At the hole below they build a pen about four feet wide and projecting ten feet from the hut; and hang a buffalo skin at the entrance of the hut for a door.

Foundations for lodges of the Pawnees, Mandans and Hidatsas were entrenched in the soil. The round mounds of Pawnee lodges were situated close to each other. The Hidatsas, Arikaras and Mandans constructed large wooden structures that were subsequently covered with earth. In Mandan villages the lodges of the most prominent people were closest to the Okipa or medicine lodge. Each Mandan lodge would be occupied by up to sixteen people for a period ranging from seven to twelve years; some of the lodges were eighty to one hundred feet wide. The large permanent Mandan lodges, used in the summer, were near the Mandan fields.

During the winter, Mandans lived in smaller villages and camps so people could more easily find adequate food. Their winter lodges were usually built in wooded bottoms along creeks and rivers, but they were not as well constructed, and they also were much smaller than the summer lodges.

Hidatsas had lodges similar to the Mandans' and also occupied them for a period from seven to twelve years.

Pawnee lodges and family at Loup, Nebraska. (William H. Jackson, 1873; National Archives, 106-INE-3)

Southern Plains people, such as the Wichitas, Caddos and their neighbors, used grass-thatched houses that were roughly fifteen or more feet in diameter. They had no smoke hole; instead, the smoke from the central fire pit was allowed to dissipate through the thatching. A number of families, who were related, occupied each of the thatched houses.

Wichitas made summer arbors by forming an arch from a sapling, which could be covered with skins, brush, grass or thatching. Later in the 1800s they used canvas coverings. Young women slept in elevated huts accessed by climbing a ladder. After girls were in the hut for the night, their mother removed the ladder. The space beneath the hut was used for food preservation including drying or slicing. Wichitas also used tipi-style lodges.

Prairies and Woodlands

Different types of dwellings were in use by Prairie and Woodland people. The Dakota tribes used hide-covered lodges similar to those of the Plains Indians. Tribes living along the Missouri River built earth lodges that were from thirty to forty feet in diameter and perhaps ten or fifteen feet high at the center. Often builders dug a foot or more of dirt from the area where the earth lodge was to be built in order to provide a solid floor. A platform made of poles surrounded the interior sides of the dwelling, serving as sleeping and seating areas. In most cases such dwellings were occupied by several families who were part of a larger extended family.

People living around the Great Lakes constructed small domed dwellings known as wigwams, which were covered with woven or sewn mats, pieces of bark and hides. Single families had individual small wigwams, while extended families had larger elliptically-shaped dwellings. Among Ojibwas, women wove plant stalks into mats, which they used to cover the wigwam frame and also to place on the floor. When the camp was moved for any reason, the women took the mats off the wigwam framework and transported them to the new camp.

The Northern Ojibwas gathered tree boughs to cover lodge floors, and in areas where the materials were available, they made mats from the inner bark of cedar or bulrushes.

Southwest

Pueblos of the Southwest were adobe structures involving several levels or tiers of housing generally arranged around a central plaza. Living quarters often faced toward the south to catch the sun, particularly during the colder winter months. Constructed of stone and adobe, the houses had thick walls that served to capture heat during the day and release it through the night. Similarly, the thick walls insulated against hot temperatures in the summer.

Pueblo dwellers such as the Zunis used the terraces formed by their living quarters as work areas where they could bake bread, dry vegetables or do other jobs such as weaving or pottery.

To protect against intruders, the ground floors of each pueblo had no exterior doors. Entry was provided through a series of ladders that led to the roofs of the buildings, and additional ladders provided access from the roof down into the room. To prevent someone who was not welcome from entering

Dancers' Rock, Walpi, Arizona, part of a Hopi pueblo including three Hopis, ladders and utensils. (John K. Hillers, 1879; National Archives, 391-JKH-3)

First terrace of Zuni pueblo, New Mexico, showing utensils and ladders. (John K. Hillers, 1879; National Archives, 391-JKH-9)

the home, the ladders simply were removed. Pots, baskets and sleeping mats were the basic items in each of the homes.

The Pueblo people were primarily matrilineal, so women owned the homes and passed them from generation to generation.

Western Apaches constructed wickiups made of a frame of bent saplings covered with grasses, while the Mescalero and Jicarilla Apaches, who hunted buffalo, had hide-covered shelters similar to the Plains lodge.

The Navajos built simple homes called hogans or "home place." They had a framework of poles that was covered with a layer of soil, especially the clay soil of the region that was easy to mold to the framework and that dried hard and substantial. The small multi-sided homes often lasted for several years. The hogan always faced with the doorway toward the east, and the Navajos considered it a sacred dwelling. Upon completion of a hogan, the Navajos would consecrate it with corn pollen. If the owner of the hogan died, the structure was usually destroyed in order to be certain that the ghost of the deceased did not return to haunt survivors. The Navajos lived in small camps of related people, with a "head mother" as the overall authority.

The Havasupais had two types of houses. Winter homes were log-and-pole frames made in a domed or conical shape and covered with thatch or dirt. Summer homes were similar, though they were often rectangular. Simple structures to provide shade also were constructed for summer use when most activity took place outside the home, which was primarily used for sleeping.

Walapai summer houses were simple structures made of branches and sticks placed against a low tree limb. By the reservation period, in the late 1800s, the Walapais constructed eight-sided hogans and tarpaper shacks.

Mohaves constructed open-sided ramadas with flat tops (called shades) for summer use. Their rectangular winter houses had four cottonwood posts and a structure of sloping poles, covered with sand and arrowgrass thatching.

Among the Pimans and Papagos, unmarried adults and each family had a house for storage of personal property and sleeping, with the dwellings grouped into household compounds generally headed by an elderly man. Other structures could be added including corrals for horses and other stock, cooking areas and menstruation huts.

ADDITIONAL READING

See references listed under chapter four Additional Reading.

Hoagland, Alison K. *Buildings of Alaska*. New York: Oxford University Press, 1993.

Laubin, Gladys. *The Indian Tipi: Its History, Construction and Use*. Norman: University of Oklahoma, 2000.

Nabokov, Peter, and Robert Easton. *Native American Architecture*. New York: Oxford University Press, 1989.

Sanford, Trent Elwood. *The Architecture of the Southwest*. Westport, CT: Greenwood Press, 1971.

Spears, Beverley. *American Adobes*. Albuquerque: University of New Mexico, Press, 1986.

CHAPTER EIGHT

TRANSPORTATION, TOOLS AND EQUIPMENT

Across Indian America the primary means of early transportation involved walking, and people from every tribe did a considerable amount of it during their lifetimes. By the 1800s most tribes had obtained horses, which they used for riding and for transporting goods. They fashioned drags from small trees or poles onto which they could place goods (or even people) for transportation. Dogs and people pulled some of the earliest drags—known as travois—but horses became the major draft animals once they were available, in part because they could haul heavier loads.

Travois were shaped from poles (for horse travois) or sticks (for dog travois) in a simple V form with the narrow end tied together and allowed to rest over the back and shoulders of the animal. The wide legs were allowed to drag on the ground. A platform made from a plank or by weaving/webbing plant or animal fibers or rawhide strips served as a place on which to pile goods. Many travois had a cage-like structure over the platform, and small children or elderly people rode there when Indians moved their camps.

Indian women in many culture areas transported babies and young children on cradleboards made of wood, hide or woven plant fibers to provide a type of "backpack." Most cradleboards had wooden frames and were highly decorated by mothers or grandmothers.

Early in the period few Indians had wheeled vehicles, though by late in the nineteenth century many had obtained wagons and carts. Those who lived along rivers or lakes relied heavily on a variety of watercraft, including rafts, dugouts, (boats shaped from a single large tree hollowed out by burning or carving), canoes, bullboats (round boats made of a willow or pole frame covered with hides), plank boats and kayaks. People living in snowy climates used sleds, toboggans and snowshoes.

American Indians tanned hides in a variety of ways. The most common method was brain tanning. They soaked the hide in water and then in a mixture of animal brains, elm bark, animal liver and sometimes sour milk. After proper soaking, the hide was wrung out and then stretched over a frame where it was allowed to dry. It became soft and pliable and could be easily cut and shaped into a variety of objects ranging from clothing and moccasins to arrow cases. Shoshone women rolled hides in ashes then soaked them in warm water for several days prior to scraping off the hair. During the scraping process the hide was repeatedly soaked in water. They then placed the hides in a tipi-like fashion over a smoldering fire to produce brown buckskin (dried over a fire of green willows), yellow buckskin (dried over smoke from a dry willow fire) or white buckskin (air dried).

Hides not tanned but with the flesh and hair removed were considered rawhides. They were sturdy and tough and used for such objects as war shields and parfleches (containers used for storing and carrying food items).

Indians seldom left the items made from either rawhide or tanned hides plain. Instead they decorated and ornamented clothing, weapons and lodges with fringe, beadwork, shellwork, quillwork and feathers. They made cloth using various weaving techniques including finger-weaving, plaiting, braiding and twining, and in some areas they also used belt-looms or true looms.

Indians made cords, ropes, rugs and rough bags from sisal, a tough cord they extracted from the agave plant. They put asphalt on baskets and cloth to make the items waterproof.

Baskets were used for threshing, to wash corn, acorns or other crops and to collect seeds. They were also used as backpacks, as fish or bird traps and for ceremonies such as funerals or weddings. Basketry techniques also found use in making hats, cradles and mats. Construction techniques included coiling, twining or plaiting such materials as rushes, yucca leaves, bear grass, cattails, willow, sumac or devil's claw (Southwest); cedar, basswood, sweet grass or hardwood (Northeast); buffalo grass or hazel (Plains); or squaw grass and cherry, spruce or cedar bark (Northwest and California). Any item that could be steamed, soaked or rubbed until it became supple could be used in basketmaking. Decorations ranged from patterns made from the natural materials themselves, to feathers, beads, fringes, shells or quills.

In the Southwest vessels were often made of clay that was coiled, twined or simply molded into shape. Such clay pots were decorated by painting or inscribing them with various designs. Though some were simply sun dried, others were fired in ovens heated with animal dung (primarily sheep). The inconsistency of the heat resulted in color striations in each pot.

Because there were many birch trees in their region, Northeastern Indians made containers of bark. White birch was the most popular type of bark used.

Apache rancheria and two men holding rifles. (Camillus S. Fly; National Archives, 111-SC-85775)

It was soaked in water and then folded into shapes ranging from simple squares or rectangles to those resembling pails. Other containers included coiled baskets, splint baskets, twined baskets and pottery.

Arctic

Aleuts used lamps filled with oil from sea mammals (such as whales or seals), and they also had small round or oval stone lamps they could light then stand over to warm themselves when traveling. In a house they seldom made a fire (they ate most of their meat raw), but when they did, they placed bird down and sulphur on a stone and ignited it by striking a flint. The fire was used to ignite dry grass for lamp wicks. Household utensils included large spoons, wooden bowls and buckets, stone knives for both men and women, often a brass kettle and a flat stone that served as a frying pan prior to obtaining frying pans and kettles from traders. Aleuts made baskets of woven plant fibers, particularly wild barley or wild rye.

Most Arctic people who lived near waterways utilized kayaks, including two-hatch and single kayaks; some were three-hole boats, called *baidaras*. Most people used the two-hatch kayak known as a umiak. Single kayaks were made to each individual user's specific body measurements. Kayakmen could travel about seven miles an hour, even in rough waters, and seldom did they encounter conditions they couldn't handle.

Kayakmen carried a variety of items with them including a wooden tube to bail with, hunting implements, a spear thrower, double-bladed paddles and domestic items such as those needed for eating and for heating. They also

CALIFORNIA BASKETRY

California Indians used baskets in almost every aspect of their lives—from gathering, preparing or storing food items to trapping animals. The Pomo Indians believed that the cultural hero Marumda, who created the world, gave women *kubum,* or the plants needed to build baskets.

The California Indians made baskets using one of two techniques: weaving (or twining) materials or coiling materials. Among the materials used were bracken fern root, redbud stalks, grass stalks, willow, spruce needles, sedge root, pine root, bear grass, maidenhair fern and porcupine quills. Though most baskets were decorated only with the various materials used to construct them, which were woven into geometric or other designs, some baskets had shells or feathers used as ornamentation.

A child was placed into a basket-woven cradleboard shortly after birth. Baskets became storage containers for clothing and other personal possessions, and basketry techniques were even used to make clothing items such as hats, raingear, belts or sandals.

Baskets came in many varieties: jar-shaped baskets with or without lids, bottle covers, flat baskets used as trays, and baskets made in myriad shapes that were used as bowls. Some basketry techniques also were used to make traps to snare woodpeckers, scoops for gathering quantities of food such as grains or acorns and even urns.

Among the largest baskets were the cone-shaped burden baskets that women used for carrying large amounts of goods such as firewood or acorns. They carried the baskets by suspending a strap called a tumpline around their foreheads and necks and attaching it around the basket, holding the basket in place against their backs. Many burden baskets were tightly woven, to prevent loss of seeds and other materials, though some were loosely woven and used for carrying roots or tubers. The loose weave made it possible for dirt on the roots to break loose and fall off as the women walked or moved the baskets.

---

carried a float made from the stomach of a sea mammal that could be used to support the person while righting an overturned kayak or making repairs to a torn kayak, or to provide lift for a boat that had a hole in it.

There is little evidence dogs were in wide use to assist in transportation—such as the pulling of sleds early in the period—though some may have been used later in the century.

The most important tool for a Bering Strait Eskimo woman was her *ulu,* a halfmoon-shaped knife used for cutting skins and fish.

California

Pomo Indians made boats of tule rushes, which they tied together. The boats easily became waterlogged, and in that case the users had to drag them to shore and allow them to dry out before again using them. Though some of the crafts were small, similar to a canoe, others were large rafts. The Choinimni, a Yokuts band, lashed the tule rafts or platforms together to form barges up to fifty feet long. They became a place for entire families to live during extended fishing trips. Tribes living near redwood forests built dugout canoes of redwood trees. Other tribes living near forested areas made dugouts of pine trees. They treated some of the boats with a mixture of tar, gravel and sand (asphalt) to make them waterproof.

Northeast and Southeast

By 1800 most tribes in the Northeast and Southeast had wide access to European weapons, including guns and iron hatchets, which they used instead of bows and arrows or wooden clubs. They also had wide access to European items such as cooking pots, and wagons or carts.

The Potawatomis moved their villages seasonally and they participated in long-distance trade, so various forms of transportation were important. On the water, the people commonly used dugout canoes. Occasionally they built large-framed canoes covered with the bark of birch, white elm or linden trees. A bark-frame canoe often reached twenty-five feet in length and was five feet wide. By 1800 many Potawatomis preferred not to use watercraft and instead relied on horses for transportation. Potawatomis used saddles made of a wooden frame (known as the tree) covered with rawhide. They had saddlebags made of rush matting in which they could carry goods ranging from clothing to food. They also used litters, similar to a travois, on which they could transport ill or elderly people as well as goods.

Great Basin

The Great Basin tribes relied on primitive tools and weapons throughout most of the period, using dogs and horses (if they had them) to transport goods on travois. They had few resources for trade and thus were among the last Indians to obtain European weapons and tools.

Interior Plateau

Bark canoes, log rafts, log dugouts and other watercraft were primary means of transportation for Plateau people who lived near rivers and lakes. Coeur d'Alenes, for example, "used doubled-ended, sharp-pointed 'sturgeon nose' cedar bark canoes," according to Gary Palmer in *Handbook of North American Indians*, vol. 12, *Plateau*.

In winter, the people used snowshoes, toboggans and various forms of sleds made from frozen bear or deer hides.

After horses became widely available, they served as the primary way to transport goods and people. Plateau people adopted many items from Plains Indian culture, including new leather clothing styles, horsehair bridles and saddles for both packing and riding, including stirrups on riding saddles. Of all the Plateau tribes, the Nez Percés had the most horses, with some families owning hundreds or even thousands of animals. The Nez Percés made horse gear including saddles that they decorated with quills, beads, dyes, rawhide, horse hair, bone or antler.

Hemp was braided and twisted into cordage, used for weaving and as tumplines.

Women wove baskets for a variety of uses including storage and carrying or preparing and serving food. Infants were sometimes bathed in large baskets. The preferred basketmaking material was red cedar, though women also used cottonwood, spruce, birch and white pine bark. Mats of cattails and tule were used as table mats and bedding. The Yakimas used cedar and spruce roots and elk and rye grass, as well as willow, cedar and alder bark and Indian hemp to make baskets, cordage, netting, rope and twine.

Among the tools used were elk horn hammers, stone mauls, beaver tooth engravers, awls and wedges made of wood and horn and needles of bone and wood (later metal). They also had earth ovens, wooden bowls and spoons made of horn, wood and bark. Thorn and fishbone needles were used in creating tattoos.

Northwest Coast

Red cedar cut in February and March went into construction of Haida canoes. The Haidas were well known for their craftsmanship, so the canoes they made were routinely traded to other people living along the Northwest Coast. The huge canoes—hewn from a single red cedar tree—could carry three tons of cargo. Propelled by up to sixty men wielding slender, highly decorated oars and sometimes by sails, the canoes had ornamentation ranging from carvings to paintings. The Haidas lashed two of the large canoes together and added a plank deck to make warships.

Kwakiutl war canoes had long, heavy, narrow hulls with a high flaring bow and a nearly vertical stern. Some earlier war canoes had the bow high and nearly vertical and the stern high and slanted, with both projected as thin fins. By the late nineteenth century, Kwakiutl canoes had a high bow and stern. Those canoes were from ten to fifty feet long and were decorated with carvings. They often had two sails made by lashing canvas or other materials to a single upright mast.

The spruce, a type of canoe, was the most common form of transportation for the Tlingit people, who sometimes added a canvas sail and who used yellow cedar oars to navigate. Southern Tlingits made canoes of red cedar, though most Tlingits preferred the large sixty-foot-long Haida canoes that had two masts and sails. Wealthy Tlingit headmen purchased such canoes and decorated them with paintings and carvings. Tlingits also used heavy-prowed canoes for sealing, and forked-prow canoes, drift-river canoes made of cottonwood, skin canoes and moon canoes made with upturned ends for sea otter hunting and fishing.

Tlingits used Eyak snowshoes that had netting only under the foot and also purchased Athapaskan snowshoes, which had wider webbing. Sometimes the Tlingits added spikes to their snowshoes, particularly when pursuing mountain goats.

Some Tlingits had tumplines, which their slaves used to carry large loads of up to two hundred pounds; others transported materials in their canoes and needed only a cord to tie around firewood or game to make it easier to move. When moving camp, goods were transported in tightly fitting boxes or waterproof bags made from seal or halibut skins. Women carried food items in large pack baskets. Occasionally the Tlingits used hand-pulled Athapascan-style sleds.

Nootkans used red cedar dugouts, war canoes and large freighters, sometimes taking pairs of canoes and bridging them with house planks in order to move large numbers of people or quantities of goods. They also employed sails to move the watercraft more easily.

Plains

The Mandans and Arikaras made boats by bending willows into a framework then stretching a fresh bison hide over it. These were known as bull boats. The method of stretching a green hide over a framework also was employed in making baskets and other receptacles for storing food and other goods. The Mandans strung rushes together to create mats, used in a variety of ways.

Traditional Plains kettles were made from a piece of rawhide dried into a kettle-like form then hung from a tripod. Water could be heated by placing hot stones into the liquid in the hide kettle. The Plains people had few clay pots and limited numbers of other pots carved from stones. They used a stone mortar and pestle to grind food.

Plains Indians relied on horses for transportation, both for themselves and their goods. As explorer Wilson Price Hunt reported in 1811, nearly every member of the Crow tribe rode horseback, including the children. In viewing one group of traveling Crows, Hunt noticed a child tied onto the back of a young horse. "He held the reins in one hand and frequently used his whip. I asked about his age and was told that he had seen two winters. He did not yet talk!"

And Hunt added, "These Indians are such excellent horsemen that they ride up and down the mountains and craggy heights as if they were galloping in a riding school."

Indians traveling on the open plains could often spot something far away. Sometimes it could be difficult to determine whether the object was moving or not. In such cases, the person would put two objects—such as two sticks— in a line and then watch the object in comparison to the line to determine the slightest movement and direction of movement.

Southern Cheyenne Stump Horn and family beside their lodge and with horsedrawn travois.
(Christian Barthelmess, 1890; National Archives, 106-INE-21)

Prairies and Woodlands

Menominees used both dugout and birchbark canoes. Birchbark covered the Ojibwa/Chippewa canoes, which were used as a primary means of transportation.

Ojibwas used fifteen-foot canoes that took two weeks to build as a joint effort involving men and women, with the former handling the woodwork and the latter sewing bark together. The canoes had a birchbark outer shell over stays, ribs, thwart and gunwales made of white cedar and floorboards of thin cedar. The women sewed the bark seams with pine roots, coating the seams with pine pitch for water resistance. The boats were large enough to be efficient, and light enough to be easily transported when portaging was necessary. In wet weather the boats were turned upside down to serve as temporary shelters or placed over the smoke holes of earth lodges to keep rain out.

Among the Northern Ojibwas, traditional common tools were stone fleshers and bone or thorn sewing needles.

Southwest

Mohaves lived along the Colorado River and were good swimmers, but they seldom used any type of boat. When crossing the river an adult might put a child into a clay pot and push it across. Sometimes the men made log rafts, or they used a single log to straddle and ride down the river. When traveling on foot, the men jog-trotted, often up to one hundred miles a day. Women hauled items in a woven basket supported by a tumpline around their foreheads.

The Cocopas built cottonwood dugouts, log-and-brush rafts and tule balsa watercraft. Children and small items were transported over water by being placed into a large pottery container known as an *olla* or into a large basket and pushed by a swimmer.

The Yaquis used cane for a variety of purposes: as sleeping mats, for roof and wall coverings, to construct fences around household compounds, and as implements and furnishings ranging from cutting instruments and spoons to shelves and even as birdcages. Cane was also used for dance wands, ceremonial headdresses and as canes of office.

ADDITIONAL READING:

See references listed under chapter four Additional Reading.
Mails, Thomas E. *Creators of the Plains.* Tulsa, OK: Council Oaks Books, 1997.

CHAPTER NINE

MEDICINE

T wo major types of sickness affected American Indians: actual diseases and illnesses (ranging from headaches to upset stomach), and spirit sicknesses, where an individual suffered from a loss or reduction of his or her spirit. Indian people believed illness could be caused by breaking taboos, by thinking evil thoughts or by harmful spirits.

Medicine men or women could often treat spirit sickness as well as diseases or other illnesses, though if a healer failed in efforts to effect a cure, the patient's family could kill the healer. In 1860–61 when there was a plague among the Pimans at Gila Crossing, "three medicine-men who were suspected of causing the disease by their magic were killed 'and nobody was sick any more.' " The role of healers involved performing rituals and casting spells during public ceremonies or over the enemy. Healers used incantations in varied aspects of Indian life: for success in war, hunting, and sports and for making rain. A spiritual healer was not a shaman. The word *shaman* originated in Asia and was applied to North American Indian healers by anthropologists, missionaries and even governmental leaders early in the 1900s, in spite of the fact that it was never a term used by any North American Indian tribe. It should not be used in reference to Indian medicine in the 1800s. Some Indian healers were herbalists; others relied on supernatural occurrences in effecting cures.

The Pimans believed there were two types of sickness: wandering sickness, which came from outside sources such as whites, Mexicans and the like, included such diseases as measles and smallpox; and staying sickness, which came only from the Pimans. Those latter types of illnesses have always existed—and always will exist for Pimans. They cannot be passed from Pimans to outsiders, and though they can be "cured," they can't truly be eliminated, so they will continue to afflict the people through the ages. People cannot get staying sicknesses from each other, but they become afflicted when they fail to properly react to certain "dangerous objects." Those objects include the badger, bee, bear, buzzard, butterfly, cat, caterpillar, cow, coyote, deer, dog, devil, eagle, frog, gila monster, hawk, horned toad, housefly, lizard, mouse, owl, peyote, quail, rattlesnake, roadrunner, rabbit, saint, turtle; datura or jimsonweed; an enemy or a whore; and lightning, the ocean and wind.

There are certain things—called ways—that people must do when they meet any one of those dangerous objects, and if they fail to act properly, they will get staying sickness. Healers must "diagnose" the sickness and then take steps to effect a cure. Sometimes they may attempt to get rid of the sickness by sucking it out of the patient. At other times—or in addition to sucking practices—they sing curing songs or perform dances.

Some examples of how dangerous objects can be harmed, thus leading to staying sickness, are these according to Donald M. Bahr in "Pima and Papago Medicine and Philosophy" in *Handbook of North American Indians,* vol. 10, *Southwest,* 1983:

> Horned toads are almost the color of the ground and they move slowly. Hence they are difficult to see. If you step on one you get sick.
>
> Rattlesnakes make their houses beneath the ground or under the brush where you can't see them. If you crush the house or burn it accidentally while burning brush in a field, that's against the 'way.'

The Hurons believed there were three types of illness, those known as desires of the soul, those caused by witchcraft and those due to natural causes such as a wound from a weapon. Cures for witchcraft and other illnesses included rituals, spells, dances and feasts held under the direction of a healer.

Medicine healers had varying treatments. They usually wore bear claw necklaces, a coyote or wolf headdress and had a deer dewclaw rattle. In a curing ceremony for the Yakimas, the medicine man sang his healing songs or power songs five times (known as the power number to that tribe; power numbers varied between tribes) while drummers beat on long planks. The doctor could then give medicine to the patient, suck out the illness or disease by placing a tube or his mouth in some location on the patient's body, or pass his hands over the patient in a massage that removed the illness. The illness could then be plunged into water where it was rendered harmless before being discarded. A Nez Percé healer would attempt to suck out a disease using a bone whistle or a small leaf funnel. Healers also sometimes predicted weather or provided prophecies.

Among the Pacific Eskimos, most healers were women who used herbs, bloodletting and extraction (sucking out the cause of illness) to effect cures.

Besides medicine men and women, there also were sorcerers, people who used black magic to cast spells. Working like witches or wizards, they were most effective when they obtained some personal item from the person on whom they intended to place a spell. Such personal items included clippings from fingernails, hair or a drop of blood.

In the Southwest, among the Navajos, witchcraft was the worst crime a person could be accused of. In the Southeast, Choctaws had great fear of witches (female) and wizards (male). If a healer failed to cure a patient, the healer might discover witchcraft and accuse some old woman of being the witch. She would immediately be chased down and killed.

Among the Indians of the Northwest Coast and the Plateau, there were two Indian medicine cults. The Indian Shakers were founded in 1882 on Puget Sound. They employed characteristics of the Roman Catholic, Indian and fundamental Christian religions believing members who would "shake" had the power to effect cures. The Feather cult started in 1904 under the direction of Jake Hunt, a Klickitat, and concentrated on in-home curing ceremonies to help people with drinking problems.

Medicines used by the Navajos in their healing or curing ceremonies included fragrant herbs such as mints (applied externally), a fumigant made of cornmeal, sulphur, herbs and birds' feathers (sprinkled on glowing coals so the fumes could be inhaled), and an emetic made of fresh herbs. An integral part of many Navajo curing rites was the making of sand paintings, a symbolic picture created on the hogan floor by trickling dry pigments between the flexed forefinger and thumb onto a background of tan-colored sand. The pigments included red, yellow and white sandstone, charcoal and mixtures to create blue, brown and pink. Sand paintings often were complex, could be prepared by one person or several and never were permanent. When completed the patient would be stripped to a breechclout (men) or a skirt (women) and then would sit on some figure in the painting, rubbing the sand from one of the bodies in the painting and adhering it to the corresponding location on the patient, in essence, providing healing, protection and power from the painting.

The traditional healer in Indian cultures was the medicine man or woman, though females could not practice medicine until after menopause. Healers relied on prayers and chants in conducting their healing ceremonies, but traditional Indian medicine also effectively used herbs and plants. Healers carried their supplies—roots, bark, animal substances, fetishes, charms and herbs—in a medicine bag. They were paid honorariums of horses, beads, clothes, skins or feathers.

> Medicine Lodge Creek [Kansas] owes its name to the superstition of the Indians, who have long considered it a favorable location to make medicine. But do not imagine that the medicine of the Indians is a potion to be swallowed, or a salve to be applied.

It is rather a charm to propitiate the spirits, good and bad, and its composition is as varied as the lively imagination of the priests or medicine-makers can invest. A great medicine lodge [is described by *Frank Leslie's Illustrated Weekly* illustrator J. E. Taylor]:

THE GREAT MEDICINE LODGE

is delightfully situated in an open prairie half a mile from the creek. It is a circular structure, composed of limbs piled up against a rude frame-work. Within are the offerings of passing Indians—such as trinkets, arrows, beads, wampum, gourds, and feathers; and the interior of the lodge presents a strange sight indeed, with those articles strewn around, some hanging high up, and others on the floor. There is also a buffalo skull, fantastically decorated.

—Frank Leslie's Illustrated Weekly, *23 November 1867, 154–1*

Medicine men or women charged high fees, but would refund them if a cure was not effected within a year. Minor complaints such as headache or upset stomach were generally treated with spoken formulas and herbal medicines. Some Hupa, Chilula and Whilkut healers resorted to sorcery in seeking cures. Among the Pomoans, people became healers through dreams (sucking doctor) or inheritance (singing doctor; someone who specialized in herbal medicines).

Bear Doctors were healers with powers to cure obtained from bears. They were most prevalent in the Lassik and Wailaki tribes in California. Among the California Indians, a primary illness related to poisoning, or the threat of poisoning. Certainly the California Indians knew of substances that could be used as poisons; some poisoning, however, was strictly magical. People could hire a professional "poisoner" at a price ranging from fifteen to one hundred shell beads. To cure someone of poisoning (either real or suspected), doctors used a variety of methods including sucking the poison from the body or singing. Among the musical instruments considered effective in curing ceremonies were a split-stick clapper, bone whistle, cocoon rattle, hollow-log foot drum and occasionally the bull-roarer (which was used more for therapeutic reasons).

Some aspects of Indian medical practice are now recognized as sophisticated techniques for treating the whole person within his environment, especially as modern medicine learns more about the relationship between psychological stress and human illness. Navajo healing ceremonies, for example, involved not only the patient, but practically all of his relatives, and had the effect of restoring the person to harmony within his community. Some aspect of this technique was a part of the practice of healers in practically every tribe.

Combined with a knowledge of the medicinal properties of plants, a knowledge gained through thousands of years of experience, and which has largely never been shared with the outside world, Indian healers were well equipped to meet the needs of their people, but were defenseless against imported diseases such as smallpox.

Nineteenth-century white observers, especially missionaries, rarely comprehended very much of what they observed regarding Indian medical practices. They tended to emphasize the supernatural aspects and be dismissive of all Indian medical practice, as they were of Indian religion.

By comparison, early nineteenth-century American doctors treated patients by bleeding "bad blood" from them and administering small doses of poisons such as mercury. For example, George Washington's doctors, in treating his pneumonia, bled him to death.

Josephine Meeker, taken captive in September 1879 when Utes attacked the White River Agency in northwest Colorado where her father N.C. Meeker served as agent, spent time with the Utes and participated in a healing ritual. In an account published in the *Weekly Rocky Mountain News*, in Denver, Colorado, 5 November 1879, she wrote:

> When their child was sick they asked me to sing, which I did. The medicineman kneels close to the sufferer, with his back to the spectators, while he sings in a series of high-keyed grunts, gradually reaching a lower and more solemn tone. The family join, and at intervals he howls so loudly that one can hear him for a mile; then his voice dies away and only a gurgling sound is heard, as if his throat were full of water. The child lies nearly stripped. The doctor presses his lips against the breast of the sufferer and repeats the gurgling sound. He sings a few minutes more, then all turn around and laugh and talk. Sometimes the ceremony is repeated all night.

INDIAN MEDICINES

Abdominal pains: Wild mint or wild verbena.

Arthritis: Peyote tea or a direct infusion of peyote was used to ease pain of arthritis.

Astringent: Wild geranium.

Bleeding: Treated with a poultice of spider webs; cauterized by placing a stem of yarrow into the wound and setting it on fire, then packing the wound with eagle down, puffballs, sumac or scrapings from animal hides.

Bowel Complaints: Sioux used roots and green fruit of the purple coneflower (echinacea); Cheyennes used a tea made from ragweed. Many tribes stripped bark from oak trees and boiled it, giving the decoction for bowel trouble, particularly among children.

Bruises and Sores: Skunk cabbage or charred honeysuckle vine in bear grease (Pacific Northwest); white fir or piñon pine pitch (Shoshone and Washoe); milkweed latex (Paiutes); white oak, boiled and used as a poultice was particularly effective on foot sores caused from wearing wet moccasins.

Cathartic: Wild rhubarb.

Colds: Eskimo healers used stinkweed or wormwood for the common cold or nasal congestion. The woods were either chewed or brewed into a tea. Yakimas made a tea from dried sagebrush, Indian rose bush leaves or chokecherry tree bark. The Lake Miwoks used sugar made from the sugar pine tree. Many tribes made a tea from dried yarrow flowers and leaves. It worked as an expectorant, helped induce sweating and was an analgesic.

Contraception: Lassik women (California tribes) drank a mixture of water and burnt seashells to prevent conception. Women controlled the timing of conception, often by abstaining from sexual activity. Some contraception occurred with use of drugs, while abortions were performed and certain tribes practiced infanticide. Blackfeet induced abortions (or speeded childbirth) by ingesting pasqueflower. Women in many tribes believed a tea made from five juniper berries drunk daily (with the berries themselves later injested) prevented conception.

Cuts and Wounds: Sutured with sinew sewn with bone needles.

Diarrhea or Upset Stomach: Cheyennes made a tea from roots of the American licorice plant. Penobscots made a tea by boiling white oak bark. Blackfeet used sagebrush tea.

Dropsical Legs: Wild tobacco leaves placed on them.

Eyewash: Poncas and Omahas used purple coneflower, black susan, comb flower and hedgehog, rubbing the eye with the plant or oil from the plant leaves.

Fever: Treated with rest, purging, sweating and restricted diet. The Delawares used a concoction made from dogwood bark.

Gas: Indian turnip.

Headache: Cherokees smoked a mixture of root of the devil's walking stick. Other tribes drank tea made from willow tree bark (aspirin).

Heart Problems: Trillium. Southwestern tribes used peyote either in the form of a direct infusion or as a tea for heart pains.

Hemorrhaging: Yakimas controlled hemorrhaging with a poultice made from the leaves of red sumac.

Hemorrhoids: Sumac root.

Insect Repellent: Leaves of the yarrow plant when rubbed on skin helped repel insects. Indians also used grease and paint on exposed portions of their bodies to provide protection from insect bites.

Listlessness: Crows ate raw bison liver.

Nasal Congestion: Yakima healers boiled sagebrush and had patients inhale the steam.

Nausea: Dakotas used willow bark tea or scarified the abdomen and spread powdered ragweed on it. Many tribes used ginger root in a tea. Omahas used ragweed by making a cut on the abdomen and then putting a dressing of bruised ragweed leaves on the cut.

Pain: Peyote bean or willow tree bark tea.

Poisoning: Algonquians used a decoction made from green cranberries to reduce effects of a poisoned arrow.

Purifier for Healing Ceremonies: Sage was burned, with the smoke allowed to drift over the patient.

Snakebite: Portions of chewed rhizomes of snakeroot were placed on the bite.

Sore Eyes: Cherokees used lotion made from wild tansy.

Sore Spots: The Lake Miwok applied a poultice of crushed angelica and the shaved bark of a tree to sore spots (but never to open sores).

Sore Throat: Algonquian healers had people gargle with a tonic made from wild blackberry root. Some people used muskrat root.

Spider Bites: A poultice made of the wet pulp created by chewing sage leaves was spread over the bite.

Stomachache: Sioux used the roots and green fruit of the purple coneflower (echinacea). Kiowas drank mint tea or chewed mint leaves.

Tonic: A general tonic made by boiling the inner bark of slippery elm (Omaha).

Toothache: Sumac root. Pain could be numbed with the use of powder derived from prickly ash roots. The Lake Miwoks used a poultice of pepperwood leaves applied to the cheek.

Urinary Problems: Juniper tea to increase flow of urine.

Venereal Disease: Lobelia seeds.

Wounds and Cuts: Micmacs made a salve from spikenard berries.

MEDICAL TIMELINE

1780–81: About 75 percent of the Arikara tribe dies in a smallpox epidemic.

1800–1: Omaha tribe sustains significant loss of life in a smallpox epidemic.

1801: Smallpox sweeps through Columbia River Basin.

1801–2: Smallpox causes many to die along the Upper Missouri, particularly among the Arikara tribe.

1816: Smallpox makes "dreadful havoc" with Comanches.

1830: Influenza sweeps through tribes in British Columbia; similar outbreaks occur in California and Oregon.

1836: Smallpox epidemic causes significant numbers of deaths among the Tlingits.

1837: Smallpox epidemic nearly decimates the Mandans and significantly impacts the Hidatsas and Arikaras.

1850–60: Cholera becomes an epidemic among tribes in the Great Basin and Southern Plains.

1867: Cholera breaks out among the Comanches with twenty to thirty people dying daily.

1883–4: Hundreds of Indians in northern Montana Territory starve to death when "the tail of the last buffalo disappeared from the plain."

1891–1901: Tuberculosis kills sixty-five members of the Sarcee tribe in Canada.

ADDITIONAL READING

Curtin, L.S.M., revisions and editing by Michael Moore. *Healing Herbs of the Upper Rio Grande: Traditional Medicine of the Southwest.* Santa Fe: Western Edge Press, 1997; originally published by the Laboratory of Anthropology, Santa Fe, 1947.

Doane, Nancy Locke. *Indian Doctor Book.* Charlotte, NC: distributed by Aerial Photography Services Inc., ND, 1983. Various remedies for ailments used by pioneers but based on Indian practices.

Gilmore, Melvin R. *Uses of Plants by the Indians of the Missouri River Region.* Lincoln: University of Nebraska Press, 1977; Bison Book edition, 1991.

Hall, Thomas B. *Medicine on the Santa Fe Trail.* Dayton, OH: Morningside Bookshop, 1971.

Hart, Jeff. *Montana Native Plants and Early Peoples.* Helena: Montana Historical Society Press, 1976, reprinted 1992.

Stockel, H. Henrietta. *The Lightning Stick: Arrows, Wounds and Indian Legends.* Reno: University of Nevada Press, 1995.

Tilford, Gregory L. *Edible and Medicinal Plants of the West.* Missoula, MT: Mountain Press Publishing, 1997.

Trennert, Robert A. *White Man's Medicine: Government Doctors and the Navajo, 1863-1955.* Albuquerque: University of New Mexico Press, 1998.

Weiner, Michael A. *Earth Medicine—Earth Food: Plant Remedies, Drugs and Natural Foods of the North American Indians.* New York: Macmillan Publishing Co., 1980.

PART THREE

AMERICAN INDIAN SOCIETY

CHAPTER TEN

ENTERTAINMENT

G ames, storytelling and dancing were major forms of entertainment for Indians throughout the 1800s. Almost every tribe engaged in all three. The tribes that lived in regions where survival took most of their time and effort had less time for entertainment than did those where there was abundant food and a mild climate. The people of the Great Basin, for example, spent most of their energies on finding food and protecting themselves from a harsh climate that was extremely hot and dry in summer and cold in the winter. Even so, they played hand games, dice games and various ball games. By comparison, Zunis, who lived in permanent homes, participated in all those entertainment forms and a variety of other amusements ranging from bean shooter and cat's cradle to shuttlecock and quoits.

Bean shooter, common in the Southeast and Northwest Coast areas, involved a stick of wood that could be used to flip mud balls, small pebbles or other similar items. The bean shooter was a child's game and was also used to cure sickness by chasing bad or evil spirits away. Cat's cradle, known to most tribes, is a game still played by children today. It involves a circle of string held between the player's hands to form a variety of shapes as one or two players pull the string into various configurations. In quoits, players have two targets—often common sticks—set in the ground separately as far apart as players can throw. They toss rings at the pegs earning points depending on how closely the ring lands to the peg (this is similar to pitching horseshoes). Shuttlecock was a game often played by girls in Northwest and Southwest areas. They created a shuttlecock by tying or attaching feathers to a cornhusk, corncob or other object. Then, using a paddle or "battledoor" made of wooden slats, another object or even a hand, they hit the shuttlecock as many times as they could to keep it in the air.

Indian games generally involved games of chance, games requiring dexterity and minor amusements. Almost every tribe involved itself in some of the games of chance and most participated in at least one game of dexterity. Besides those games, storytelling and dancing were popular forms of entertainment in almost every tribe, though storytelling and dancing had cultural significance beyond entertainment.

GAMES OF CHANCE

The various games of chance included dice games (the most popular game of all), stick games, hand games, a four-stick game and the hidden ball or Moccasin game.

Dice Games

Indians throughout North America including both men and women participated in dice games, though they seldom played each other. The dice games involved two basic game parts: dice and something to keep count. Dice generally had two sides with colors and markings and were made of such items as walnut shells, peach and plum stones or pits, split canes, wooden staves or blocks, bone pieces, pottery, shell or brass disks, bone staves and beaver or woodchuck teeth. They were tossed by hand or in a basket or bowl. Basket games were more common among women. When dice were thrown by hand, they were tossed in the air and allowed to fall freely to land upon the ground, or perhaps on a blanket or hide; sometimes they were allowed to stick into the ground. To keep count, Indians used sticks or twigs, or something similar to an abacus with the winning person being handed the sticks or twigs (or having beads on the abacus moved). Once an individual (or perhaps a team of individuals) had all the sticks, he or she had won the game.

Ethnologist George Bird Grinnell provided this description of a basket dice game:

> I have seen this game played among the Pawnee, Arikara and Cheyenne, and substantially the same way everywhere. The Pawnee do not use a bowl to throw the seeds, but hold them in a flat wicker basket about the size and shape of an ordinary tea plate. The woman who makes the throw holds the basket in front of her, close to the ground, gives the stones a sudden toss into the air, and then moves the basket smartly down against the ground, and the stones fall into it. They are not thrown high, but the movement of the basket is quick, and it is brought down hard on the ground, so that

Four Nuaguntit Paiutes gambling, southwestern Nevada. (John K. Hillers, 1873; National Archives, 57-PE-71)

the sound of the slapping is easily heard. The plum stones are always five in number, blackened and variously marked on one side. The women who are gambling sit in a line opposite one another, and usually each woman bets with the one sitting opposite her, and the points are counted by sticks placed on the ground between them, the wager always being on the game and not on the different throws.

Stick Games

Sticks (or sometimes flat disks), specifically marked to represent totem animals or in some other manner so that they could be distinguished from each other, were the main game pieces. Generally there were from ten to one hundred sticks used in a single game. The sticks were divided into two bundles (one of which may have one more stick than the other). The primary object of the game was to guess the location of a specific stick or bundle containing the odd number of sticks. The bundles of sticks could be hidden in places, like a mass of shredded cedar bark for Indians on the Northwest Coast or in a leather pouch, or they could be held openly in the hands.

Crees played the game this way, according to an account by collector J.A. Mitchell of the Field Columbian Museum in Chicago:

> Played by both men and women or by either separately. Players are divided into two parties, seated opposite each other. Stakes of money, clothing, etc., are then put up in a common lot. The person inviting the players begins the game by secretly dividing the bundle of twenty-five sticks into two lots, holding one bundle in either hand. If his opponent chooses the bundle containing the even number of sticks, he wins; if the odd bundle, he loses, and the play passes to the next couple. Play is kept up until either one or the other party desires to stop, when the wagered articles are taken possession of by the party having made the most points and are divided among all that party. The game is sometimes kept up for several days and nights.

Hand Game

Many tribes played this simple game. It was particularly popular when people of different tribes met because it was played with actions and motions so players didn't need to speak the same language; instead, they could use simple sign language to communicate. To keep count of the times an individual won, pointed sticks were placed before the players, and the sticks were moved to reflect winning guesses. Though there certainly were variations, the game was generally played like this description of a Chinook game given by James G. Swan, nineteenth-century collector of Indian game material for the Free Museum of Science and Art at the University of Pennsylvania:

> Another game is played by little sticks or stones, which are rapidly thrown from hand to hand with the skill of experienced jugglers, accompanied all the while by some song adapted to the occasion, the winning or losing the game depending on being able to guess correctly which hand the stick is in. This game can be played by any number of persons and is usually resorted to when the members of two different tribes meet, and is a sort of trial of superiority. Before

commencing the game the betting begins, and each article staked is put before the (players), and whoever wins takes the whole pile.

Four-Stick Game

Only a few tribes played the four-stick game, including the Klamath, Modoc, Paiute, Washo, Achomawi and perhaps the Chinook. Like the hand game, the count is kept with pointed sticks that are stuck in the ground. In the Klamath game the four sticks include two larger sticks, perhaps about twelve and a half inches long called *solchise*, and two smaller sticks about eleven and a quarter inches long designated as *skotus*. Klamath Indian Agent L.S. Dyar provided this description of the game:

> The game is played by two persons, who sit upon the ground facing each other. The round mat, puh-lah, is used as a cover to hide the four rods, two each of the sol-chise and sko-tus. The person performing with these places them side by side on the ground under the mat, and the other guesses [where] their relative position is, whether the large ones are on the outside or in the middle, or if they alternate, etc., and his guess is indicted by certain motions of the hand and fingers. After one guesses a certain number of times he takes the mat and another guesses. The small sharp sticks, kice, are used for the same purpose as points or buttons in billiards, and the other two sticks, te-ow-tis, are stuck in the ground and used to indicate the progress of the game.

Hidden Ball or Moccasin Game

For the hidden ball game, players hid something in one of several places (usually four) such as cane tubes, wooden cups made from canes, or moccasins. The objects into which the ball (or other item) was to be hidden were placed before the players. While singing to divert the attention of the players, one person deposited the ball or other item in one of the tubes, cups or moccasins. The players then guessed where the object had been hidden, similar to our shell game or three-card monte. The moccasin game was often played as a part of mourning rituals.

Among the Missisauga, according to author George Copway, who researched the Ojibwas and wrote in 1851, "the Moccasin play is simple, and can be played by two or three. Three moccasins are used for the purpose of hiding the bullets which are employed in the game. So deeply interesting does this play sometimes become, that an Indian will stake first, his gun; next, his steel-traps; then his implements of war; then his clothing; and, lastly, his tobacco and pipe, leaving him, as we say, 'Nuh-bau-wan-yah-ze-yaid,' 'a piece of cloth with a string around his waist.' "

GAMES OF SKILL

Hoop and pole was the most popular game of dexterity or skill, and most tribes played it in some form. Other games requiring skill included archery, snow-snake, ring and pin, racket or lacrosse, shinny, chunky, double ball, ball race, hand-and-football and tossed ball.

Hoop and Pole

Played by all Indian tribes, hoop and pole involved shooting arrows or throwing spears through a hoop or circle. The hoops varied among the tribes, but often they had spokes or strands similar to a spider web with the counting done by determining which hole the arrow or spear passed through. Hoops were made of net, rawhide, bark and corn husks or twined with cord or beads. (Many of the hoops resembled the spider-web style of ornament known as a dream-catcher.) There were also rings of stone made from such materials as lava or quartzite. Men played the game; there is no evidence women ever did. For the game, players (generally two) shot arrows or tossed spears at the hoop as it rolled in front of them. Most tribes played on a level field that they sometimes prepared just for the game. The Mandans had a wooden playing field and the Creeks played on courts, which were surrounded by seating areas for spectators. Players gambled various objects—ranging from the arrows and spears they used in the game itself to other personal possessions.

This description of the Chiricahua Apache hoop-and-pole game comes from observer E.W. Davis, who saw it played in 1889:

> The hoops were ordinary pieces of flexible wood, tied into a circle of about 12 inches with leather thongs, and the poles were reeds 10 or 12 feet long. A little heap of hay was placed on the ground and parted in the center. The players stood about 15 feet away, and each in his turn would roll his hoop into the little valley in the hay mount. Waiting until the hoop had nearly reached the hay so that it might encircle the end of the pole when the hoop reached the hay. This game was very difficult and misses were more frequent than scores.

The hoop-and-stick game, popular among almost all tribes, had some variations in equipment and scoring, but generally it involved throwing a spear or shooting an arrow at a hoop or ring. The Upper Missouri tribes played the game on a large playing field using long sticks to catch the target rings and flat clay targets that they also sometimes used. The sticks looked somewhat like billiard cues.

Sgt. John Ordway provided this description of the Mandan game:

> They had feattish [flat] rings made out of clay Stone & two men had Sticks about 4 feet long with 2 Short peaces across the fore end of it, and neathing on the other end, in Such a manner that

they would Slide Some distance. They had a place fixed across about 50 yards to the 2 chiefs lodge, which was Smothe as a house floor. They had a Battery fixed for the rings to Stop against. Two men would run at a time with Each a Stick & one carried a ring. They run about half way and then Slide their Sticks after the ring.

Archery

Indian archers used their bows and arrows for hunting, warfare and occasionally in games. They seldom competed by aiming at a specific target; instead they more often shot their arrows at such targets as a bundle of hay or bark, an upright stick or another arrow or a ball of grass.

Snow-Snake

The game of snow-snake involved hurling a spear, dart or arrow across snow or ice in a competition to see who could toss theirs the farthest. Men, women and children played the game. Often it involved teams. The thrown spears, darts or arrows were known as snow-snakes, and they were often intricately carved, sometimes with feathers attached to them. In some versions, the snow-snake was not thrown, but instead was allowed to simply slide down an icy chute of its own weight; the one moving the farthest was the winner.

Anthropologist Walter J. Hoffman described the snow-snake game of the Menominee Indians:

> It was played during the winter, either in the snow or on the ice, and the only article necessary consisted of a piece of hard wood, from 5 to 6 feet long and from one-half to three-fourths of an inch thick. The head was bulb-like and shaped like a snake, with eyes and a cross cut to denote the mouth. This round end permitted it to pass over slight irregularities in its forward movements. The player would grasp the end, or tail, of the snake by putting the index finger against the end and the thumb on one side, opposite to which would be the remaining three fingers; then stooping toward the ground the snake was held horizontally from right to left and forced forward in the direction of the head, skimming [along] rapidly for a considerable distance.

Ring and Pin

Similar to hoop and pole, ring and pin involved trying to get one object to pass through another; in this case, however, the ring, or the target, and the pin were attached by a cord, piece of rawhide or other material. The game is like the European cup and ball game where the player attempts to catch a ball in a cup. In ring and pin, the player tried to get the ring to land on the pin.

Racket or Lacrosse

Men played this game in most cultural areas, but it was not played by Indians in the Southwest or by all California tribes. In both racket and lacrosse, players had a ball (wood or perhaps buckskin stuffed with hair or other materials) that they attempted to drive through goals (two sets of posts or poles at opposite ends of the field) using short sticks or rackets to move the ball. It was commonly played both by members of the same tribe and also as intertribal contests. It was played by the Cherokees in the summer and by the Santee Sioux in the spring and winter. The Hurons played it as a remedy for sickness. In almost all cases, wagering was a part of the game and sometimes several hundred Indians were involved in a game.

Among the Choctaws, according to nineteenth-century artist George Catlin:

> It is no uncommon occurrence for six or eight hundred or a thousand of these young men to engage in a game of ball, with five or six times that number of spectators, of men, women, and children, surrounding the ground and looking on.

Shinny

This game was similar to racket or lacrosse and was played by men and women together, or by segregated teams of men and women. The ball was batted or kicked and could not be touched with the hands. Both wooden and buckskin balls were used. Bats were generally carved and wider at the striking end, sometimes being painted as well. The goal could be a single post, a line marked on the ground or two posts set at opposite ends of the playing field. Unlike racket or lacrosse, shinny was played by most tribes, including those in the Southwest culture area.

Chunky

Eastern Indians played this game with a round stone or boulder rolled down a slope. Men threw their spears to the point where they thought the stone would stop. When the Iroquois played the game, they used a hollow wooden frame rather than the stone, aiming their spears at the frame itself rather than the place where it was expected to stop (similar to hoop and pole).

Ball Games

Indians played a variety of ball games including double ball (where two balls were tied together so they could be thrown with a curved stick); ball race (in which players kicked an object then ran around a playing field and back to the starting place); hand-and-football, or tossed ball (where players kicked or threw balls toward a goal); and ball juggling.

One popular Crow game involved two teams kicking a ball. A youth from one team put a ball on his or her foot and then kicked it up in the air, continuing to kick it until he or she missed (similar to hacky sack). Then a player on the other side did the same thing. This continued until all players had a chance to kick the ball. The side that had kept the ball in the air the longest—or for the most kicks—won the game. At the end of the game the winners would touch the losers on their foreheads with their hands. One Crow child, Pretty-Shield, had a ball painted red and blue, made from the thin skin of a buffalo heart that was stuffed with antelope hair.

Indians also participated in minor amusements that included such games and activities as shuttlecock, tipcat, quoits, stone throwing, jackstraws, swing, stilts, tops, bull-roarer, buzz, popgun, bean shooter, and cat's cradle. Crow children made sleds of buffalo briskets that were held in shape with cords from the neck of a buffalo. They placed a buffalo robe on the sled to make it more comfortable to ride.

MUSIC AND DANCE

Songs served as prayer for most Indians, and songs were part of daily activities, rituals and ceremonies. Indian people had songs for birth, death, puberty, marriage and every other life stage, and the songs often included animal sounds or bird calls. Their music included spirit songs and dances, medicine songs and dances, and those involved with ceremonies or social situations.

Songs were considered personal property—therefore, they could be bought or sold. They existed for a variety of reasons: love, curing, and luck in fishing, hunting, gambling or war. Songs were often short—lasting only a half a minute or less—and many times were repetitive.

Though lullabies or work songs seldom had instrumental accompaniment, most other songs included instrumentation, ranging from sounds made by clappers; rattles made of such items as deer hooves, pottery, turtle shells and gourds; to whistles made of bones. Rhythm was also provided by a variety of drums, or something as simple as a plank struck routinely with a hand or other item, or two sticks struck together.

Two instruments, the musical bow and the flute, provided music without the need for singing. The musical bow was a stringed instrument made of a thin strip of wood with a string stretched between the two ends so it resembled a hunting bow. The musician played it by plucking the string or by tapping it with fingers, a stick or a piece of bone to create a low sound. Indians played the musical bow for individual enjoyment since it made little sound.

The flute was the most common musical instrument in use among tribes across the country. It was generally a wooden or cane tube held horizontally with a row of holes that could be alternatively covered or uncovered to produce different sounds.

A bull-roarer—considered a child's toy in many situations—produced a unique sound and was often heard during ceremonial rituals. It was a flat stick with one end pointed and a buckskin thong attached to the other that could be whirled to make sound. Among the California tribes the Pomo and Yuki tribes believed it symbolized thunder. People in the Cahto tribe twirled it to bring rain or fair weather.

Arctic

Both men and women danced at Arctic festivals and gatherings. The women often accompanied their dancing by shaking a rattle made from placing stones or teeth in or on the stomach, bladder or piece of intestine of a sea mammal.

California

Men gambled by using a small group of sticks including one with a ring around the middle. They shuffled the sticks (Indian cards) behind their backs and the opponent had to guess which hand held the stick with the ring on it. The game generally involved music such as singing and drumming, said to bring luck to the players.

Northeast and Southeast

These tribes had flutes and whistles, which they usually played separately. Tribal members provided rhythm for singers by using rattles, drums and sticks that they struck together. Some of their dances were performed by individuals and others involved groups of dancers.

Great Basin

These tribes had the simplest forms of music. Songs were short and usually repeated twice. Instruments included rattles, sticks that could be struck together and drums.

Interior Plateau

Among Plateau tribes there were three major types of songs: personal songs, ancestral/cultural songs and songs that came from prophets. They had "touching" or "kissing" songs, and songs for seasonal ceremonies including those for first game, first fruits, first salmon and first roots.

Songs served roles related to personal power, communication with natural forces, healing and protection. Though some songs were tribal in nature, others were personal songs, to be sung only by their owner (or perhaps by others with consent of the owner). Youths received their guardian spirit songs when they spent several days and nights alone seeking communication with the supernatural. Several years after receiving them, they revealed their personal songs at the Winter Dance, a major Plateau religious ceremony.

Plateau music included sacred songs performed for religious reasons, such as songs associated with the Prophet Dance, in the 1820s and 1830s; the Washat, in the 1850s; the Earth-lodge cult, Klamath Ghost Dance and Dream Dance from the period 1870 to 1890; and the Yakima Indian Shakers of 1890. That music had its roots in the pre-white-contact traditions in which dreamers or prophets sang of events expected to alter their world.

In 1805 William Clark wrote of music among the Columbia River tribes: "About 200 men singing and beeting on their drums and keeping time to the music they formed a half circle around us and sung for some time."

The elderberry courting flute was the only melody instrument that all Plateau tribes had. Such flutes generally had six finger holes and possibly one extra hole to provide a sweeter tone. Other instruments used for Plateau songs and to accompany dances were hand drums made of deerhide stretched over wooden frames, deer hooves—and in later years trade bells—on a stick used as rattles, and wooden rods pounded on a plank.

The Molalas participated in summer dances, medicine healers' initiation dances and girls' coming of age dances. For the summer "fun" dances, both men and women wore feathered and beaded regalia. They used rattle drums made of deer dewclaws as they danced in a circular motion.

Northwest Coast

These tribes had flutes, horns and whistles, all of which were often beautifully carved or painted. They also had percussion instruments such as drums made of planks as well as rattles, clappers and rasps. Individuals sang and so did groups. Some of the group songs had multi-voice harmonies.

Plains

Musical instruments among the Teton Sioux in 1804 included a tambourine-like instrument made of skin stretched over a willow hoop and rattles made from a stick with deer and elk hooves tied to it.

Protestant missionary Henry Spalding in 1836 wrote this description of Indian music at the Green River Rendezvous:

> . . . a few striking words oft repeated, but sung in a plaintive tone, in which they were joined by a large band of young women, riding in an extended column behind, their wonderfully sweet voices keeping most excellent time, floating far through the air . . . (dresses) hung with hawk-bells and steel top thimbles, and fine bead work, hung with phylacteries of elk teeth and tin coils, producing a regular, loud, but not harsh jingle, as their fiery steeds pranced slowly along . . . and all accompanied by the constant pounding of a great number of Rocky Mountain gongs, or Indian drums, the terrific screams of a number of whistles made of leg-bone of the grey eagle and swan, the constant jingle of the 'medicine rattle box' and heavy clang of hawk-bells, tin coils, bear claws and human bones trimmed with human scalps hanging upon every horse . . . interrupted now and then by a terrific battle-yell, bounding off in a vibrating war-whoop, almost sufficient to curdle the blood in our veins. . . . They are seen already collected in a thick group hard by, bounding up and down in the scalp dance, all as

one being, first upon one leg and then the other, taking three steps, keeping the most perfect time with the beat of the drum and the voices of the singers.

Prairies and Woodlands

Some tribes in this region had songs that included a call and then a response, which is unique among Indian groups. They emphasized the complex rhythms of their songs by using of rattles and drums or by striking sticks together. They played flutes and whistles as solo instruments.

Southwest

Musical instruments of the Cocopas included cane flutes and whistles, gourd rattles, drummed baskets and the bull-roarer, a flat stick with one end pointed and a buckskin thong attached to the other, which can be whirled to sound like thunder.

Among the Navajos casual songs included lullabies, farewell songs and occupational songs such as the corn-grinding songs, which were sung by men to encourage women as they went about their routine task of grinding corn.

Some sacred songs of the Navajos were not connected to ceremonies, and they included those like the moccasin game songs, which were to be sung only in the wintertime. By far the majority of Navajo songs were affiliated with ceremonies. Some of the ceremonies lasted from three to nine nights, and the songs or chants often had long epic sequences.

STORYTELLING

Though often considered a form of entertainment, storytelling was much more to Indian people, as it also served as their way to preserve their history. The stories of the North American Indians are both simple and complex. Because many of them involved the traditional stories of tribes and people, they also became part of the customs handed down from generation to generation. See more information about storytelling on page 225.

ADDITIONAL READING

See references listed under chapter four Additional Reading.

Culin, Stewart. *Games of the North American Indians.* Vol. 1, *Games of Chance.* Lincoln: University of Nebraska Press, Bison Books, 1992; originally published as 24th Annual Report of the Bureau of American Ethnology, 1902–1903, Smithsonian Institution, 1907. Detailed explanations of various types of games for different tribes make this a valuable reference work.

———. *Games of the North American Indians.* Vol. 2, *Games of Skill.* Lincoln: University of Nebraska Press, Bison Books, 1992; originally published as 24th

Annual Report of the Bureau of American Ethnology, 1902–1903, Smithsonian Institution, 1907. Detailed explanations make this a valuable reference work.

Densmore, Frances. *Teton Sioux Music and Culture.* Lincoln: University of Nebraska Press, 1992.

Macfarlan, Allan and Paulette. *Handbook of American Indian Games.* Toronto: General Publishing Company, Ltd., 1958; Mineoloa, NY, Dover Publications, reprint, 1985. Though written to show people today how to play Indian games, there is much detail on each of the games that includes rules, numbers of players and equipment needed.

CHAPTER ELEVEN

LANGUAGE

Across North America Indians spoke one of six language types. Three were major—the Algonquian, Athapascan (or Athabascan) and Siouian—and these formed the basis of language for many tribes (though each tribe had variations). The other types formed language for fewer tribes and included Eskimo-Aleut in the Arctic region, Uto-Aztecan in the western desert regions, and Penutian of the West Coast. There were other minor variations of language as well, including Muskogean in the Southeast, Shoshonean in the Uto-Aztecan region, Caddoan on the Southern Plains and in the Dakotas, and three separate languages among the Pueblo people: Zuni, Keresan and Tanoan. Even within those Pueblo types there are further subjugations of language. Tanoan, for example, is divided into Towa, Tiwa and Tewa, while Eastern Keresan differs from Western Keresan.

As a result of the language differences, though the root came from the same place for many people, neighboring tribes couldn't necessarily communicate easily with each other, not even if they were technically blood relatives. However, because the various tribes routinely traded with each other, they developed ways to do so.

People of the Plains developed a universal sign language that involved hand motions to represent words and phrases. They had no written language but used signs to record events and deeds. And they kept track of important periods in tribal life through drawings. Known as "wintercounts," the drawings portrayed significant events in individual or tribal life. Those wintercounts were most often kept on a bison or other hide.

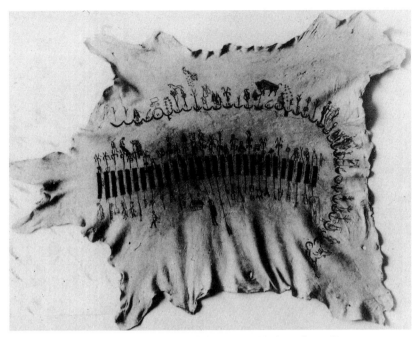

Calendar of thirty-seven months, 1889–92, kept on a skin by Anko, a Kiowa man. (National Archives, 106-IN-78)

To facilitate trade and other relations in Northwest Coastal areas, Chinook Trade Jargon developed as a pidgin language with a small vocabulary and simple grammar. It served as a common language for people from different tribes. Earlier the tribes in the Lower Columbia River region and along the Northwest Coast also relied on a local sign language. Later, as trade extended to broader areas, Northwest and Plateau tribes began to use Plains Indian Sign Language in addition to the Chinook Trade Jargon. Indians throughout a large part of the Southeast used a trade language called Mobilian Trade Jargon, which was a simplified form of Choctaw.

In the Southwest, to facilitate trade, people used their native language, a common third language and sign language. The most common languages used by people in that region were Spanish and Navajo.

Many tribes, such as the Pimas and Maricopas used calendar sticks and stories to record their history. A calendar stick—like the wintercount hides of the Plains Indians—had symbols and images that represented important events that occurred in a given year. The keeper or owner of the calendar stick was expected to remember the events of the year.

A listing of some tribal names is as follows:

Apache: The English word comes from the Spanish *Apache*, first used by Juan

Animal skin with pictorial history of Shoshone Chief Washakie's combats. (National Archives, 111-SC-83538)

de Oñate in the late 1500s at San Juan Pueblo, referring to both the people who came to be known as Apaches and also Navajos. Variations of the name include Tineh, Tinde, Diné, Inde (N'de), Deman and Haisndayin, all of which mean "the people."

Arapaho: *Inuna-ina* "our people."

Arikara: Sometimes called the Arikaree (or Rees), their name is thought to mean "horns." Other versions of the name are Sanish or *Star-ra-he-as.*

Assiniboine: Nakota Sioux sometimes called Stoney.

Athapascan: Sometimes spelled Athapaskan or Athabascan.

Blackfeet: *Nitzitapi* included these Blackfeet confederation tribes: Blackfeet proper (Siksika, "those with black-dyed moccasins"), Piegan (Pikuni or sometimes Pigunni, "poorly dressed"), Blood (Kainai) and Small Robes.

Caddo: *Kadohadacho* "real chiefs." Also called Prairie Caddos.

Cayuse: One variation of the name is "pony." Modern Cayuses (the tribe) refer to themselves as *waeiletpu* (waiilatpu), "people of the shady place."

Cherokee: *Ani-Yun'wiya* ("principle people"). The Choctaws called them *Tsalagi*, "people of the land of caves." The Creek word for them was *Tisolki* or *Tciloki*, "people of a different speech."

Cheyenne, Northern: *Tsistsistas*, or *Dzitsistas* (Beautiful People). Cheyenne was the Sioux name for the tribe.

Cheyenne, Southern: *Tsctschastahase.*

Chickasaw: "To leave."

Chippewa: Primarily used in the United States. Also known as the Ojibway, Ojibwa or Ojibwe (particularly in Canada); native name is *Anishinabe* "first people."

Chiricahua Apache: Named for the mountains, also "red paint people."

Choctaw: The name is likely derived from the Spanish word *chato* for flat, or perhaps from the native name for the Pearl River, *Haccha.*

Coeur d'Alene: "Heart of an awl" or "pointed hearts."

Comanche: *Nermurnuh*, "true human being," with variations including the Spanish *Camino Ancho*, "main road," and the Ute *Komon'teia* or *kohmaths*, "one who wants to fight me."

Cree: *Kenistenoag.*

Cree, Plains: *Natimiwiyiniwuk.*

Crow: *Apsaalooke*, "children of the large beaked bird"; also Absaroka.

Dakota: Santee (*Isanti*), Yankton (*Ikanktonwan*) and Yanktonai (*Ihanktonwanna*). Divisions of the Sioux.

Delaware: Often referred to as the Delaware Indians, the tribe is properly Lenni Lenape, "real people" or "people of the standard," or sometimes Lenape, "the people."

Dirt-Lodges: Crow name for the Gros Ventres.

Flathead: Salish (*Selis*), Pend d'Oreilles and Kutenai. First called Flatheads by Lewis and Clark.

Fox: Also known as the Red Earths.

Gros Ventre: *A'aini'* or Atsina and Hidatsa. The native name is *Ah-ah-nee-nin*, "white clay people." They were a part of the Blackfoot Confederacy.

Haida: *Kaigani*, "people."

Hidatsa: *Nuxbaaga* or Atsina or Minnetaree (Minitaris), "willows."

Hopi: A short version of *Hopituh*, "peaceful ones."

Hualapai: Singular for *Walapai*.

Hupa: *Natinook-wa* "where the trails return."

Huron: Wyandot or Wendat or Guyandot, "peninsula dwellers" or "islanders." Huron is normally used in connection with the tribe in Canada; Wyandot is generally used in reference to the tribe in the United States.

Illinois: *Ilaniawaki* or *Illinok*; sometimes *Illini*.

Inuit: Almost always called Eskimo during the nineteenth century.

Ioway or Iowa: *Pahodja* or *Paxoje*, "dusty noses" is the tribal name, though the Sioux name for them is *ayuhwa*, "sleepy ones," or perhaps *ai'yuwe*, "squash."

Iroquois: *Ireohkwa*, "real adders," or *Haudenosaunee*, "people of the longhouse."

Jicarilla Apache: From the name of a peak or hill called Cerro de la Xicarilla, "little-chocolate-cup-(shaped) peak." The Jicarillas call themselves *haisndayin*, "people who came from below."

Kalispel: "Camas," also known as the *Pend d'Oreille* (French for earrings). Nez Percés referred to them as the "camas people."

Kansa: Kaw, "people of the south wind."

Kickapoo: *Kiikaapoa* or *Kiwegapaw*, "he who moves about, standing now here, now there."

Kiowa: *Kaigwu*, "main people," or *Gaigwa*.

Kiowa-Apache: "Knife-whetting men."

Klamath: Formerly known as *maqlaqs*, "people" or "community." The name Klamath is borrowed from Upper Chinookan and means "they of the river, they who have a river."

Kutenai: Also spelled Kootenay (preferred in Canada), Kootenaes, or Kootenai. Montana Kootenais use the term *ksanka* "standing arrow."

Lakota: Pte Oyate, Titonwan, Teton or Western Sioux. Divisions of the Lakota: Oglala, Brûlé (Sicangu) Miniconjou, Hunkpapa, Sans Arc (Itazipacola), Two Kettle (Oohenunpa), and Sihasapa (Blackfeet). *See also* Sioux.

Lillooet: "Lake people" or "clear-water people."

Mahican: *Mu-he-con-ne-ok,* "people of the waters that are never still." This tribe is sometimes confused with Mohegan, which is from *Mingan,* "wolf," and both names have been used as Mohican since publication of James Fenimore Cooper's 1826 novel *Last of the Mohicans.*

Mescalero Apache: "People of the mescal" (referring to the agave plant, not mescal beans). Tonkawas called them the "turned up moccasins." Along with the Jicarilla and Chiricahua Apaches they are called the "eastern people."

Modoc: Probably derived from their name for Tule Lake "in the extreme south." Other tribes knew them as "fish people," "those above the lakes," and "tule eaters." When grouped with the Klamath and Northern Paiute tribes on the Klamath Reservation, they were known as "people of the chipmunk" or "cottontail rabbit people."

Mohave: *Hamakha v,* perhaps translated as "people who live along the water" or "three mountains."

Mohawk: *Kanienkahagen,* "people of the place of flint." The name Mohawk came from *mohowawog,* "eaters of men."

Navajo: *Dineh* or *Diné,* "the people" or "human beings." *See also* Apache.

Nez Percé: From the French for pierced noses. Tribal members refer to themselves as *Ni mi pu* or *nimi pu,* "the people."

Ojibwa: Preferred name in Canada; known also as Chippewa (United States), Anishinaabe, Bungi or Saulteaux.

Oneida: *Onayotekaona,* "people of the upright stone."

Onondaga: "People of the hills."

Osage: *Ni-U-Ko'n-Ska,* "people of the middle waters."

Ottawa: "To trade" or "at-home-anywhere people." An alternate spelling is *Odawa* (singular) or *Odawak* (plural).

Paiute: "True ute" or "water ute." Spelled *Piute* by the tribe in the nineteenth century.

Palouse: *Paluus* or *peluss,* "what is standing up in the water."

Papago: "Desert Pimans." *See also* Pima.

Pawnee: The name might come from *pariki,* "horn," or from *parisu,* "hunter." Chahiksichahiks; divided into four major tribal groups Chaui (Grand), Pita-hawirate, Kitkahahki (Republican), and Skiri (Skidi or Panismaha).

Penobscot: *Panawahpskek,* "rocky place" or "where the rocks spread out."

Pequot: "Destroyers."

Pima: Pimas and Papagos refer to themselves as "tribesman, person, human," "bean people" or as "river people."

Ponca: "Sacred head."

Potawatomi: Also spelled Pottawatami, Potawatami, or Pottawatomie.

Quapaw: Also called the Arkansas. Quapaw is from the Siouan *ugakhpa*, "downstream people."

Quechan: "Those who descended" or sometimes "those who descended by way of the water" or "those who descended by a different way." The Spanish name for the tribe was Yuma.

Sauk: Also spelled *Sac*, both from the Algonquian word *Asa ki waki* "yellow earth people" or "yellow earths."

Seminole: Lexicographers invariably say this name comes from the Spanish word *cimarron*, "wild" or "runaway," but the Seminole people say it comes from a similar word in their native language meaning "free people."

Seneca: *Onondowagah* or *Nundawaono*, "people of the great hill." They are also called *Osininka*, "people of the stone."

Shawnee: *Chawunagi*, "southerners."

Shoshone: *Aqui-Dika* (sometimes spelled Shoshoni).

Sioux: *Oce'ti Sakowin* (Seven Council Fires of the Sioux) include the Teton, Yankton, Yanktonai and four Santee groups. There are three major groups of Sioux: Nakota, Dakota and Lakota. Bands within the Teton or Lakota are the Oglala, Brûlé (Sigangu) Hunkpapa, Miniconjou, Oohenunpa (Two Kettle), Itazipcola (Sans Arcs) and Sihasapa. The four bands of the Santees or Dakota are Sisseton, Wahpeton, Wahpekute and Mdewakanton. The Yankton (Ihanktonwan) or Nakota, had only one band, the Yankton, while the Yanktonai (Ihanktonwanna) also Nakota, has three bands: Yanktonai, Hunkpatina and Assiniboine. The name *Sioux* comes from the Chippewa word for them: *Nadouessioux* "adders." Sioux was in use throughout the nineteenth century; Lakota, Dakota or Nakota are preferred now.

Tlingit or Tlinkit: "People." Russians called them *Kolush*.

Tonkawa: "They all stay together."

Tuscarora: *Ska-Ruh-Reh*, "shirt-wearing people."

Umatilla: "Salmon people."

Ute: "High up" or "land of the sun."

Walapai: "Pine person" or "pine tree people." In singular form spelled Hual-pais, other nineteenth century spellings include Hualapais, Huallapais, Huali-pais, Hualopais and Huallopi.

Walla Walla: "Little rivers."

Wampanoag: *Pokanoket,* "place of the clear land."

Wasco: "Those of the dipper."

Wichita: Kichais, Taovayas, Tawakonis, Wacos and Wichita Proper.

Winnebago: *Ho-Chunk, Hotcangara* or *Hochungra,* "people of the parent speech" or "people of the first voice." Also *Wonkshiek* "first people of the old island."

Yakima or Yakama: There are variations of the name including those translated as "narrow river people," "a growing family," or "black bear." Spellings vary. Both Yakima and Yakama were in use during the nineteenth century; Yakama is presently the preferred use (since 1994).

Yavapai: "People of the sun" or "people living in the direction of the sunrise."

Zuni: *Ashiwi,* "the flesh."

MEASUREMENT OF TIME

Native Americans gauged time by the moons and each tribe referred to the months of the Euro-Americans by varying names. For Arapaho Indians the calendar went like this:

January—First Moon—Moon When the Snow Blows Like Spirits in the Wind
February—Second Moon—Moon of Frost Sparkling on the Sun
March—Third Moon—Moon of Buffalo Dropping Their Calves
April—Fourth Moon—Moon of Ice Breaking in the River
May—Fifth Moon—Moon When the Ponies Shed Their Shaggy Hair
June—Sixth Moon—Moon When the Hot Weather Begins
July—Seventh Moon—Moon When the Buffalo Bellow
Late July—Eighth Moon—Moon When the Chokecherries Begin to Ripen
August—Ninth Moon—Moon When the Geese Shed Their Feathers
September—Tenth Moon—Moon of Drying Grass
October—Eleventh Moon—Moon of Falling Leaves
November—Twelfth Moon—Moon When the Rivers Start to Freeze
December—Thirteenth Moon—Moon of Popping Trees
—Source, McLain, *The Indian Way*

Part of the Crow Calendar According to Pretty-Shield
March—Moon When the Ice Goes Out of Rivers
April—Moon When the Sage-Hens Dance
May—Moon When Leaves Were Showing
June—Moon When the Leaves Are Fully Grown
July—Moon When the Berries Begin to Turn Red
September—Moon When Plums Fall
November—Moon When the Leaves Are on the Ground

Oto Calendar
January—The little young bear comes down the tree
February—Raccoon's rutting season
March—Big clouds
April—Little frogs croak
May—To get ready for plowing and planting
June—Hoeing corn
July—Buffalo rutting season
August—All the elk call
September—Spider-web on the ground at dawn
October—Deer rutting season
November—Every buck loses his horns
December—Cold month

Hopi Lunar Calendar
Mid-October–mid-November: Initiates' Moon
November–December: Dangerous Moon
December–January: Water Moon (sometimes Prayer Stick Moon, Play Moon or Foolish Moon)
January–February: Purification Moon
February–March: Whistling or Cactus Moon
March–April: Windbreak Moon
April–May: Waiting Moon (also called Sweet-corn-planting Moon)
May–June: Planting Moon
June–July: nameless moon, traditional name *ka-miyaw*
July–August: nameless moon, traditional name *pa-miyaw*
August–September: nameless moon, traditional name *powamiyaw*
(September): Feasting Moon or Harvest Moon. This moon is the intercalary moon necessary every two to three years to keep the lunar year with its twelve months of about 354 days in step with the solar year of about 365 days).
September–October: Autumn Moon (also Basket-Carrying Moon)

Southern Cheyenne Seasons
Autumn—Leaves turn yellow
Winter—It is getting colder
Spring—Grass is becoming green
Summer—Hot weather

ADDITIONAL READING

See references listed under chapter four Additional Reading.

Blevins, Winfred. *Dictionary of the American West*. New York: Facts on File, 1993.

Clark, W.P. *The Indian Sign Language*. Lincoln: University of Nebraska Press, 1982. Originally written for army use in 1882.

Coward, John M. *The Newspaper Indian: Native American Identity in the Press, 1820–90*. Urbana: The University of Illinois Press, 1999. This is an important book for the sense of how European-ancestry people and the American press perceived Indians. Details about Indian removal, the Sand Creek and Fetterman massacres, and the "Indian as villain."

Drechsel, Emanuel. *Mobilian Jargon: Linguistic and Sociohistorical Aspects of a Native American Pidgin*. New York: Oxford University Press, 1997.

Eagle/Walking Turtle. *Indian America*. 4th ed. Santa Fe: John Muir Publications, 1995. Primarily a guidebook to contemporary Indian museums, reservations and other sites; quotes from Indian people and various tribal names/ meanings are included.

McLain, Gary. *The Indian Way*. Santa Fe: John Muir Publications, 1990.

Stoutenburgh, John. *Dictionary of the American Indian*. New York: Philosophical Library, 1960.

CHAPTER TWELVE

CUSTOMS AND RELIGION

Two types of religious activities predominated in Indian belief: guardian spirit complex including winter sings and curing, vision quests and the sweat lodge; and the traditional Indian Longhouse religion, known as Washut.

Washut involved community celebrations for a variety of reasons including first fruit or food (such as the Green Corn Ceremony) and funerals. It was practiced by tribes in the Arctic, California, Northeast, Southeast, Northwest Coast, Prairie and Woodland and among Pueblo tribes in the Southwest.

Guardian spirit belief was more individualized and included such activities as participation in vision quests, Sun Dances, the sweat lodge, dreams and winter sings. Most tribes in the 1800s participated in some type of guardian spirit belief, but it was most common among the Arctic, California, Great Basin, Plateau, Plains and Southwest cultural groups, with some use by the Northeast culture groups (particularly under teachings of Handsome Lake's Longhouse religion to the Iroquois League).

Indian people knew spiritual beings by differing names. For the Algonquians it was *manitou*. The Iroquois called them *orenda* and the Sioux knew them as *wakan* or *wakonda*. Though referred to here in past tense, many of these religious practices are still in use among Indian people.

Not all Indian people believed in a supreme being. Among those who did were the Teton Sioux who believed in Wakan Tanka (The Great God), the Pomos of California who believed in Madunda, the Mohaves who believed in Matavilya and the Eskimos who believed in Raven. The Pueblo people believed either Spider Grandmother or Thought Woman created the world, while the Five Civilized Tribes (Choctaw, Creek, Cherokee, Seminole and Chickasaw) attributed creation to Breath-Holder or the Master of Breath. In most cases the creator god was one of many spiritual beings important in the beliefs of people from each tribe, and many of them took the shape of animals, reptiles, birds or even inanimate objects such as the sun, moon, mountains or bodies of water.

Worship could occur in both private situations and in public events such as those held in a medicine lodge or longhouse. Almost always the main entrance to such structures faced east, toward the rising sun, and the structures had a sacred fire.

The areas of worship for Pueblo people were circular structures extending below the earth, known as *kivas*. Though all kivas were used for religious ceremonies, some were also used as general clubhouses, as a meeting location to debate war or other important tribal matters, and even as a cool place to spend some time during hot summer days. Kivas were largely the realm of men, though women could be invited in during special ceremonies. Kivas were accessed by climbing a ladder. They remain in use in the Southwest.

VISION QUESTS

For American Indians, spirituality—religion—was (and still is) an intensely personal journey often first taken by youngsters as they near or reach puberty. Indian people generally believed that spirits were present throughout their lives, and at all times of the day and night. In an effort to identify spirit helpers, youths isolated themselves for a period—lasting from one to several days, and usually for four days among the Plains tribes—fasting, praying and seeking guidance. Usually, but not always, they received a message on such outings, which are commonly called vision quests. From the point in their lives when a spirit helper made its presence known, the individual relied on that helper. Some of the powers received during vision quests in the 1800s included those for use in hunting, war, fishing, love, curing, gambling, clairvoyance, finding lost items or people and on rare occasions, producing rain. A person could receive more than one power, but seldom did anyone receive more than four powers during a lifetime.

SWEAT LODGE

Sweat lodge was powerful because it could restore both spiritual and physical purity by curing disease, and provided such traits as skill and strength for use in various pursuits such as fishing, hunting and even courting. Among the Yakimas, the sweat lodge ground was covered with cedar or green fir boughs. Stones were heated in a fire then sprinkled with water to create steam, which would purify the individuals taking part.

STORYTELLING AND WINTER SINGS

Many recorded narratives of Indian people are traditional stories, which present a view of how events happened to create the world and the people, animals and objects in it. Others describe customs. Both narrative types have spiritual connotations.

These traditional stories and tales are known today because of the oral traditions of Indian people. For them, storytelling was both entertainment and education. It was the way they handed down their traditions and how they maintained the records of their lives. Though anyone could participate in storytelling, there were, of course, some individuals who were particularly skilled raconteurs, and it is those people who provided the continuation of Indian history from one generation to the next.

The winter months, when people were in their lodges and homes for longer periods of time, were filled with storytelling, particularly during the time of the Winter Spirit Dances in the Northwest and Plateau regions. Sometimes a narrative begun one evening would be expanded and continued over several days. Raconteurs used such techniques as repetition and word patterns in telling their stories, and they added such elements as intonation and gestures. Though stories were told more during the winter months, such storytelling occurred, at least in part, because during the winter months the people needed stories to strengthen their spirit or overcome what they called "spirit sickness." During the summer, people were closer to nature and thus they naturally received spiritual powers and meanings.

Many narratives were laced with moral messages about how to live a better life or how to be a better person, though often the message was oblique, rather than direct, giving individuals an opportunity to discover it for themselves. Children listened to the stories and learned the history and ways of their people, as well as moral values.

SUN DANCE

Many Plains tribes celebrated the Sun Dance, held in summer, generally around the time of the summer solstice (mid-June). The Sun Dance was most elaborate among northern Plains tribes including the Sioux, Cheyenne and Mandan, but many tribes participated in Sun Dances. The principal ceremony generally lasted three days, during which time the people erected a sun pole (or buffalo pole) and a sun lodge. During the final days of the Sun Dance, those participating were involved in a ritual known as *okipa*, which had four major elements representing a warrior's capture, torture, captivity and deliverance.

To begin, participants in okipa had wooden skewers thrust through the skin and muscles of their backs or chests. Then they were attached to the sun pole within the sun lodge by rawhide thongs tied to the skewers. Once that had been done they were raised up so that their skin and muscles strained and tore. The warriors involved in the Sun Dance faced the sun with their eyes open. As they moved and struggled against the skewers that held them, they heard the songs and drums of bystanders, who were a part of the ceremony as well. Eventually each warrior tore loose from the skewers.

Not all Sun Dances involved the okipa and its torturous elements.

DREAMS

Indians recognized the value and importance of dreams in obtaining spiritual guidance and power. Among the techniques considered beneficial in obtaining dreams or visions were torture (such as the Sun Dance), fasting, wild dancing, swallowing emetics, taking sweat baths, and isolation in dark places, on mountain tops or in the desert. Dreaming was not reserved for adults. Children were encouraged to fast or isolate themselves in order to dream.

TOBACCO

Of all the practices, the most universal for American Indians was the use of tobacco in rituals. Though smoked for relaxation, tobacco also had a religious element to its use. In regions where tobacco was cultivated, there were ceremonies for its planting and harvest. The tobacco pouches, the tobacco itself and the pipe in which it was smoked were all considered sacred. Among the Mandans, where women did all the farming, men cultivated and harvested tobacco. Among other Plains tribes, which abandoned farming when they obtained the horse, tobacco is the one crop they continued to cultivate.

Most tobacco was not smoked plain, but rather was mixed with herbs and sweet grasses. Plains people mixed tobacco with laurel, squaw bush and maple bush, and the inner bark of cherry, red willow, poplar, birch, dogwood, or arrowwood. Occasionally they mixed it with bison dung (which of course had grasses in it).

Most people smoked tobacco using various types of pipes (known as calumets, from the French *chalumuau* meaning reed or reed pipe), such as the small smoking tubes, elbow-pipes and "cloud-blowers" of the Pimas to those made of clay, or cut from soapstone or catlinite. The catlinite (most often a dark red color, though sometimes black) existed in only a few locations, primarily in what is now Minnesota (Pipestem National Monument) and became an important trade item. When first quarried the catlinite is a soft material that can be carved and shaped rather easily, but it becomes harder with age and exposure to the air.

Men also chewed tobacco and ground it for use as snuff. The tribes of the Southwest and Great Basin rolled it in cornhusks to smoke like a modern cigar or cigarette. Indians in the area of present Nevada and California ground tobacco and mixed it with water and lime, subsequently swallowing the concoction. (See also page 135.)

EUROPEAN RELIGIONS/MISSIONS

Though Indian people had their own spiritual beliefs, European influences eventually reached them. Spanish missionaries first impacted tribes in the Southwest. French and English missionaries started in the Northeast and then spread toward the west, in some cases using converts from Northeastern tribes to approach the Western Indians.

As early as the 1820s some Western tribes were approached by outside religious influences. Big Ignace, a lay apostle and a member of a band of Iroquois from the Caughnaquga Mission near Montreal, Canada, made his way into the Plateau area in the 1820s. He began teaching the Indians there about Christianity. He showed them how to make the sign of the cross and taught them the words to the Lord's Prayer.

In 1825 four Spokane boys left their tribe en route to Canada with missionaries, where they were taught about Christianity at the Red River Mission at Fort Garry. Four years later the boys returned to their tribe. They had cut their hair short and wore the clothes of white men. They had also become Christians, and they returned not only knowing—but actually spreading—European ways and their knowledge of the Church of England's Book of Common Prayer and the Bible. Additional boys were sent to the Red River Mission in 1830, furthering the spread of Christianity among the Spokanes and ultimately among other Northwest and Plateau tribes.

French Canadians built the first Roman Catholic Church in the region in 1836 in Champoeg (Oregon). Two years later, in 1838, the first priest arrived at the church, where he routinely said Mass and conducted baptisms. Additional missions were established at Cowlitz and at Fort Vancouver.

In part due to the teachings of Big Ignace, the Flathead Indians appealed to the Jesuit Society, asking the Black Robes—as they called the priests—to come to their country. A Flathead delegation made its way to St. Louis to ask for Black Robes as early as the 1830s, but not until 1840 was their request answered. That year Father Pierre De Smet, a Belgian member of the Society of Jesuits, crossed the plains to participate in the fur rendezvous on the Green River in present northwest Wyoming, where he preached the first Catholic Mass in that area—"La Praire de la Masse"—on 5 July 1840. Father De Smet traveled to the rendezvous and subsequently into present northwest Montana. In 1841 he established the St. Mary Mission in the Bitterroot Valley. Subsequently, in 1854, he established the St. Ignatius Mission, also in present-day northwestern Montana, in a region that became known as the Mission Valley.

By 1863 De Smet appealed for teachers to serve the Flathead Indians. The Sisters of Charity of Providence responded, and the first four sisters from the order arrived at St. Ignatius on 17 October 1864, to become the first Catholic sisters in what became Montana. They established the Providence Holy Family School and a hospital.

The missions not only taught the Indians about Christianity, they also were encouraged to become farmers. In October 1841 De Smet met with Indians at Fort Colville, baptizing 190 of them. When he returned to St. Mary's Mission, he had seeds for beans, onions, carrots, lettuce, wheat, potatoes and oats. Those became the first crops of the mission farm.

The Catholic priests "were convinced that it was necessary to change the secular as well as the spiritual lives of the Indian people. They often imposed new social and political structures on the Indian communities in which they worked," according to Deward E. Walker Jr. and Roderick Sprague in "History until 1846," a chapter in the *Handbook of North American Indians*, vol. 12, *Plateau*. As part of that philosophy Indians were "required to abandon all dances, potlatching, . . . and gambling."

The Protestant mission began in 1837, in response to appeals from Plateau tribes for "The Book." The Protestants rushed to establish missions because they didn't want the Catholics to have the advantage. The first Protestants to make their way into the Plateau were Marcus Whitman, a doctor who wanted to work among the Indians, and the Rev. Henry Spalding who met Nez Percé and Flathead people in 1836. Those two men traveled with their wives, Narcissa Whitman and Eliza Spalding, and a fur brigade as far as the fur trapper rendez-vous on the Green River. From there they continued west to establish the Whitman Mission at Waiilatpu.

Besides taking their wives, Whitman and Spalding also took wagons over the route. Though they eventually abandoned the wagons, cutting one down into a cart before subsequently leaving it as well, the Whitmans and Spaldings demonstrated that not only men but also *women* could travel the western trail. This led eventually to hoards of people following their route to Oregon, begin-ning in 1841 with the first small party and swelling in 1843, the first year of major emigration to Oregon.

Narcissa Whitman and Eliza Spalding, then, not only took religion to the Indians, but also unknowingly forged the way for other white women and even-tually for the families who ultimately displaced most of the Indian people.

At Waiilatpu, the Whitmans and Spaldings and others proceeded with their missionary work until 1847 when the Cayuses attacked and killed most of the whites at the mission. The attack was in retaliation for white diseases—specifically measles—which had killed many Indian children and adults, though partially in response to the increased emigration to the Oregon country. Killed in the Whit-man massacre were both Narcissa and Marcus Whitman. The Spaldings and other missionaries subsequently left for the Willamette Valley, and Protestant missionary work declined until 1870 when Henry Spalding established a Presbyterian mission at Lapwai.

TRIBAL PRACTICES

Arctic

Eskimo-Aleut religion had five categories of interacting powers: magic formu-las, charms, talismans and amulets; souls of men and animals that were immortal or perpetually reincarnated; demonic earth and air spirits; the "persons" of places, creatures and things; and the spirit-powers that direct the universe. As part of their religion the people had public ceremonies and personal spirit guardians.

The first Russian Orthodox missions were established in 1824 on Unalaska, and in 1825 on Atka Island and thereafter, the Aleuts were involved with Russian religion along with their traditional practices. A place such as a cave, cliff or high rock near every village served as a sacred site where adult men made offerings of objects (usually animal skins or feathers) as they sought power. Young males and all females were prohibited from approaching the sacred sites.

Aleut spiritual leaders provided mediation between the present and the spirit worlds through drumming, singing and dancing. Two particularly prized items among Aleuts were a bicolored hollow pebble amulet seldom found on the beach and kept hidden by the owner to draw sea otters to him, and a girdle (that could be inherited) of plaited grasses and sinews worn under clothing to protect the wearer from death.

Several types of dances and celebrations were held including those for war party planning, memorial feasts for the dead, invitational potlatches and trading, succession of a chief and various first events in a person's life. At most celebrations both men and women danced, the men often wearing masks representing animals or humans. At certain times one village would entertain another village and competition evolved as the villages attempted to outdo each other. The largest ceremonial of all occurred at the end of a forty-day mourning period. Winter festivals also were large with varied entertainment.

Ceremonies

Bladder Festival: Held in the fall for propitiation of seals and other game.

Messenger Feast: A trading festival at year's end where land and sea products were exchanged by all mainland tribes. Known as *nilga*, chiefs organized the event but it was not held until late in the century.

California

Only men participated in activities in the sweat house, and women weren't allowed to participate in religious rites as freely as men could. Women did participate in Memorials for the Dead in Southern California, but in other areas they were severely restricted when it came to religious activities. Pomo men held dances of spirit-impersonating ceremonies, known as Ghost and Kuksa, in an earth-covered dance house, which young boys and women could not enter. The dances were held in part to terrify women. Female participation in the Acorn Ceremony of the Hupas, held each fall, was limited to grinding the acorns needed for the ritual.

The most elaborate ritual in northwestern California was "World Renewal" or "Big Time," which involved dancing, displays of tools and other goods, and recitations. The dances included the Jumping Dance and the White Deerskin Dance.

Major ceremonies included the Deerskin Dance or White Deerskin Dance, Boat Dance, Jumping Dance, First Salmon Rite and Acorn Feast.

The Wiyot held the Brush Dance to cure a sick child and Victory Dances after the death of an enemy. Many tribes restricted dancing by women in Victory Dances, but the Wiyot women participated in that activity.

Among the Miwok tribes, there were four different types of spiritual leaders or doctors: deer doctors who could locate deer and assist with success in hunting; weather doctors who could control wind and rain as well as other weather occurrences; rattlesnake doctors who performed at rattlesnake ceremonies; and bear doctors who had bears as their guardian spirits. The Miwoks generally engaged in two types of ceremonies, those considered sacred, and which had elaborate costumes and also the potential to harm dancers if they didn't properly handle paraphernalia needed for the ceremonies, and the profane dances that were primarily entertainment and presented little or no risk to those involved.

Northeast

By 1800 much of the traditional life of the Northeast Indians, particularly those of the Iroquois Longhouse (Seneca, Cayuga, Onondaga, Mohawk and Oneida), had been affected by development and treaties as well as establishment of reservations. Though the traditional governing by the Council of Chiefs no longer remained in full effect, many of the ceremonial traditions continued, including the two most important ones: Midwinter and Green Corn ceremonials.

Midwinter was the longest Iroquois ceremonial, held in January or February and lasting at least a week. To begin the ceremony, messengers—called Our Uncles or Big Heads—entered houses, stirring ashes and announcing the start of Midwinter ceremonial. Several days devoted to renewal and fulfillment of dreams, dances and games were part of the rite, which concluded with performance of the Four Sacred Rituals (Feather Dance, Thanksgiving Dance, Personal Chant and Bowl Game). Traditionally the people sacrificed two large white dogs at the beginning of the ceremony, burning them later.

The Green Corn Ceremony coincided with the harvest of the first ears of corn and also involved the Four Sacred Rituals and Our Life Supporter Dances, which honored corn, beans and squash.

Other Iroquois rituals were the Strawberry, Maple, Planting, Bean, Harvest, Thunder, Moon and Sun ceremonies. Activities varied, but often there was a Thanksgiving speech, tobacco invocation and special dances or games. A feast followed most ceremonies, though often the food was prepared and brought to the ceremony to be distributed for consumption in individual homes.

The Feast for the Dead or Condolence Ceremony was an important part of

Iroquois tradition. (See page 94.)

Delawares had two basic types of ceremonies: family feasts and vision recitals. The major tribal ceremony was a combination of harvest and corn-planting ceremonies, held in the fall and known as the Big House Ceremony. It involved storytelling, singing, dancing and a ritual meal. The Big House Ceremony sometimes lasted six or eight nights, but occasionally extended over twelve nights. Family feasts in the nineteenth century included Grease-Drinking Ceremonies, where a bear or hog was devoured, the grease drunk and some thrown into the fire for the vision recitation. In the latter part of the 1800s, some Oklahoma Delawares became involved in the peyote ritual. (See page 240.)

Longhouse Religion: Following the American Revolution, people of the Iroquois League found themselves facing significant changes in their lifestyle, particularly as chiefs agreed to treaties that established reservations. By the mid-1790s, many of the Iroquois people were feeling the effects of white influence, including proliferation of alcoholic beverages, loss of land use and reduction in military and diplomatic power. People traveled to places like Pittsburgh, Pennsylvania, or other markets to trade for goods and services, and they began operating blacksmith shops, sawmills and gristmills. In 1798 Quakers established a mission among the Allegany band of Iroquois, with a stated goal not of religious change but rather of education. They wanted the Indian people to learn to read and write English, to learn mathematics and to learn how to better handle business dealings including the marketing of their products.

Restrictions on hunting and trading rendered men relatively powerless; women continued in a life similar to what they had always known by tending crops and households. As the men lost their power and became virtually unemployed, they became involved in feuds. Sexual jealousies led to increased divorce.

Subsequently Handsome Lake, a League chief, had visions that led him to organize the Longhouse religion. Handsome Lake advocated a moral code outlawing drunkenness, sexual promiscuity, quarreling, gambling, wife beating and witchcraft. He called for renewal of traditional rites including particularly the Strawberry Ceremony and the Midwinter Ceremony.

Following Handsome Lake's death, his nephew helped continue the Longhouse religion, and it remained in use throughout the nineteenth century. Children as young as age seven undertook vision quests among the Shawnees (see information on vision quests on page 224).

The Shawnees recognized several ceremonial events. They held the Spring Bread Dance to request an abundant harvest, while the Fall Bread Dance was an opportunity to express thanksgiving and to request that game be plentiful. During both dances, the people held a feast with a dozen men killing the game and a dozen women preparing the food. The hunters and cooks held their positions for life, though they could be removed for misconduct. The Green Corn Dance took place in August, where individuals were absolved of misconduct and where any injury would be forgiven, with the exception of murder. The Men's Dance or War Dance also occurred in August.

Missions: During the nineteenth century, a variety of Quaker and Christian missions were established among the Northeast Indians, and increasing numbers of Indians began attending their functions, ranging from religious services to schools. The small one-room schools with white teachers became common, and children who did not attend them commonly attended boarding schools such as the Thomas Indian School on the Cattaraugus Reservation or the Carlisle Indian School in Pennsylvania.

Southeast

Origin of the world stories with some Southeastern Indians involved three tiers: the Upper World where deities and spirits lived, the Middle World where Indians and most animals lived and the Lower World where abnormal life forms and spirits resided. A great variety of supernatural beings were present in the lives of Southeastern Indians, and the two most common were the Immortals (who were usually invisible and who paid little attention to natural laws) and the Little People (small individuals who played pranks, liked to be with children and who can be likened to Irish leprechauns). To see one of the Little People could be an omen of impending death.

Southeast Indians recognized the bear as an important culture hero in part because of sacrifices made by bears (whom the Creeks believed were their relatives) in order to help the Creek people survive during a period when they were short on food. The bears sacrificed themselves to become food for a people that did not normally eat bear meat. Cherokees also had specific tribal rituals related to hunting of bears. Though Creeks and Cherokees hunted bears, they always paused to give thanks for the sacrifice of the bears.

Corn Maiden was a similar culture hero, in some stories arising from the sacrifice of a woman who obtained corn from a mystical source for her twin sons. When the sons found out where she got the corn, she told them she had to die, but before she did she instructed them to scatter her remains over the fields, that they might produce corn for the people. Nearly every tribe has a different story about how they received the gift of corn.

Ceremonies

Black Drink Ceremony: Choctaw, Creek and Cherokee tribal members took part in this purification ceremony that involved brewing and ingesting a drink made from a holly species. Known as the Black Drink, it was a stimulant and diuretic that resulted in sweating and vomiting.

Green Corn Dance: Common to all Southeastern tribes, the Green Corn Dance or Ceremony involved ritual cleaning of homes and public areas. It also involved purification rites for both physical and mental difficulties. Among the

Creeks the Green Corn Dance or Busk, provided for absolution of transgressions, including murder.

Great Basin

Wolf, who was believed to have created the solar system and people, became known as Father by many tribes in the Great Basin including the Northern Shoshone, Bannock, Ute, and some Southern Paiute and Western Shoshone tribal members. The Eastern Shoshones called Wolf *Pia Apo*, Big Father, while Coyote was *Tei Apo*, Little Father. For the Northern Paiutes, *Numuna*, Gray Wolf, was the creator.

An overriding element in the beliefs of Basin tribes was that powerful spirits were elements of nature and not separate deities. The Utes and Southern Paiutes believed that a snow white being living high in the mountains controlled deer, mountain sheep, bears and elk. Meanwhile Thunder Badger reacted when the land became too dry by digging into the ground and throwing up clouds and thunder curses.

Dances and Ceremonies

Bear Dance: Bear, believed to provide hunting and sexual prowess, was honored with the Bear Dance held during late winter.

Mourning Cry: The Southern Paiutes considered this their most important ceremony of the year. Held to end formal mourning periods, it involved ritual washing of mourners who had not bathed since the death of a loved one.

Round Dances: For many Basin tribes, who spent most of their energies on survival, the Round Dance was the most important (sometimes the only) ceremony conducted each year. It was held to give thanks for the first antelope hunt in the spring and the pinon harvest or the first rabbit drive in the fall. Bannocks and Northern Shoshones held Round Dances in early spring, both prior to the arrival of the salmon (in an effort to entice the salmon) and after the fish had arrived (as thanksgiving). The Round Dances involved clockwise movement around a tree or pole as the people held hands. Besides the thanksgiving and prayer aspects of the Round Dance, it also became an opportunity for courting. Some Round Dances also were held as part of rainmaking ceremonies, and they later became the Ghost Dance (see page 241).

Sun Dance: Eastern Shoshones held Sun Dances most years.

Interior Plateau

Coyote was one of the endearing images of Plateau stories, the people believed that he preceded them to the region, ridding it of (most) evil and preparing it for people. Coyote was cunning, naïve, a trickster, a creator and a transformer. He brought meaning and spiritual authority to the world.

Coyote was just one of many cultural figures in the Plateau stories. Most were animals, like Raccoon, Eagle, Fox, Grizzly Bear, Salmon and the Swallow Sisters, but some were plants or objects such as Sweat Lodge. These cultural figures lived in villages. They hunted, fished and dressed in ways that made them appear human, and they had human traits like generosity, bravery, jealousy, greed and even vengeance. They had, as the Salish referred to it, *sumix* or "sacred power." Of all the Plateau culture figures, Coyote was the one who best illustrated the spiritual power of the supernatural beings. He could change himself into different forms, he slew monsters (though sometimes with the help of Fox) and he gave the people food.

Plateau people believed Coyote gave them salmon when he made his way up the Columbia River and its tributaries, naming landforms and streams. Coyote disguised himself as a child near the Celilo Falls, where culture figures, The Sisters, had made a dam keeping all the fish from migrating upstream. In his disguise, Coyote broke the dam, releasing the fish, then he told The Sisters that they would be turned into birds. The Sanpoils called them Dove Sisters; the Kutenais called them Nighthawk and Snipe. For the Wishrams, Wascos and Sahaptins they were Swallows who announced the arrival of the salmon each spring.

The Klamaths believed Bear Power could help provide clairvoyant spirits; Dog Power could help find lost items; Eagle or Weasel Power could help predict what would happen in an impending fight. People with special training were relied upon to affect weather by calling on various spirits such as Thunder, Rain or West Wind.

Ceremonies

Blanket Ceremony or Conjuring Ceremony of the Kutenai: In the evening two or three blanket spiritual leaders directed this ceremonial meeting with various spirits. They covered the entrance to a tipi or frame house with a blanket, allowed participants to enter, then darkened the area and lit a juniper smudge, which filled the space with smoke. The singing of spirit songs enticed the various spirits to join the gathering. The leaders of the ceremony offered tobacco to the spirits then asked questions in order to give aid to those who were in attendance.

Bluejay Dance: A ceremony conducted at night for spiritual healing, prediction of the future and the chance to increase power. Those participating often "transformed" themselves into Bluejays so they could use curing or clairvoyant powers. Kutenai, Spokane and Kalispel tribes held similar ceremonies.

Chinook Dances or Weather Dances: Ceremonies held to entice the spirits to melt the snow or bring rain. Popular among the Northern Okanagan, Lakes, Colville and Kalispel tribes.

First Salmon Ceremony: Conducted by two spiritual leaders to recognize and give thanks for the first chinook salmon caught at a communal weir.

Jump Dance: Several Plateau tribes including Kutenai, Flathead and Pend d'Oreille, held this observance (similar to Winter Spirit Dances) where people prayed for good fortune for the coming year.

Spirit Dances: Held by the Salish and similar to the Bluejay Dance.

Sun Dance: Kutenai and Spokane tribal members held spring dances that were similar to Plains Sun Dances.

Sweat Lodge Ceremony: To obtain ritual purity and healing, Kutenai men and women participated in sweat lodge ceremonies. They entered the small sweat lodge on three to seven consecutive evenings to pray, pour cold water onto hot rocks to create steam and periodically take plunges into cold water lakes or streams.

Winter Spirit Dances: Conducted to give thanks for the previous year, to cure illness and to seek protection and luck in the future. Almost all Plateau tribes had some form of winter dances; many times they began with the winter solstice.

Other ceremonies of the Northern Okanagan, Lakes and Colville tribes included the War Dance, Scalp Dance, Religious Dance and the Guardian-spirit Dance.

Northwest Coast

A tradition of some Northwest Coast tribes, who were generally among the most prosperous of all Indian people in the 1800s, involved potlatch, a ceremonial feast held for a variety of reasons: death, recognition of a girl reaching puberty, marriage or even the building of a new longhouse. The word *potlatch* is from the Chinook tribe, but the practice spread up and down the Northwest Coast as chiefs attempted to impress people with their wealth and generosity. The primary elements of a potlatch involved inviting visitors to a home or village then bestowing gifts upon them. Sometimes so many gifts were given that the chief and his family were left nearly destitute. Among the items given were blankets, jewelry, food, household goods, furs, skins and even ships or boats.

Rival chiefs might hold a joint potlatch to see who had the most wealth to dispose. The chief with items left when the other had nothing was declared the winner in such contests. Often items given away were subsequently destroyed— either by burning or breaking them, or by throwing them into the sea. Though a potlatch could leave a chief, his family and the people of his village with few posessions, the most lavish (and therefore the more successful) potlatch would be remembered for years and brought honor to the organizers.

The Memorial Potlatch lasted four, eight or more days, involving four joy feasts and culminating in the potlatch, held primarily to honor the dead, but it also provided a way to add prestige to people or to get repairs made to a house. For the potlatch, relatives of the wife of the chief host donated items that would eventually be returned to them. The wife also gave her belongings and the husband's clanmates gave items as well. Throughout the several-day ceremony, repairs were made to homes (or the chief's home) and at the end of the period the host chief gave "gifts" to those who had assisted. The gifts included the items people had earlier provided at the request of the chief's wife. People considered their participation in a potlatch as a way to ensure their reputations.

Three important ceremonies of the Tlingits were a feast for the children, memorial potlatches and funeral feasts.

Plains

For some Plains Indians the number four was sacred, so many of their rituals were conducted over four-day periods. For some tribes the number seven was sacred, as in the seven sacred ceremonies of the Sioux.

Arikara life centered on the medicine lodge, a ritual lodge that generally was the largest earth structure in the village. It could be fifty or sixty feet in diameter, though it was generally octagonal in shape. The medicine lodge had an altar (often a low platform) at the opposite end from the entrance, where ritual offerings could be left. Known as the Magic Performance, the medicine fraternity rite lasted from midsummer into the fall and involved singing, dancing and other rituals every afternoon and evening.

Mandans had a cedar post in the center of their village with an open plaza around it. The post represented the primary Mandan culture hero, Lone Man. To the north side of the plaza stood the Okipa (or medicine) lodge, which had effigies representing various spirits hanging outside it. Those families with the most influence lived nearest to the Mandan Okipa lodge.

Individuals "bought" their way into the Mandan organizations. The beginning society for males was the Fox Society, and from there youths could purchase songs and dances with a variety of items, such as horses or other personal possessions and services, exchanged to advance to other societies. Those included the Half-sheared Society, Make Mouth Black, Dog Society, Buffalo Bull Society and finally the Black-tail Deer Society, which involved the older men who had achieved much during their lifetimes. Mandan females belonged to the Skunk Society for young girls, Creek Woman Society for young unmarried women, Goose Society for married women and the White Buffalo Society for old women. They also purchased entry into societies with personal possessions.

Bear Cult: This cult had three major functions: to conduct ceremonies honoring the bear, to participate in war parties and to doctor the sick. Bear Cult members from the Assiniboine tribe carried a "bear knife," which was broad, flat and double-edged metal attached to the jaw of a bear. Members wore distinctive clothing, carried bear shields and painted bears on their lodges.

Ceremonies

Cheyenne Buffalo Ceremony: The rite included ritualistic prayers and songs seeking favor from the spirits of the earth, sky, animals, four winds and all growing things. Participants were members of the animal societies.

Cheyenne Sacred Arrow Ceremony: Divine sources gave the Cheyennes four arrows and instructions about their use, which was the central feature of the tribe's religious thought. The giving of the arrows occurred at a sacred mountain, but its precise location is uncertain. The tribe migrated from the east, and some consider the sacred mountain Nuwawus, which is located in the Black Hills (South Dakota), as the origin. Only participants in the Arrow rite could see or touch the arrows, and no woman ever could. The arrows were kept in a bundle in a lodge near the home of the arrow keeper, and only the arrow keeper (who served for life) could enter the lodge where the sacred bundle was placed. It included a coyote hide quiver for the arrows and a bison skin to wrap around other sacred objects.

When traveling the arrow keeper walked, carrying the sacred bundle on his back, with guards watching him at all times. In the evening the arrow lodge would be quickly erected so the arrow keeper could enter. The Sacred Arrow Ceremony was conducted infrequently and only when necessary. If a Cheyenne killed another Cheyenne, the ceremony was held to remove the evil that threatened the tribe. The ceremony lasted four days, during which everyone in the camp was quiet. Incense fires burned during the ceremony, most of which was conducted in secrecy. After the Cheyennes divided into Northern and Southern branches, the sacred arrows were kept with the Southern Cheyennes. They were subsequently captured by enemy raiders, though the Cheyennes retrieved some of them.

Mandan Buffalo-Calling Ceremony: In this ceremony young married women had sex with old hunters in the belief that intercourse would transfer spiritual power from one person to another. In this way the power of the older hunters, which would draw animals closer and lead to good kills, was passed on to the young hunters by their wives.

Pawnee Captive Girl or Morning Star Sacrifice: The ceremony was held in the spring to ensure fertility for crops. It was dedicated to Morning Star (because Morning Star's mating with Evening Star brought light and warmth to the world). During the four-day preparation period Pawnee warriors captured a thirteen-year-old girl from an enemy tribe, bringing her to the camp where they treated her well, providing her with special foods and clothing. For the four-day sacrificial ceremony the men gathered four types of wood: willow, elder, cottonwood and elm, each symbolizing a point on the compass and a sacred animal (wolf, mountain lion, wildcat and bear), to use in constructing a scaffold.

Wearing a painted buffalo robe the captive girl was taken to the scaffold.

The left side of her body was painted black for the night, and the right side was painted red, representing the day and the Morning Star. After a ritual smoking of tobacco, all the people of the tribe changed clothes while four priests joined the girl on the scaffold, tying her in an upright but spread-eagled fashion to the scaffold. As the rays of Morning Star greeted the day, a warrior killed the girl by shooting an arrow into her heart. Another warrior cut an incision over her heart, putting her blood on his face and allowing some to drop to an offering of buffalo meat in the pit below the scaffold. The people then ate the consecrated buffalo meat in addition to dancing, singing, praising Morning Star and Mother Corn, engaging in mock battles and even indulging in unrestrained sex.

In 1816 Pitalesharo (Man Chief), the son of the chief, Lachelesharo (Knife Chief), cut the captive girl free just before the fatal arrow could be unleashed, ending the traditional sacrificial ceremony for the Pawnees. Though his people believed the Morning Star would strike down Pitalesharo (because they believed he was exchanging his life for that of the girl), he lived to ultimately become chief of the tribe. Like the Sun Dance, the sacrifice was held so the people would obtain power from the sun, moon, thunder, lightning, wind and other such elements.

The Comanches had few ceremonies and they relied little on religious and spiritual customs, according to Edward S. Curtis who photographed and studied Indian tribes across the country. As Curtis reported, the Comanche elders told him they "were so active in warfare, so constantly on the move, that they had little time to give thought to the origin and purpose of their existence; in fact, they seemingly took pride in not doing so."

And David G. Burnet, a lawyer and store manager in Natchitoches, Texas, who lived with the Comanches for a time, wrote in 1847:

> The Comanches had no definite idea of their own origin. Their loose tradition, is that their ancestors came from the north; but they have no precise conception of the time when, or from what particular region. . . . They believe in, or have some indefinite traditional idea of, the Great Spirit; but I have never discovered any distinct mode or semblance of worship among them. I frequently observed, early in the morning, a shield, such as they use in war, elevated at the point of a javelin (the hilt on the ground) and invariably facing the east.

The Comanches did have a Sun Dance, and they also held the Big Tail Medicine Ceremony, a healing ritual conducted in an oblong tipi with a deep trench on the north side symbolizing the underground runway of the beaver. A pool of water stood in the middle of the tipi with an earth mound formed like a beaver near the entrance. The patient was placed against that mound. During the ceremony the healer whirled his bull-roarer, and he healed by incantation, body manipulation and sucking the disease out of the person's body.

Principal ceremonies of the Sioux included the Sun Dance, Vision Cry, Buffalo Chant (a puberty ceremony for girls), Ghost Keeper and Foster-parent Chant. The Sioux had no ritualistic healing ceremony, though medicine men provided services as directed by their spirit helpers.

Dances of the Plains Indians included the Bear Dance, Dance of the Crazy Dogs, Eagle Dance, Dance of the Scalped Ones (Pawnee) and the Sun Dance, a ritual (described on pages 225-226) held so warriors would gain strength and power from such elements as the sun, wind, thunder and the like.

Prairies and Woodlands

The Foxes had two major ceremonies each year, one in winter that was small and another in summer that involved songs and prayers, dances and a feast. Both were to remind the manitous (spirits the Foxes believed in) of promises made to the people.

The Kickapoos held a number of public rituals, and they found both tobacco and the thunderers important messengers for communicating with the manitous or supernatural beings. Among the tribal ceremonies were religious feasts such as the Green Corn Dance, held during the maize harvest, and family feasts or rituals such as the feast for the dead and adoption and naming ceremonies.

Among the Illinois, young boys who preferred implements used by women were dressed as females and became transvestites. They were considered manitous (spirits) and as such were invited to council meetings so their valued advice could be heard. They participated in war parties, but used only clubs to fight with, rather than bows and arrows as other males would do.

The most sacred items of the Winnebagos were their war bundles, which belonged to the clans and were the focus of important ceremonies. Spiritual direction could lead to development of new bundles or the addition of items to existing bundles. Each bundle ceremony involved ritual offerings to supernatural beings that were associated with war. Such rituals could include the Victory Dance (often called the Scalp Dance) in which four scalps were given to individuals who placed them as grave offerings. Four-night wakes, in which warriors recounted their part in battles, involved wagering the souls of slain enemies, with the winners turning the souls over to the deceased Winnebagos to help them on their way to the next world.

Menominees had religious groups including the Medicine Lodge Society, with membership by invitation or inheritance, and the Dream Dance or Drum Dance, which had fairly open membership. Medicine Lodge rituals involved those to prolong life and good health. The Dream Dance was held so individuals could obtain supernatural power in order to properly carry out activities, respect others and maintain good relationships with their source of power.

The Chippewas recognized a supernatural world filled with many spirits including both animate and inanimate objects. The Midewiwin, or Medicine Dance, was the most important ceremony of the Medicine Lodge Society (also called the Midewiwin Society). The society was for curative purposes and required initiation, instruction and payment of high fees from those involved. The Midewiwin was held twice annually, in the spring and fall, lasting from two to five days. Each member ultimately received a medicine bag (which was buried with him or her) for use in curative rites. The medicine bags, containing personal power items such as amulets, were made of various materials depending on the degree of involvement of the individual. First-degree bags were of mink, otter, beaver or muskrat; second-degree bags were of owl or hawk; third-degree bags were of snake, fox or wildcat claw; and fourth-degree bags were cub bear or bear paw.

Other Chippewa Rituals

Bear Ceremony: Held when hunters killed a bear, this involved a feast and speeches of respect to the bear.

Chief Dance: Initially held before a war party left the village to protect those who would engage in battle, or an entire community.

Curing Rituals and Practices: Used widely by Chippewas to treat disease and various ailments. Practitioners always received pay and many were also Midewiwin priests.

Drum Dance: Originating on the plains, this dance was not in use among the Chippewas until the 1870s. There was some belief that performing it would lead to peace between Indians and whites. It was a four-day event, held after the Midewiwin and involved drumming and dancing in a special lodge or outdoor area. A number of activities could occur during Drum Dance including marriages, divorces or the lifting of mourning.

Peyote Ritual: Used as a curative ritual late in the nineteenth century and more extensively in the twentieth century. Once prosecuted by the U.S. government, it is now a legalized practice of the Native American Church.

Southwest

By 1800 Southwest tribes had been under Spanish influence for nearly two hundred years. There were fewer Franciscan missionaries among the Pueblo Indians, though some remained who performed their ecclesiastical duties perfunctorily. The Pueblo tribes generally followed some outward practices of Christianity while maintaining their traditional ceremonies.

Western Pueblos had heavy involvement with the kachina religion (see page 244) and in those pueblos individuals were all affiliated with kivas (see page 224), though only men danced. In some areas where there was no involvement with the kachina ceremonies, the people were involved in medicine societies. Some societies were extremely complex. The Zunis, for example, had twelve matrilineal clans, thirteen medicine societies, a masked dance society for all males, a series of priesthoods with high-ranking officials comprising the religious government, and a secular government comprised of elected officials. Later there were four mission churches and three public schools.

The Roman Catholic Church also played a part in religious life for most of the Pueblos in the 1800s, with some impacts from Protestant churches after 1850.

Taos Pueblo, in north-central New Mexico, is divided into two sides: North and South. The North side kivas are Big Earring People, Day People and Knife People. The South side kivas are Feather People, Water People and Old Axe People.

Pueblo dances included the Pine Tree Dance, Butterfly Dance, Deer Dance, Turkey Dance and Snake Dance.

The Ghost Dance, which started in 1889 among the tribes in the Great Basin and spread to other cultural groups in the West, had two ideological goals: removal of whites from Indian country and resurrection of ancestors. The Walapais held their final Ghost Dance in 1895.

For the Hopis certain colors were aligned with certain directions: north—yellow; south—red; east—white; west—blue; above—black; below—all colors. Ritual acts were associated with numbers, with "four" and "six" predominating and chants being repeated either four or six times.

Among the Yavapais, each of the directions was associated with a color; for example, the east was associated with yellow cattail pollen, which was used in all rituals and prayers. They believed that white and turquoise beads provided protection against bad luck and sickness and that the bald eagle and golden eagle were messengers from the spirit worlds. Their down and feathers were essential for most rituals and were carried to obtain special knowledge. Only men used the sweat lodge. Music and dance were a form of prayer and therefore a part of all Yavapai rituals. Medicine men used the rattle and the pot drum in healing ceremonies. They used a flute or bull-roarer on various occasions, but primarily when seeking rain.

Mohaves believed that religion centered on dreams, which started when a child was still in its mother's womb, though the child forgot an early dream upon birth and generally dreamed it again as an adolescent. Only a few people (chiefs, warriors, healers, singers and funeral orators) received "great dreams" or "good dreams." Proper dreaming for all people, however, could lead to success at a variety of activities ranging from lovemaking to warfare.

Pima and Papago rituals that took place as part of the "Ceremonial Cycle" included these: Corn Harvest and Deer Hunting, called *ma amaga*; Early Winter and "prayerstick" ritual called *wi gida*; a summer cactus wine feast, a "naming ceremony" and purification rights for warfare, eagle killing and salt expeditions to the Gulf of California. Private ceremonies and rituals included a purification ceremony upon the birth of a child, puberty dances for girls and ritual curing for illness.

Jesuits impacted the Yaquis after 1617, but by 1767 the Yaquis had forced the Jesuit priests to leave their area and afterward they formed three men's sodalities: The Horsemen, dedicated to the Child Jesus; Judases, dedicated to Christ crucified; and Matachines, dedicated to the Virgin Mary. They also had two women's sodalities: "singers" and "altar-tenders." The Yaquis recognized Lent and Holy Week and the sodalities took control of church and town activities each year. The male sodalities established and enforced taboos related to both Lent and to sexual acts, and they conducted burials.

In Apache traditional stories there were two culture heroes—one associated with water and the other associated with sun or fire—who were able to slay or vanquish any monsters that might threaten the people's survival. Religion combined priestcraft with ritual healing. Some rites were established based on visions, while others could be handed down through training. Like the Pimas, the Apaches, believed they could become ill if they angered a natural source such as owl, bear, coyote or lightning.

The Chiricahua Apaches vaguely believed in "Life Giver" and addressed prayers to him, but they also called on the culture heroine White-Painted Woman and her son, Child of the Water, as well as mountain spirits who lived in the high ground of Chiricahua territory. Most ceremonial practices revolved around the acquisition and use of supernatural power by individuals, with the power obtained from a number of sources including plants, animals and celestial bodies. A healer sometimes served as an intermediary to obtain such power, using a variety of rituals such as smoking, singing and prayer; marking the central figure with red or yellow ocher, charcoal, white clay or iron ore; sucking at an afflicted spot with a tube; rubbing or brushing with feathers; and administering special foods or herbal decoctions. Payment was necessary for such intervention and came in the form of horses, buckskins or meat.

Mescalero Apaches also believed in White-Painted Woman and Child of the Water.

Jicarilla Apaches classified rites either as personal (healing rituals) or as traditional (long-life). Under personal rites, an individual derived power from an animal, celestial body or natural phenomenon. Traditional or long-life ceremonies came from the emergence stories, which tell of how people came to live on earth, and do not require a person to have a direct encounter with the supernatural; rather they can be taught what they need to know. The Holiness Rite or Bear Dance, a curing rite, was the most difficult of the long-life ceremonies. Usually beginning three days prior to a full moon, and lasting four days, the ceremony took place in an enclosure made of piñon, spruce or pine, with an eastern entrance. Patients who needed to be cured of Bear or Snake sickness were placed in a tipi within the enclosure and on the first night a bear appeared. If the bear frightened the people, that was evidence that someone with the illnesses was being cured. Healers presided, singing songs. Sacred clowns appeared on the fourth night, demonstrating obscene and grotesque language and behavior as they prayed for guidance and for a cure for the patients. Women were involved in dancing, and they also served food and drinks to all who attended. At the culmination of the ceremony, people exited the enclosure and ailments were "deposited" on a tree the medicine man had specially prepared.

Among the Western Apaches curing ceremonies varied from tribe to tribe, but there were some common elements: use of turquoise beads, drums, cattail pollen to bless the patient, eagle feathers and objects and colors which represented the four directions. People sang chants representing Deer, Bear and Lightning and offered prayers to Life Giver, Sun and Changing Woman.

Navajo Ceremonies

Most Navajo ceremonies were held for curing diseases, thus they were highly individualized. For Navajos, personalized powers had forms that were somewhat like humans, and therefore they were conceived of as people; thus the Navajos had Snake People, Bear People, Cactus People, Deer People, Ant People, Wind People or Thunder People. The most loved deity of the Navajos was Changing Woman. She, along with her twin children, Born for Water and Monster Slayer, and their father, Sun, were the "holy family" of the Navajos. Two of the main ceremonials of the Navajos were the Blessingway, which dealt with harmony, peace and good things, and the Enemyway, which dealt with war, violence and ugliness.

Blessingway: the backbone of Navajo religion—was used to bless a new hogan, to protect livestock, aid childbirth, to install a tribal officer and to consecrate a marriage, among other practices. Blessingway rites also were used to summon positive blessings, for good luck, to turn away misfortune and to protect or increase possessions. The only essential item needed to conduct a Blessingway rite was the mountain soil bundle, a piece of buckskin that contained soil from the summits of the sacred mountains as well as stone objects. Most Blessingway singers also had talking prayersticks and sacks of pollen. In a Blessingway rite, pollen—usually from the tassels of corn—was eaten in conjunction with prayer. The pollen prayer involved placing a small amount of pollen in the mouth, on top of the head and scattering some into the air.

Enemyway: an ancient war ceremonial—was started to protect warriors from the ghosts of slain enemies. It lasted three or five nights with various portions conducted in different locations by more than one singer, or ritual leader. This was considered an Evilway ceremonial.

Chantways used to prevent illness or for curing comprised the largest group of Navajo song ceremonials. They were dominated by one of three rituals: Holyway, Evilway and Lifeway. The Holy People, generally in two-night, five-night, and sometimes nine-night forms, directed Holyway rituals.

Among the items in a singer's bundle were rawhide, gourds, bison or deer hoof rattles, a bull-roarer, feathered wands, smooth canes or digging sticks (used to remove medicines from pouches), eagle quill feathers, talking prayersticks of stone or wood, chant tokens known as tie-ons, an eagle wing bone whistle used to summon or signal the Holy People, a fire drill, abalone or turtle shell medicine cups, small sacks of cornmeal, pollen, paints, herbal medicines, stones, fossils, quartz crystals, animal figurines and a stone club (Monster Slayer's weapon).

Kachinas

Kachinas were the benevolent beings who lived in mountains, springs and lakes and who brought blessings such as rain, crops and healing (particularly among the Eastern Pueblos). Usually the focal point of the kachina regalia was a mask (not all Kachinas wore masks). It was treated reverently and sometimes fed cornmeal or other sacred foods. Kachinas generally arrived at Hopi villages in January and remained there until July, when they returned to their homes in the San Francisco Peaks. The kachinas served as messengers between the Hopis and the gods who provided rain, controlled weather and reinforced social and religious laws. There were more than 250 different Hopi kachinas, both male and female.

ADDITIONAL READING

See references listed under chapter four Additional Reading.

Arnold, A. James, ed. *Monsters, Tricksters and Sacred Cows: Animal Tales and American Identities.* Charlottesville: The University Press of Virginia, 1996.

Bierhorst, John, ed. *The Sacred Path: Spells, Prayers & Power Songs of the American Indians.* New York: Quill, 1984. A variety of pieces representing tribes across the continent.

Bucko, Raymond. *The Lakota Ritual of the Sweat Lodge.* Lincoln: University of Nebraska Press, 1998.

Caduto, Michael J., and Joseph Bruchac. *Keepers of the Animals.* Golden, CO: Fulcrum Publishing, 1991. This book written as a story and activity guide for children includes many cultural stories and legends.

———. *Keepers of the Earth.* Golden, CO: Fulcrum Publishing, 1988. This book written as a story and activity guide for children includes many cultural stories and legends.

Coleman, William S. *Voices of Wounded Knee.* Lincoln: University of Nebraska Press, 2000. Includes reminiscenses of individuals involved with the Ghost Dance religion and Wounded Knee.

Dorsey, George A. *The Pawnee Mythology.* Lincoln: University of Nebraska Press, Bison Books, 1997.

———. *Traditions of the Arapaho.* Lincoln: University of Nebraska Press, Bison Books, 1998.

———. *Traditions of the Caddo.* Lincoln: University of Nebraska Press, Bison Books, 1997.

Eastman, Charles A. *The Soul of the Indian.* Lincoln: University of Nebraska Press, 1980.

Fletcher, Alice C. with James R. Murie. *The Hako: Song, Pipe, and Unity in a*

Pawnee Calumet Ceremony. Lincoln: University of Nebraska Press, 1996.

Garter Snake. *The Seven Visions of Bull Lodge, As Told to His Daughter.* Edited by George Horse Capture. Lincoln: University of Nebraska Press, Bison Books, 1992. The record of the spiritual life of Gros Ventre Bull Lodge (1802–1886), including detail about fasting, sacrifices, visions and healing.

Grinnell, George Bird. *By Cheyenne Campfires.* Lincoln: University of Nebraska Press, Bison Books, 1971; originally published by Yale University Press, New Haven, CT, 1926.

Hardin, Terri, ed. *Legends & Lore of the American Indians.* New York: Barnes & Noble Books, 1993.

Hittman, Michael, edited by Don Lynch. *Wovoka and the Ghost Dance.* Lincoln: University of Nebraska Press, Bison Books, 1997.

Hultkrantz, Ake. *Native Religions of North America.* San Francisco: Harper & Row, 1987.

Irwin, Lee. *The Dream Seekers: Native American Visionary Traditions of the Great Plains.* Norman: University Press of Oklahoma, 1994.

Johnston, Basil. *Ojibway Ceremonies.* Lincoln: University of Nebraska Press, 1990.

———. *Ojibway Heritage.* Lincoln: University of Nebraska Press, 1990.

Judson, Katharine Berry, ed. *Myths and Legends of California and the Old Southwest.* Lincoln: University of Nebraska Press, Bison Books, 1994. Includes cultural tales of Zuni, Pima, Paiute, Shastika and Miwok tribes.

———. *Myths and Legends of the Pacific Northwest.* Lincoln: University of Nebraska Press, Bison Books, 1997. Includes cultural tales and legends of Klamath, Nez Percé, Modoc, Tillamook, Shastan, Chinook, Flathead, Clatsop and other tribes.

Malotki, Ekkehart, ed. *Hopi Animal Tales.* Lincoln: University of Nebraska Press, 1998.

McGaa, Ed Eagle Man. *Native Wisdom.* Minneapolis: Four Directions Publishing, 1995. This is a contemporary account of spiritual matters by a member of the Oglala Sioux Nation.

McLaughlin, Marie L. *Myths and Legends of the Sioux.* Lincoln: University of Nebraska Press, 1990.

Mooney, James. *The Ghost-Dance Religion and the Sioux Outbreak of 1890.* Lincoln: University of Nebraska Press, 1991.

Neihardt, John G. *Black Elk Speaks.* New York: Pocket Books, 1975; originally published by W. Morrow & Co., 1932; reprinted by University of Nebraska Press, Bison Books, Lincoln, 1961. The story of Oglala holy man Black Elk that tells his holy vision.

Opler, Morris Edward. *Myths and Tales of the Chiricahua Apache Indians.* Lincoln: University of Nebraska Press, 1994.

———. *Myths and Tales of the Jicarilla Apache Indians.* Lincoln: University of Nebraska Press, 1994.

Parker, Arthur C. *Seneca Myths and Folk Tales.* Lincoln: University of Nebraska Press, Bison Books, 1989.

Parks, Douglas R., ed. *Myths and Traditions of the Arikara Indians.* Lincoln: University of Nebraska Press, 1996.

Parsons, Elsie Clews. *Pueblo Indian Religion.* 2 vols. Lincoln: University of Nebraska Press, 1996.

Ruby, Robert H., and John A. Brown. *John Slocum and the Indian Shaker Church.* Norman: University of Oklahoma Press, 1996.

Speck, Frank G. *Midwinter Rites of the Cayuga Long House.* Lincoln: University of Nebraska Press, Bison Books, 1995.

Taylor, Colin F., ed. consultant. *Native American Myths and Legends.* New York: Smithmark, 1994. A concise book with limited information about all cultural groups.

Walker, Deward E. Jr. *Blood of the Monster: The Nez Perce Coyote Cycle.* Worland, WY: High Plains Publishing Company, 1994.

Walker, James R. *Lakota Belief and Ritual.* Edited by Raymond J. DeMallie and Elaine A. Jahner. Lincoln: University of Nebraska Press, 1991.

———. *Lakota Myth.* Edited by Elaine A. Jahner. Lincoln: University of Nebraska Press, 1983.

Wissler, Clark, and D.C. Duvall. *Mythology of the Blackfoot Indians.* Lincoln: University of Nebraska Press, 1995.

CHRONOLOGY

1802   Congress provides funds to "educate and civilize" Indians.

1802   16 June—Creeks cede land in the Treaty of Fort Wilkinson.

1803   30 April—President Thomas P. Jefferson purchases Louisiana.

1804   Meriwether Lewis and William Clark along with their Corps of Discovery begin the explorations of the Louisiana Purchase; the first American exploration of the lands west of the Mississippi river.

1804   Louisiana Territory Act launches intent to remove Eastern Indians to new areas west of the Mississippi River.

1806   Cherokees cede territory in Tennessee and Alabama.

1806   The War Department establishes the Office of Superintendent of Indian Trade to oversee federal trading houses with the Indians.

1808   Osages cede much of their land in Missouri and Arkansas.

1809   Treaty of Fort Wayne leads Tecumseh to take up arms against the United States as policies implemented by Indiana Gov. William Henry Harrison lead to loss of 2.5 million acres of Indian territories.

1811   Tecumseh tries to recruit the large Southern tribes, but is opposed by Choctaw Chief Pushmataha. In a meeting of a Choctaw grand council, Tecumseh is expelled from the Choctaw country. In the War of 1812 Tecumseh will be commissioned a brigadier general in the British army and lead hundreds of Indians in battle in the Great Lakes region, while Pushmataha will be commissioned a brigadier general and lead up to eight hundred Choctaws in Andrew Jackson's U.S army in the South in battles against the Creeks, the Seminoles and the British.

1812   War of 1812 begins; most Indians align themselves with the British.

1813   Creek War begins involving a variety of conflicts with American forces. The war extends into 1814 and involves such major conflicts as the Battle of Horseshoe Bend (27 March 1814) where eight hundred Creeks die in the fighting. The war ends with the Treaty of Fort Jackson (9 August 1814) when the tribe cedes twenty-two million acres.

1815   January 8—Choctaws led by Chief Pushmataha assist American troops to defeat the British at the Battle of New Orleans.

1816   Metis and settlers in Canada's Red River Valley clash over farmland in a conflict that becomes known as the Selkirk incident.

1817   First Seminole war begins.

1818   First Protestant missionaries arrive among the Choctaws and establish schools, a total of eleven by 1830 (the schools are quickly reestablished after removal by 1835). By the early nineteenth century, Choctaws already have influential, educated, mixed-blood families descended from white traders who intermarried within the tribe. The mixed-blood families produce tribal leaders who are loyal Choctaw patriots in disputes and negotiations with the United States throughout the nineteenth century.

1819	Gold is discovered in the Cherokee Nation, starting the Southern Gold Rush and causing Georgia to demand Cherokee removal.
1819	18 October—Choctaws exchange some land in Mississippi for land west of the Mississippi River under the Treaty of Doak's Stand.
1821	Sequoyah finalizes the Cherokee alphabet.
1824	President John C. Calhoun establishes the Bureau of Indian Affairs under the War Department; Congress ultimately recognizes it in 1832.
1824	First Choctaw lawyer, James Lawrence McDonald, is admitted to the bar, after studying law in the office of Judge John McLean in Ohio (who later became a justice of the Supreme Court). The Choctaws had sent McDonald to the East when he was fourteen to be privately tutored by the Rev. Dr. Carnahan (who later became president of Princeton College). McDonald negotiates the Treaty of Washington of January 1825 for the Choctaws, prompting Commissioner of Indian Affairs Thomas McKinney to say, "I found him so skilled in the business of his mission . . . as to make it more of an up-hill business than I had ever before experienced in negotiating with Indians. I believe Mr. Calhoun [U.S. Secretary of War] thought so too." McDonald refused to listen to new U.S. treaty demands until the government had first fulfilled all its unmet obligations from previous Choctaw treaties, many of which were satisfied by new monetary awards to support Choctaw schools.
1825	Treaties are negotiated with many tribes including the Creeks, who cede land in Georgia and Alabama; the Kansas, who cede land in what becomes Kansas and Nebraska; and the Arikaras, Mandans, Hidatsas, Crows, Missourias, Pawnees, Mahas and Otos, who agree to keep the peace. The Osage and Kansa Indians also agree to permit roadbuilding.
1825	A young Choctaw named Peter Perkins Pitchlynn (who will become Principal Chief of the Choctaw Nation in 1864) leads the first group of Choctaw boys on horseback to the Choctaw Academy in Kentucky (operated by Col. Richard M. Johnson, who will later become vice president of the United States). There many future Choctaw leaders will be educated until 1841, when the Choctaws begin building nine similar academies in the Choctaw Nation in Indian Territory for both boys and girls. Choctaws send their most promising graduates to Dartmouth, Union, Yale and other colleges.
1827	Cherokees adopt a constitution similar to the U.S. Constitution.

1829	Andrew Jackson argues for removal of Indians from the Southeast.
1829	29 August—Winnebagos cede land in the Treaty of the Prairie du Chien.
1830	15 July—Another treaty at Prairie du Chien involves land cessions by the Sauk and Fox Indians.
1830	President Andrew Jackson enacts the Indian Removal Act, which calls for instant removal of southeastern tribes to Indian Territory.
1830	27 September—Choctaws cede lands east of the Mississippi River in the Treaty of Dancing Rabbit Creek.
1831–34	Two-thirds of the members of the Choctaw Nation and many Chickasaws remove to Indian Territory, each receiving as compensation thirteen dollars and a blanket.
1832	In exchange for fifteen thousand dollars Seminoles and Creeks agree to remove to Indian Territory under the Treaty of Payne's Landing.
1834	The American Fur Company begins operating a trading post at Fort Laramie.
1835	Seminoles begin their second war to remain in Florida.
1835	29 March—Cherokee Treaty Party agrees to leave the Southeast and move to Oklahoma.
1835	29 December—Cherokees cede most of their homeland in the Treaty of New Echota.
1835	Texas declares its independence from Mexico and subsequently organizes the Texas Rangers to lead attacks against the Comanches.
1835–42	Second Seminole War.
1837	Pueblo Indians defeat the Mexican militia in the Battle of La Canada, New Mexican territory.
1838	Cherokees are confined to stockades and subsequently forced to march west on the Trail of Tears.
1839	22 June—Cherokees assassinate John Ridge and Elias Boudinot, leaders of the Cherokee treaty party, for treason as a result of their roles in ceding tribal lands in the Southeast.
1840s– 1850s	The wealthiest Choctaw, Robert M. Jones, owns five large Red River plantations (the largest more than five thousand acres), more than five hundred slaves, a trading house at Doaksville and a number of steamboats.
1841	Jesuit Fr. Pierre De Smet begins the St. Mary's Mission in what becomes Montana, to launch the mission era in the Northwest.
1843	The first mission school for Eskimos is established by the Russian-Greek Orthodox Church.
1844	The *Cherokee Advocate* begins publication in Oklahoma; federal troops confiscate the press.
1844	Jonathan E. Dwight, a Choctaw educated at Yale, begins teaching at Spencer Academy in the Choctaw Nation. The academy teaches

English and Latin, arithmetic, geography, natural philosophy, United States history and algebra.

1845   Klamath Indians and troops under leadership of Lt. John C. Frémont clash in early fighting over California.

1847   Mormons settle a state they call Deseret, but which becomes Utah, forging friendly relations with the resident Ute and Paiute Indians.

1847   19 January—Indians at Taos Pueblo revolt against white leadership killing New Mexico Gov. Charles Bent, but subsequently suffer significant losses when troops attack the Pueblo church where Indian men, women and children had sought refuge.

1847   29 November—Cayuse Indians attack the Whitman Mission, killing Marcus and Narcissa Whitman and a dozen others, including women and children. The Indians capture fifty-six prisoners, but subsequently release them.

1848   24 January—John Marshall discovers gold in California leading to a subsequent rush to the area by thousands of miners and the ultimate destruction of California Indians; many tribes become extinct within a matter of years.

1848   The first commercial whalers arrive in what becomes Alaska.

1849   Bureau of Indian Affairs transfers from the U.S. Department of War and merges with the U. S. Department of the Interior.

1851   Plains tribes cede enormous amounts of territory in the Treaty of Fort Laramie, which also gives a right-of-way to the Oregon-California-Mormon Road.

1853–57 The United States negotiates fifty-two different treaties and subsequently acquires 157 million acres of Indian lands; it ultimately fails to honor any of the treaties, but retains the land.

1854   Oregon territorial legislature makes it illegal to sell firearms or ammunition to Indians, and people with at least one-half or more of Indian blood are prohibited from testifying in court.

1855–58 Third Seminole War.

1860   12 May—Paiutes attack miners near Pyramid Lake (Nevada) setting off subsequent reprisals.

1861–63 Apaches led by Mangas Coloradas and Cochise fight numerous battles with U.S. troops.

1862   President Abraham Lincoln signs the Homestead Act, opening western lands to settlement.

1862–63 Santee Sioux revolt killing Minnesota settlers; troops arrest and subsequently hang thirty-eight Indians in a mass execution in Mankato, Minnesota.

1864   6 January—Troops led by Kit Carson attack and subdue Navajos in the Battle of Canyon de Chelly, subsequently removing the Indians to Bosque Redondo near Fort Sumner, New Mexico, in an exodus known as The Long Walk.

| 1864 | Kit Carson and New Mexico Volunteers clash with Kiowas and Comanches in the Battle of Adobe Walls. |

1864   Kit Carson and New Mexico Volunteers clash with Kiowas and Comanches in the Battle of Adobe Walls.

1864   John Bozeman and John Jacobs pioneer a road from Fort Fetterman (Wyoming) to Virginia City (Montana) called the Bozeman Trail, but better known as the Bloody Bozeman for the conflict that occurred with various tribes, particularly the Sioux, Cheyenne and Arapaho people.

1864   29 November—Col. John Chivington leads a dawn attack on the peaceful village of Cheyenne and Arapaho Indians led by Black Kettle at Sand Creek, Colorado, killing more than one hundred. Known as the Sand Creek Massacre, this sets off retaliatory raids by the Cheyenne and Sioux tribes.

1865   The Bloody Year on the Plains begins 7 January when Cheyenne Indians raid Julesburg, Colorado, in retaliation for Sand Creek. Subsequent fighting breaks out all across the northern and southern Plains.

1865   Ute Indians led by Black Hawk begin what becomes a twenty-year conflict with Mormons.

1866–68 The First Sioux War, known as Red Cloud's War, takes place, fought primarily in the Powder River basin (Wyoming and Montana) over the Bozeman Trail.

1866   U.S. military establishes three forts to protect the Bozeman Trail: 13 July—Fort Phil Kearny; 28 July—Fort Reno; 12 August—Fort C.F. Smith.

1866   21 December—Eighty troops led by Lt. William J. Fetterman die in an attack by Sioux just north of Fort Phil Kearny.

1868   Navajos are allowed to return to their homelands, ending The Long Walk and their exile in southern New Mexico at Bosque Redondo.

1868   6 November—Treaty negotiations at Fort Laramie lead to abandonment of forts Phil Kearny, Reno and C.F. Smith along the Bozeman Trail. Troops leave the forts, which are subsequently burned by Sioux Indians and their allies.

1868   27 November—Lt. Col. George A. Custer leads troops against Cheyenne fighters in the Battle of the Washita; many of Custer's troops are killed when he abandons them during the battle.

1869   President Andrew Johnson establishes the Santee Sioux Reservation near Niobrara, Nebraska.

1869   Brig. Gen. Ely Parker, a Seneca, takes over as commissioner of Indian Affairs, the first Indian to hold that position; he serves until 1871.

1869   Metis along the Red River in Canada engage in the First Riel Rebellion.

1871   U.S. Congress declares an end to all treaty making with Indian tribes.

1872   Persuasion by Gen. Oliver O. Howard leads Chiricahua Apaches to move to a reservation.

1873   Modocs in northern California and southern Oregon begin a war, murdering peace commissioners.

1873   The government establishes the Red Cloud and Spotted Tail Indian Agencies in northwestern Nebraska to distribute annuities to the Sioux and Cheyenne Indians.

Investigation of Fraud at the Red Cloud Agency

We found the system of keeping accounts at the Red Cloud Agency exceedingly loose and defective, and for much of this the Indian Office is justly censurable. It is only within the last few weeks that the Government has supplied the books to the agent and required the adoption of a system calculated to exhibit clearly the state of his accounts. Prior to that time the agent furnished his own books, and made all his accounts in a loose and irregular manner; and when his agency expired, carried off all the books and papers as his private property.

—Frank Leslie's Illustrated Weekly, 6 November 1875, 130-2

1874   Red River War breaks out involving Kiowas and Comanches with major fights, including the Battle of Adobe Walls on 27 June where buffalo hunters repel seven hundred Kiowas, Comanches and Cheyennes, using their powerful buffalo guns (Sharps .50 caliber known as Big 50s).

1874   Lt. Col. George A. Custer leads a military reconnaissance of the Black Hills finding gold in the process. The land, though set aside for the Sioux, is subsequently the scene of a rush of gold miners.

1874–76 Second Sioux War, known as Crazy Horse's War.

1875   May—Sioux chiefs reject a six million dollar government offer for the Black Hills.

1875   September—Thousands of members of the Sioux Nation watch as the Allison Commission fails to purchase the Black Hills.

1876   When Sitting Bull indicates he wanted to purchase supplies from the Fort Peck Indian Agency, Montana Territory, the response to the agent is: "Inform Sitting Bull that the only condition of peace is his surrender, when he will be treated as a prisoner of war. Issue no rations except after such surrender, and when fully satisfied that the Indians can be held at the agency. Make early preparation to defend the agency stores and property. The military will cooperate as far as possible."

1876   Canadian government passes the Canadian Indian Act, defining Indian policy and allowing Indians to become Canadian citizens by renouncing rights and privileges as Indians.

1876   17 June—Sioux and Cheyenne warriors defeat Gen. George Crook's troops in the Battle of the Rosebud.

1876   25 June—Lt. Col. George A. Custer and his entire troop of cavalry-men are killed by a combined force of Sioux and Cheyenne warriors in the Battle of the Little Bighorn (called the Battle of the Greasy Grass by the Sioux). Subsequent battles include the Battle of Warbonnet Creek, 17 July, where the Fifth Cavalry defeats the Cheyennes; the Battle of Slim Buttes, 9 September, where troops attack Crazy Horse's village; and the Dull Knife Battle, 25 November, on Red Fork of the Powder River, when Lt. Ranald Mackenzie attacks the Cheyenne camp of Dull Knife.

1877   Washington Territory establishes fishing seasons, with some periods of the year closed.

1877   Nez Percé war breaks out and the tribe flees toward Canada, engaging in fighting with U.S. troops at White Bird Canyon, 17 June; the Clearwater River, 11–12 July; the Big Hole, 9 August; Camas Meadows, 20 August; Canyon Creek, 13 September; Cow Island, 23 September and culminating in a siege at Bear Paw 30 September–5 October where Chief Joseph surrendered the tribe just forty miles short of refuge in Canada.

1878   Oregon Territory establishes fishing seasons.

1878   U.S. Congress authorizes Indian Police units.

1879   Following the Meeker Massacre in northern Colorado, Utes relinquish their Colorado lands and move to a reservation in Utah.

> COLORADO—The Utes, of Colorado, have agreed to give up the San Juan mining region, about which there has long been contention between miners and Indians.
> —Frank Leslie's Illustrated Weekly, *4 October 1873, 59-4*

1879   Carlisle Indian School opens.

1879   Cheyennes break away from their reservation in Indian Territory, fleeing to their homeland on the northern plains; they are subsequently captured and incarcerated at Fort Robinson, Nebraska. Ultimately a reservation for some is established in Montana Territory.

1879   Groups proclaiming their friendship for Indians organize including the Indian Rights Association, National Indian Defense Association, Indian Protection Committee and the Women's National Indian Association.

1879–85   Apaches continue resistance with raids led by Victorio, Nana and Geronimo.

1883   U.S. Congress approves the Court of Indian Offenses, giving tribal units authority to administer justice for all but major crimes; the 1885 Major Crimes Act subsequently gives federal courts jurisdiction over major Indian offenses.

1884   Congress outlaws Northwest Indian potlatch ceremonies.

1885	Metis along Canada's Red River engage in the Second Riel Rebellion.
1886	Geronimo surrenders, but subsequently escapes. He is then recaptured (4 September) and the Apache Wars effectively end.
1887	8 February—President Grover Cleveland approves the Dawes Severalty Act, named for its sponsor, Massachusetts Senator Henry Dawes. The act dissolves Indian tribes as legal entities and divides tribal lands, giving heads of Indian households 160 acres, single Indian people 80 acres, and minor Indians 40 acres. The Indians agree to farm their land and that they will not sell it to non-Indians for at least twenty-five years. Subsequent changes in the act weaken it.
1889	The Ghost Dance religion, first taught by Paiute Wovoka, begins.
1889	Congress purchases two million acres in Indian Territory to be subsequently granted to homesteaders in the first Oklahoma land run.
1890	U.S. Bureau of the Census declares there is no longer an American Frontier.
1890	29 December 29—The Seventh Cavalry kills 150 Sioux men, women and children in the Wounded Knee Massacre.
1895	Bannock and Shoshone Indians protest hunting license provisions in Wyoming, taking the case to the state supreme court, which affirms the state's ownership of wild game.
1898	Six soldiers die in an attack by Chippewa Indians at the Battle of Leech Lake, Minnesota.
1898	Congress approves the Curtis Act that dissolves tribal governments, requires Indians to submit to allotment, and authorizes civil government for Indian Territory.

ADDITIONAL READING

Flanagan, Mike. *The Old West: Day By Day.* New York: Facts on File, 1995.

Heard, J. Norman. *Handbook of the American Frontier: Four Centuries of Indian-White Relationships.* Metuchen, NJ: Scarecrow Press. vol. I, *Southeastern Woodlands,* 1987; vol. II, *Northeastern Woodlands,* 1990; vol. III. *The Great Plains,* 1993; vol. IV, *The Far West,* 1997; vol. V, *Chronology, Bibliography, Index,* 1998.

GLOSSARY

Berdache: A Plains Indian man who acted and dressed like a woman.

Brave: A white term for a warrior.

Breath-feathers: The downy feathers of an eagle or other bird.

Breechclout: An article of male clothing, breechclouts usually hung below the waist with flaps in the front and back. Sometimes they were styled as kilts or aprons.

Bride Service: Payment made for a woman when she married, similar to a dowry.

Bull-roarer: A flat stick with one end pointed and a buckskin thong attached to the other, which can be whirled to sound like thunder. Used as a musical instrument and in certain rituals, particularly among the Navajos.

Calumet: A prairie term for a pipe used to smoke tobacco in both religious and secular situations. A calumet was generally a reed or tube-shaped piece of wood that had an elbow-shaped pipe bowl into which tobacco could be placed for smoking. It looked like any elbow-shaped pipe, except the stem was generally much longer.

Canoe, parts of: Ribs (curved pieces of wood to form the basic shape), stays (stiffened pieces of wood or other material to help hold the canoe shape), thwart (the seat in the canoe), gunwale (the upper edge of the canoe).

Counting Coup: Touching or striking an enemy without killing him. It was an important act of bravery for Plains Indians and a recognized war honor.

Coyote: A term for "everything low" among the Paiutes. According to Sarah Winnemucca Hopkins: "Coyote is the name of a mean, crafty little animal, half wolf, half dog, and stands for everything low. It is the greatest term of reproach one Indian has for another. Indians do not swear. . . . The worst they call each other is 'bad' or 'coyote.' "

Decoration Day: Another name for Memorial Day, which Indian children at boarding schools were required to celebrate.

Deerskin Dance: A major ceremonial of the California tribes.

Genizaro: A term used in New Mexico during the nineteenth century referring to American Indians of mixed tribal blood who had Spanish surnames, Christian names obtained during baptism, who spoke simple Spanish and who lived in special communities or in Hispanic towns. They were almost always the children of individuals captured from Plains tribes, most often female and very rarely male captives. They were subsequently "adopted" or "ransomed" by the Spanish, who turned them into virtual slaves, giving them their own surname.

Ghost Dance: The Ghost Dance, which started in 1889 among the tribes in the Great Basin and spread to other cultural groups in the West, had two ideological goals: removal of whites from Indian country and resurrection of ancestors. Participants wore special shirts they believed made them impervious to bullets and other attacks.

Kinnikinnik: Algonquian for "that which is mixed," generally referring to mixtures of barks and seeds from Canada and the Eastern United States.

Kubum: A general term of California Indians indicating the types of plants that could be used in making baskets.

Labret: An elliptical piece of wood, ivory or bone inserted into the lower lip.

Mestizo: People who were the mixed-race offspring of Southwest Indians and non-Indians.

Metis: (Slotas) French-speaking offspring of fur traders and Indians primarily from the Cree and Ojibwa tribes who made their home along Canada's Red River.

Potlatch: A ceremonial feast held for a variety of reasons: death, recognition of a girl reaching puberty, marriage or even the building of a new longhouse. The word *potlatch* is from the Chinook tribe.

Puha: Power.

Pul: The name given to a Cahuilla medicine woman.

Scalp Lock: A portion of hair at the top of the head that could be cut away and taken by enemy raiders.

Smoking: Word also meaning "to have a meeting" in Southwest cultural groups.

Squaw: A corruption of the Narraganset word for *woman*, which has derogatory connotations. Nevertheless, whites commonly used the word throughout the 1800s.

Travois: A drag made of poles or large sticks attached to a dog or horse and used to transport goods or people, particularly the elderly and children.

Tumpline: A strap used for hauling burdens. Most often it was placed around the forehead and attached to a load carried on the back in a basket. Tumplines could also be used to tie bundles of firewood, furs or other materials to make transporting them easier.

Wampum: Tubes or disks of shell strung together like belts or necklaces and used as currency or a trade item.

Yellow-eyes: The second name for whites among the Crows. The Crow version is *masta-cheeda*. The first name for whites among the Crows was *beta-awk-a-wah-cha*, meaning "Sits-on-the-water," because the first white people the Crows met came in canoes.

BIBLIOGRAPHY

Bataille, Gretchen M. and Kathleen Mullen Sands. *American Indian Women Telling Their Lives.* Lincoln, NE: University of Nebraska Press, 1984.

Birchfield, D.L., ed. *Encyclopedia of North American Indians.* New York: Marshall Cavendish Corp., 1997.

Bleed, Ann, and Charles Flowerday, eds. *An Atlas of the Sand Hills.* Lincoln: Conservation and Survey Division, Institute of Agriculture and Natural Resources, University of Nebraska Press, Lincoln, 1990.

Blouet, Brian W., and Frederick C. Luebke, eds. *The Great Plains: Environment and Culture.* Lincoln, NE: University of Nebraska Press, 1979.

Brown, Dee. *Wondrous Times on the Frontier.* Little Rock: August House Publishers, 1991.

Clark, Robert. *River of the West.* New York: HarperCollins West, 1995.

Crum, Sally. *People of the Red Earth: American Indians of Colorado.* Santa Fe: Ancient City Press, 1996. A concise volume about Indians who lived in what is now Colorado.

Curtis, Edward S. *The North American Indians.* New York: Johnson Reprint Corp., 1970; originally published Cambridge, MA: University Press, vol. 1, 1907; vol. 2, 1908; vol. 3, 1908; vol. 4, 1909; vol. 5, 1909; vol. 6, 1911; vol. 7, 1911; vol. 8, 1911; vol. 9, 1913; vol. 10, 1915; vol. 11, 1916; vol. 12, 1922; vol. 13, 1924; vol. 14, 1924; vol. 15, 1926; vol. 16, 1926; vol. 17, 1926; vol. 18, 1928; vol. 19, 1930; vol. 20, 1930.

Dary, David. *Buffalo Book: The Full Saga of the American Animal.* Athens, OH: Swallow Press/University of Ohio Press, 1989.

Debo, Angie. *A History of the Indians of the United States.* Norman: University of Oklahoma Press, 1970.

DeGraf, Anna. *Pioneering on the Yukon, 1892–1917.* Edited by Roger S. Brown. Hamden, CT: Archon Books, 1992.

Dick, Everett. *Conquering the Great American Desert.* Lincoln, NE: Nebraska State Historical Society, 1975.

Dickason, Olive Patricia. *Canada's First Nations: A History of Founding People From Earliest Times.* Norman, OK: University of Oklahoma Press, 1992.

Driver, Harold E. *Indians of North America*, 2d ed., rev. Chicago: The University of Chicago Press, 1969; originally published University of Chicago Press, 1961. This is an excellent resource book including details about food, clothing, architecture, lifestyle and family relationships.

Eagle Walking Turtle. *Indian America: A Traveler's Companion.* 4th edition. Santa Fe: John Muir Publications, 1995.

Ewers, John C. *Indian Life on the Upper Missouri.* Norman, OK: University of Oklahoma Press, 1968; paperback, 1988.

———. *Plains Indian History and Culture: Essays of Continuity and Change.* Norman, OK: University of Oklahoma Press, 1997.

Foote, Cheryl J. *Women of the New Mexico Frontier, 1846–1912*. Niwot, CO: University Press of Colorado, 1990.

Foreman, Grant. *The Five Civilized Tribes—Cherokee, Chickasaw, Choctaw, Creek, Seminole*. Norman, OK: University of Oklahoma Press, 1989.

Franchere, Hoyt C., trans. and ed. *The Overland Diary of Wilson Price Hunt*. Ashland, OR: Oregon Book Society, 1973.

Greager, Howard E. *We Shall Fall as the Leaves*. No Place: Howard E. Greager publisher, 1996. Contemporary accounts related to banishment of the Uncompahgre and Northern Utes from their ancestral homeland in Colorado.

Greeley, Horace. *An Overland Journey From New York to San Francisco in the Summer of 1859*. New York: Knopf, 1964.

Haines, Francis. *The Buffalo: The Story of American Bison and Their Hunters from Prehistoric Times to the Present*. Norman, OK: University of Oklahoma Press, 1995.

Hays, Robert G. *A Race at Bay: New York Times Editorials on "The Indian Problem," 1860–1900*. Carbondale, IL: Southern Illinois University Press, 1997.

Heard, J. Norman. *Handbook of the American Frontier: Four Centuries of Indian-White Relationships*. Metuchen, NJ: Scarecrow Press. vol. I, *Southeastern Woodlands*, 1987; vol. II, *Northeastern Woodlands*, 1990; vol. III, *The Great Plains*, 1993; vol. IV, *The Far West*, 1997; vol. V, *Chronology, Bibliography, Index*, 1998.

Heizer, Robert E., ed. *The Destruction of California Indians*. Lincoln, NE: University of Nebraska Press, 1993.

Holder, Preston. *The Hoe and the Horse on the Plains: A Study of Cultural Development Among North American Indians*. Lincoln, NE: University of Nebraska Press, 1991.

Hopkins, Sarah Winnemucca. *Life Among the Paiutes: Their wrongs and claims*. Edited by Mrs. Horace Mann. Boston: Cupples, Upham & Co., G.P. Putnam's sons, NY, 1883.

Hoxie, Frederick E., ed. *Encyclopedia of North American Indians*. Boston: Houghton Mifflin Company, 1996.

Klein, Laura F., and Lillian A. Ackerman, eds. *Women and Power in Native North America*. Norman, OK: University of Oklahoma Press, 1995.

Lee, Wayne C., and Howard C. Raynesferd. *Trails of the Smoky Hill: From Coronado to the Cow Towns*. Caldwell, ID: Caxton Printers Ltd., 1980.

Luchetti, Cathy, and Carol Olwell. *Women of the West*. New York: Orion, 1992.

Mayer, Melanie J. *Klondike Women: True Tales of the 1897–98 Gold Rush*. Athens, OH: Swallow Press/Ohio University Press, 1989.

McBride, Bunny. *Women of the Dawn*. Lincoln, NE: University of Nebraska Press, 1999.

Neiderman, Sharon. *A Quilt of Words: Women's Diaries, Letters & Original Accounts of Life in the Southwest, 1860–1960*. Boulder, CO: Johnston Books, 1988.

Nelson, Richard K. *Make Prayers to the Raven: A Koyukon View of the Northern Forest*. Chicago: University of Chicago Press, 1983. An account of origins and lifestyle of Koyukons, who follow traditional lives in the Alaskan boreal forest.

Nerburn, Kent, ed. *The Wisdom of the Native Americans.* Novato, CA: New World Library, 1999. Includes quotations and speeches from Indian leaders; an excellent resource to hear the "voices" of American Indians.

Parins, James W. *John Rollin Ridge: His Life and Works.* Lincoln, NE: University of Nebraska Press, 1991. A biography of the Cherokee leader.

Peavy, Linda and Ursula Smith. *Women in Waiting in the Westward Movement.* Norman, OK: University of Oklahoma Press, 1994.

Peterson, Nancy M. *People of the Moonshell: A Western River Journal.* Frederick, CO: Renaissance House Publishers, 1984.

———. *People of the Old Missury: Years of Conflict.* Frederick, CO: Renaissance House Publishers, 1989.

Poling-Kempes, Lesley. *Valley of Shining Stone: The Story of Abiquiu.* Tucson: University of Arizona Press, 1997.

Rawls, James J. *Indians of California: The Changing Image.* Norman, OK: University of Oklahoma Press, 1984.

Riley, Glenda. *Women and Indians on the Frontier, 1825–1915.* Albuquerque: University of New Mexico, 1984.

Ronda, James P. *Lewis and Clark Among the Indians.* Lincoln, NE: University of Nebraska Press, 1984; Bison Books edition, 1988.

Ruby, Robert H., and John A. Brown. *A Guide to the Indian Tribes of the Pacific Northwest.* Norman: University of Oklahoma Press, 1986.

Sage, Rufus G. *Rocky Mountain Life.* Lincoln, OK: University of Nebraska Press, Bison Books, 1982; originally published 1846.

Sandoz, Mari. *Crazy Horse: The Strange Man of the Oglalas.* Lincoln, NE: University of Nebraska Press, Bison Books, 1992; originally published by Alfred A. Knopf, New York, 1942.

———. *Love Song to the Plains.* Lincoln, NE: University of Nebraska Press, Bison Books, 1966; originally published by Harper, New York, 1961.

Schoolcraft, H. R. *Indian Tribes of the United States,* vol. I. Philadelphia, 1860.

Slatta, Richard W. *Comparing Cowboys and Frontiers.* Norman, OK: University of Oklahoma Press, 1997.

Sneve, Virginia Driving Hawk. *Completing the Circle.* Lincoln: University of Nebraska Press, 1995.

Sturtevant, William C., gen. ed. *Handbook of North American Indians.* Washington: Smithsonian Institution. This twenty-volume encyclopedia (still being published) is invaluable for its information about specific tribes. The volumes are: Wilcomb E. Washburn, ed., vol. 4, *History of Indian-White Relations,* 1988; Damas, David, ed., vol. 5, *Arctic.* 1984; Helm, June, ed., vol. 6, *Subarctic,* 1981; Suttles, Wayne, ed., vol. 7, *Northwest Coast,* 1990; Heizer, Robert F., ed., vol. 8, *California,* 1978; Ortiz, Alfonso, ed., vol. 9, *Southwest,* 1979; Ortiz, Alfonso, ed., vol. 10, *Southwest,* 1983; D'Azevedo, Warren L., ed., vol. 11, *Great Basin,* 1986; Walker, Deward E., Jr., ed., vol. 12, *Plateau,* 1998; Trigger, Bruce G., ed., vol. 15, *Northeast,* 1978. Sturtevant, William C., ed., vol. 17, *Languages,* 1996. Forthcoming volumes are: vol. 1, *Introduction;* vol. 2, *Indians in Contemporary Society*; vol. 3, *Environment, Origins, and Population*; vol. 13, *Plains*, Wilcomb Washburn, ed.; vol. 14, *Southeast*; vol. 15, *Technology and Visual Arts*; vol. 18 and vol. 19, *Biographical Dictionary*; vol. 20, *Index*.

Terrell, John Upton. *American Indian Almanac: The Authoritative Reference and Chronicle*. New York: World Publishing Co., 1971.

Thrapp, Dan. L. *Encyclopedia of Frontier Biography*. Lincoln: University of Nebraska Press, '95 for CD, '91 for 3 vol; Originally published by Arthur H. Clark and Company, Glendale, CA, 1988–1994.

Time-Life eds. *The American Story: Defiant Chiefs*. Alexandria, VA: Time-Life Books. 1997.

Tremblay, William *The June Rise: The Aprocryphal Letters of Joseph Antoine Janis*. Logan, UT: Utah State University Press, 1994.

Van Bruggen, Theodore. *Wildflowers, Grasses and Other Plants of the Northern Plains and Black Hills*. Interior, SD: Badlands Natural History Association 4th printing, 1992.

Waldman, Carl. *Encyclopedia of Native American Tribes* rev. ed. New York: Facts on File. 1999; originally published, 1988.

Weatherford, Jack. *Indian Givers: How The Indians of the Americas Transformed the World*. New York: Crown Publishers, 1988. A good resource including details about food, trade, leadership and Indian medicine.

———. *Native Roots: How The Indians Enriched America*. New York: Crown Publishers, 1991. An excellent resource with details about food, architecture, trade, warfare and language. Though not written just with the nineteenth century in mind, this is an important work for an understanding of the contributions by Indians to American life and society.

Webb, Walter Prescott. *The Great Plains*. Boston: Ginn & Company, 1931.

Webber, Bert. *Indians Along the Oregon Trail*. Medford, OR.: Webb Research Group, 1989.

White, John Manchip. *Everyday Life of the North American Indian*. New York: Holmes & Meier Publishers, 1979.

Woodhead, Henry, series ed. *The American Indians*, Alexandria, VA: Time-Life Books. *The First Americans*, 1992; *The Spirit World*, 1992; *The European Challenge*, 1992; *People of the Desert*, 1993; *The Buffalo Hunters*, 1993; *Keepers of the Totem*. 1993; *Realm of the Iroquois*, 1993; *The Mighty Chieftains*, 1993; *The Way of the Warrior*, 1993; *War for the Plains*, 1994; *People of the Lakes*, 1994; *Cycles of Life*, 1994; *People of the Ice and Snow*, 1994; *The Indians of California*, 1994; *Tribes of the Southern Woodlands*, 1994; *Algonquians of the East Coast*, 1995; *Hunters of the Northern Forest*, 1995; *Tribes of the Southern Plains*, 1995; *The Woman's Way*,1995; *People of the Western Range*, 1995; *The Reservations*, 1995; *Winds of Renewal*, 1996.

Wright, J. Leitch, Jr. *The Only Land They Knew: American Indians in the Old South*. Lincoln, NE: University of Nebraska Press, 1999. An account of Southeastern Indians from arrival of the Spanish to removal in the 1830s.

INDEX

Look for These Other Fascinating Histories From the Everyday Life Series!

Everyday Life in the 1800s is a superb reference for writers, researchers, students and teachers. Laid out dictionary-style, this book examines everyday life decade by decade. You'll find hundreds of otherwise obscure facts about popular slang, fashions and style, courtship and marriage rituals, popular food and drink—including brand names and costs—plus information on furnishing a farmhouse or outfitting a barn! *1-58297-063-7, paperback, 320 pages*

Everyday Life in the Middle Ages uncovers the startling reality behind all those tales of English crusaders and Viking raiders. In it you'll find a massive overview of life in Northwestern Europe from 500 to 1500, including fascinating details on medieval food and dining habits, clothing for lords and ladies, medicine for rich and poor, the royalty, heraldry, arms and armor, the brutality of war and the honor of chivalry. You'll also find facts on saints, popes, religious orders, festivals and the roles of men, women and children in all areas of medieval life. *1-58297-001-7, paperback, 240 pages*

Everyday Life During the Civil War takes you back to the sweeping events and standard practices that shaped this fascinating era. From soldiers to Southern belles, you'll learn what people wore, what they ate, their diversions from combat, and much more. Discover the social and economic realities of daily life in the Union and Confederacy, the hardships of military life, common dialects, weaponry, and quick reference timelines that make it easy to pinpoint historical events before, during and after the war. It's all here in one spectacular volume! *0-89879-922-8, paperback, 288 pages*

The Writer's Guide to Everyday Life in the Wild West shows you firsthand what it was like to tame the prairies, fight the battles and build the boomtowns. From things people ate (including boudins and buffalo humps) to what they wore (such as linsey-woolsey, calico and duck), this book is packed with historical accounts, maps and photographs to give you a complete perspective on this fascinating era. More than a reference book, this guide is like a trip back to the Old West. *0-89879-870-1, hardcover, 336 pages*

The Writer's Guide to Everyday Life in Renaissance England explores the large tapestry of often-elusive day-to-day details that bring the period fully to life. You'll journey back to 1485–1649 England and discover what people ate, what they wore, table customs, the details of family life and the Royal Court. You'll also find details about life in the cities and rural areas, as well as information on religion, piracy, crime and punishment. *0-89879-752-7, hardcover, 288 pages*

The Writer's Guide to Everyday Life in Regency and Victorian England captures all the details that made life in 19th-century England so fascinating. You'll find everything from slice-of-life facts, anecdotes and firsthand accounts, to sweeping timelines and major historical events. Learn what people ate, how couples married and divorced, and the rules honored by "decent" society. Want to know what people did for work? For entertainment? The meaning of common slang from the period? It's all here! *0-89879-812-4, hardcover, 256 pages*

The Writer's Guide to Everyday Life in Colonial America illuminates the events that framed Colonial American life, from existing under England's dominion and clashing with Native Americans to finally tearing away from the mother country. You'll find a comprehensive overview of each colonial region, including what colonists ate, the details of food preparation, geography, religion, politics, attitudes about sex and marriage, Colonial fashion, etiquette, earning a living and the events leading up to the Revolution. *0-89879-942-2, paperback, 304 pages*